The BRONTË FAMILY

The BRONTË FAMILY

Sibling Rivalry and a Burial in Paradise

CATHERINE RAYNER

PEN & SWORD
HISTORY

AN IMPRINT OF PEN & SWORD BOOKS LTD.
YORKSHIRE - PHILADELPHIA

First published in Great Britain in 2025 by
PEN AND SWORD HISTORY
An imprint of
Pen & Sword Books Ltd
Yorkshire – Philadelphia

Copyright © Catherine Rayner, 2025

ISBN 978 1 03612 904 0

The right of Catherine Rayner to be identified as Author of this work has been asserted by her in accordance with the Copyright, Designs and Patents Act 1988.

A CIP catalogue record for this book is available from the British Library.

All rights reserved. No part of this book may be reproduced, transmitted, downloaded, decompiled or reverse engineered in any form or by any means, electronic or mechanical including photocopying, recording or by any information storage and retrieval system, without permission from the Publisher in writing. NO AI TRAINING: Without in any way limiting the Author's and Publisher's exclusive rights under copyright, any use of this publication to "train" generative artificial intelligence (AI) technologies to generate text is expressly prohibited. The Author and Publisher reserve all rights to license uses of this work for generative AI training and development of machine learning language models.

Typeset in Times New Roman 10.5/13 by
SJmagic DESIGN SERVICES, India.
Printed and bound in the UK by CPI Group (UK) Ltd.

The Publisher's authorised representative in the EU for product safety is Authorised Rep Compliance Ltd., Ground Floor, 71 Lower Baggot Street, Dublin D02 P593, Ireland.
www.arccompliance.com

For a complete list of Pen & Sword titles please contact
PEN & SWORD BOOKS LIMITED
George House, Units 12 & 13, Beevor Street, Off Pontefract Road, Barnsley, South Yorkshire, S71 1HN, England
E-mail: enquiries@pen-and-sword.co.uk
Website: www.pen-and-sword.co.uk

or

PEN AND SWORD BOOKS
1950 Lawrence Rd, Havertown, PA 19083, USA
E-mail: uspen-and-sword@casematepublishers.com
Website: www.penandswordbooks.com

Contents

Acknowledgements		vi
Glossary of Religious People and Places		vii
Foreword		xi
Other books by Catherine Rayner		xii
Unquiet Slumbers		xiii
Chapter One	The Birth Order and Genetic Inheritance of the Brontë Siblings	1
Chapter Two	The Lasting Effects of Maternal Deprivation	17
Chapter Three	Death and the Family	34
Chapter Four	The Return of Tragedy: A Vale of Tears	48
Chapter Five	Confined and Contained: 1825–1831	64
Chapter Six	Anne Brontë: Learning to Be the Youngest	77
Chapter Seven	The Brontës and Mental Health	90
Chapter Eight	'Mushrooms Growing in a Cellar'	102
Chapter Nine	'The Dark Side of Sisterhood'	114
Chapter Ten	Anne as Governess: The Conflict of Experience	130
Chapter Eleven	Thorp Green: 'A Patient and Persecuted Stranger'	144
Chapter Twelve	*Agnes Grey*: The Autobiography of a Governess	160
Chapter Thirteen	*The Tenant of Wildfell Hall*: 'She Will Not Preach, She Will Exhibit'	173
Chapter Fourteen	The Final Separation	185
The Denouement		200
References		201
Bibliography		212

Acknowledgements

Any book on the Brontë family owes a huge debt to Dr Juliet Barker's amazing works. With regards especially to Anne, Dr Edward Chitham is the leading authority. I thank them both for allowing me to quote from them in this edition.

It was Scarborough historian and lecturer, Marie Belfitt (1935–2017) who alerted me to the old name of Paradise, assigned long ago to the area where Anne Brontë is buried. I hope that she would have approved of this book

In the twenty-first century, Anne's place as a Brontë novelist, poet and hymnist has become far more recognised. New writers, with new ideas, are blossoming and I thank them all, especially John Hennessey for his wonderful book on the Brontës and their music and Samantha Ellis for her insight and forward thinking.

The Anne Brontë Association in Scarborough and the Brontë Birthplace Trust are new and exciting additions to the Brontë extended collective. I am now involved with both and they are fast gaining an important and special role in the ever-evolving Brontë story.

I have involved my family, as always, in proofreading my work and adding comments. They have been, as ever, kind, helpful and forthcoming and have all, in their own way, taught me a great deal about sibling rivalry!

Glossary of Religious People and Places

The following is a list and brief outline of some of the religious denominations and leaders that are part of the Christian churches.

Adventists: Founded in the USA in 1863. Part of the Protestant Christian Denomination. Worship the Sabbath on a Saturday, according to the Hebrew calendar, and advocate the second coming of Christ.

Agnostic: A person who deems that knowledge of a supreme being is impossible.

Anglican: A member of the Church of England.

Arminianism: Began in the seventeenth century. It arose in Protestant Christianity as a liberal reaction to the Calvinistic doctrine of predestination. It denies the chosen 'elect' and believes that God chose the believing Church for salvation.

Atheist: A person who does not believe in a God or Gods.

Baptist: A person of any Christian sect who believes in baptism as a necessary rite.

Bishop: Spiritual head of a Church or diocese.

Calvinist: Followers of John Calvin who believe in predestination and of an 'elect' number of people who will enter heaven.

Canon: One of several priests organising a Church.

Cathedral: A church that contains the *Cathedra* (Latin for seat) of a bishop. Thus, serving as the central church in a diocese or episcopate.

Catholic: Is the Roman Catholic Church and the largest Christian Church in the World, with over 1.5 billion baptised members. The belief is in the Holy Trinity, Jesus as the son of God, the crucifixion, the resurrection and the ascension of Jesus as the work of the Holy Spirit.

Chapel: A non-conformist place of worship, or a place set aside for individual prayer.

Christian: A follower and believer in Jesus Christ.

Church: A building designated for public worship, especially for Christians.

Church of England: Church and belief that is separated from the Church of Rome.

Clergyman: A member of the clergy, i.e. a churchman.

Congregational: Protestant Church in the Reformed tradition practising congregational government. Each congregation, independently and autonomously, runs its own affairs.

Curate: A clergyman appointed to assist a priest or vicar.

Dean: The head of a chapter of canons.

Denomination: Divided into sects and follow particular religious tenets.

Diocese: District under the jurisdiction of a bishop.

Ecclesiastic: Clergymen or others in holy orders associated with a Christian Church.

Episcopal: Belief that a Church should be governed by bishops.

Episcopate: the office and status of a bishop or bishops.

Evangelical: The practice of spreading the Christian gospel, e.g. missionaries or itinerant preachers.

Jehovah's Witness: Founded in the USA in 1879. A non-political Christian-based religion, but does not celebrate religious festivals. Refusal of blood products. Belief in Armageddon as imminent. Practice baptism. They 'witness' by distributing literature and personal evangelism. Belief in a chosen number of people attaining heaven and the Bible as God's message.

Lutheran: Followers of Martin Luther, who believed in religious justification by faith alone.

Methodist: System of faith and practice initiated by John Wesley in the eighteenth century. Part of Protestant Christianity, it became non-conformist as it became a separate Church that did not conform to the rules of the Established Church of England. Belief in God as a loving deity. Condemns vices of alcohol and gambling.

Minster: A person authorised to conduct religious worship. A member of the clergy.

Moravian: Protestantism originating in Moravia. Links with Luther. Belief in universal salvation. Everyone is equal and has salvation in Christ. Promotes Christian unity in all denominations.

Mormon: Founded in the USA in the nineteenth century with a religious tradition of the latter-day saints. Unique view of cosmology and that people are the spiritual children of God.

Non-conformist: Protestant Christians whose members 'dissent' from the established Church and do not conform to its beliefs and practices. Also known as Dissenters.

Parson: A Church of England parish priest.

Pastor: An ordained churchman who is the leader of a Christian congregation and who also gives advice and counselling within the community and congregation.

Pentecostal: A charismatic religious movement founded in the USA in the twentieth century. Belief in a personal experience with God through 'baptism with the Holy Spirit'.

Presbyterian: A teaching elder adhering to a modified version of Calvinism.

Priest: An ordained person in the Catholic or Church of England faiths who acts as a mediator between God and man.

Protestant: Non-Catholic. Separated from the Roman Catholic Church.

Roman Catholic: A Catholic who is a member of the Roman rite. Involves Mass, veneration of the Virgin Mary and saints. A body of dogma that believes in papal infallibility.

Sectarianism: Members of a sect who are intolerant of any other sect or religion.

The Oxford Movement: Centred on Oxford University in the nineteenth century. It strove to revive and renew Catholicism within the Church of England, in opposition to the Protestant tendencies. Anglo-Catholicism.

Unitarianism: Branch of Christianity that believes in God as the singular and unique creator. They believe that no one religion has the answer and that all have something to teach.

United Reform Church: A united group of congregational sects.

Vicar: A clergyman appointed to act as representative of the head of his diocese, who receives the revenues from the Church and is awarded a stipend. He leads his Church in worship and prayer and performs communion, baptisms, weddings and funerals, often aided by a curate.

Wesleyan: Includes Methodist theology and is a Protestant Christian tradition based on the evangelical reforms and teachings of John and Charles Wesley. Asserts the primary authority of the scriptures and has a doctrine of unlimited atonement for everyone. Belief in faith as necessary for salvation.

Foreword

Since I first became interested in the Brontës' works and later their lives, I could never understand why Anne Brontë was buried separately, seventy miles away from her family. Her grave lies in the churchyard of St Mary and the Apostles parish church, Scarborough, just below Scarborough Castle, in an area known for centuries as 'Paradise'.

Paradise was, and still is, the local name for this area above Scarborough 'old town' because it was once occupied by a monastery with its accompanying graveyard and walled garden.

Many writers, researchers and historians have always maintained that Anne was buried here because 'she loved Scarborough'. However, I do not believe that Anne wanted to be separated from her family, her pets and her beloved moorland home, in life or in death, and that the decision was not hers, but her sister Charlotte's.

This book seeks to explain why I am sure that the lives of the Brontë siblings were greatly upset and irrevocably altered when Charlotte became the eldest child and how this and their birth order eventually led to the choice of Anne's final resting place, away from Haworth and all of her family.

Other books by Catherine Rayner

Wild Imaginings: A Bronte Childhood. Austin Macauley Publishers Ltd., 2018.

The Bronte Sisters: Life, Loss and Literature. Pen and Sword History, 2018.

Haworth and the Brontes: Literary Trails. Pen and Sword History, 2018.

Essay on Anne Brontë entitled 'Buried in Paradise', in *Walking with Anne Brontë: Insights and Reflections.* An Anthology edited by Tim Whittome, Xlibris, USA, 2023.

'Domestic Distress and the Uncanny as Aspects of Emily Bronte's Life and her Parsonage Home' in *Bronte Transactions*, Volume 19, Part 6, pp.245–250, 1988.

Socio History: A Course Reader. Co-authored with Professor Eric Sigsworth, 1983.

Unquiet Slumbers

Three gifted sisters, in their shared abode;
Cast in a mould that blends the mind with mystery of genetic kind
Their thoughts and actions intertwined,
They bore life's weary load.

Fame, what did it cost? Fortune only frowned;
No riches gained to guild their art, no lover's kiss, no cupid's dart.
Death's arrow shot each harassed heart
And laid it in the ground.

They were three sisters, How separated?
In life so close, so bound so loyal, in death one lies in foreign soil;
A Scarborough grave holds Haworth's spoil
A vacant place created.

But one of the dead, a lonely vigil keeps.
A sister who can never rest without the one she loved the best,
She longs to flee that awful nest
And find the soul she seeks.

Simpler than a child, stronger than a man,
Disturbed and restless in her tomb, encased within death's
dungeon room,
Laid deep within St Michael's womb,
She longs for gentle Anne.

Lonely spirit held, struggling to be free;
If anyone could ever rise, to stalk the hills and cross the skies,
To break the chains and gain her prize,
It would be Emily.

The Brontë Family: Sibling Rivalry and a Burial in Paradise

Moving shadow glides, brave and tireless soul.
Through Yorkshire clay and fields of chalk, the empty Wolds,
the Vale of York,
For seventy lonely miles she'll walk
To reach her precious goal.

Finally she comes, silent is her tread,
And there beside the grave she stands, clasps ancient stone with
trembling hands
And pleading with the night demands
The right to claim her dead.

Pounding waves below, raging skies above.
All through the night her frantic calls reverberate round castle
walls
On crumbling graves their echo falls
Sad cries for Emily's love.

No-one ever hears, no lost voice replies.
So sinking down upon the grave she weeps for one she cannot save,
Nor bear away to Haworth's knave
To share her deep demise.

Sorrow bound she goes, bleak and dark the span.
Returning to her resting place, turns to the wall her saddened
face
And in the dust her fingers trace
The cherished name of Anne.

On her gentle slope, high above the sea
Sweet sister lies in her domain, quite unaware of Emily's pain.
In Paradise she will remain
For all eternity.

(Erin Ray)

Chapter One

The Birth Order and Genetic Inheritance of the Brontë Siblings

In this book, my intention is to take a look at the Brontë siblings from the perspective of their birth order and its resulting rivalry. I am doing this in order to understand and explain the behaviour and consequences that this engendered in the entire family, but with a specific focus on Anne. This is not a new idea generally, but it is a neglected area of Brontë studies which has never been fully explored. We have accepted many versions of the Brontës' lives as facts because servants, friends and eye witnesses have reported their observations. However, the bulk of information is in the form of letters, written mostly by Patrick and Charlotte and their friends and acquaintances. Added to this are the hundreds of books and articles which have reported and repeated years of unprovable 'facts'. This has led to very little actual criticism of the family as a unit or individually. Once a person has been labelled a genius, very few biographers are prepared to challenge or even question the information they glean from the books and letters of others.

It is not my intention to investigate the merits of the Brontës' works or criticise their writings, although I will make some references to their novels and poetry, especially Anne's. My focus is to look further into their motivations and behaviour in the light of common family traits and sibling interaction. The Brontës were not a straightforward or typical family of their time and they follow some very different social experiences to their neighbours. One can link some, if not the majority, of their behaviour and characteristics to their inherited genes, their gender and the order in which they were born, along with the losses and depravation they suffered in both childhood and adulthood.

When we are born, we are the latest version of our families, in a long line that goes back millennia – to the very beginnings of life. Even so, we tend to focus on our immediate parents and grandparents as having the most profound influence. It is their abilities and experiences that are usually put into practice during our upbringing.

Our birth is an inescapable dilemma for us which cannot be altered. All of our history brings us to that one child, that one result of generations of interbreeding that makes each child a unique product of their genetic inheritance. No-one can alter these remarkable facts of existence and no-one can re-live their lives. We are totally at the mercy of our genes and the people who nurture us. Their behaviour towards us and the environment in which we discover ourselves, together provide the building blocks of our development from infant to adult. What, I maintain, is especially important to note is that we are not born with inherited religion, evil, good, prejudice or morals, any more than any other animal. These are taught by our carers, teachers, circumstances and lifestyles long before we have the knowledge and ability to choose. These may or may not alter as we learn to distinguish and decide what route we wish to take throughout our lives, although by adulthood, it is often too late as we may, in many areas, already be indoctrinated, for better or worse. Unfortunately, labelling of children also begins at birth and what may seem benign names, at first, can develop into traits and personalities that the child develops growing up. For example: sensitive, noisy, shy, pretty, stupid, slow, silly, funny, serious, difficult, etc.

In her book *Birth Order Blues*, Meri Wallace stresses the importance of not labelling or comparing one's children. She states that:

> *It is important to avoid inadvertently setting up a competition between (your children) by using labels, or by playing favourites with one child.*[1]

I maintain that labelling children can become an effective and damaging way of affecting their natural growth and development. Tell a child that it is slow and stupid, as I have heard people do, and you can get an adverse reaction that will reinforce that label or cause an anti-social reaction. All children are different individuals and all develop at different rates. Siblings, even twins, are not the same and all have differing reactions to their childhood even within the same family structure and upbringing. To compare the Brontë siblings with each other, or anyone else, is, I suggest, a useless and unproductive exercise. They may have been like each other at times and looked or behaved in similar ways, but they were, like all of us, different and unique. When Ellen Nussey described Emily and Anne as 'like twins', she set in motion a false labelling that has endured over the last 200 years. I will demonstrate in later chapters how very different all the sisters were and the reasons why.

Inherited genes are not the only influence on a child and it has long been a debate as to the effects of nature and nurture on the growing infant. By the time most children have reached beyond their early years, the pattern of their personality and experience are fairly well established. It was that wise Greek philosopher, Aristotle, writing in the third century BC, who stated:

Give me a child until he is seven and I will show you the man.[2]

This philosophy is still held today and coincides with the physical and mental changes that occur roughly every seven years as the child develops into an adult. A child's brain, from birth to the age of five, develops at a greater rate than at any other time in its life. This stage has a lasting impact on its ability to learn. Aristotle is observing that the first seven years are when the child develops most of its abilities, personality and characteristics, which it will then carry through life.

A further and important issue arises also from the whereabouts in the family hierarchy a child is born. There has been intensive debate around the issue of birth order and its effects on the child, its siblings and its parents or primary carers. Research into birth order has suggested a number of outcomes. The focus lies on the eldest, the youngest, the first boy and the first girl and the only child. It also examines how this affects other children who do not carry any of these titles. As I shall demonstrate, in the Brontë family the natural birth order dissolved on the deaths of the two eldest girls and upset the attitudes and behaviour of the remaining four children for the rest of their lives.

In the third edition of *The Birth Order Book* by Dr Kevin Leman, he states that:

The intimate relationships that develop in the family can be found nowhere else on earth. And these relationships are created in great part by your order of birth... The relationship between you and your parent is fluid, dynamic, and all-important.[3]

Before I examine these statements, it is important to place the Brontë and Branwell families in context and show how the Brontës' parents developed as children themselves and how their differences and similarities brought them together. How our parents met and produced offspring is, in Western culture, almost always accidental, although often the result of a limited social circle or common interests. People meet in all manner of circumstances and that chance chemical reaction between two people produces the next generation with all its mixed ancestry.

I find it important to mention the history of the Brontë family, both in Ireland, where their father Patrick Prunty/Brunty was born and raised, and in Cornwall, the birthplace and childhood home of their mother, Maria Branwell. It is interesting to note that Patrick was the eldest of ten children and that Maria, although the eleventh of twelve children, was the youngest child for six years before the twelfth and final child was born.

A major study on child care reported by John Bowlby in the 1950s and 1960s in Britain was an important and enlightened step forward in understanding the development of children under adverse conditions. One of Bowlby's findings suggested that social workers and psychiatrists look to the childhood of the parents when assessing the behaviour and development of their children. We do not know all of the circumstances of the Brontë children's parents and grandparents, but we know a little. We can examine the recent forebears of Patrick and Maria and better understand the circumstances in which they came to rear their own children and a little of their education and beliefs. This couple had parents of widely different backgrounds but had an instant attraction to each other on first meeting in the summer of 1812, in West Yorkshire, England. Whilst it is not my intention to rewrite the well documented lives of Patrick and Maria before their marriage, the following is a potted version which can highlight the gulfs and similarities between them.

Patrick Prunty, or Brunty, as the family name was then spelt or spoken, was born to an impoverished couple, Hugh and Eleanor (also known as Alice, nee McCory) in a tiny, two-roomed cottage near Drumballyrooney in County Down, north-east Ireland, on St Patrick's day, March 17, 1777. There is dispute as to Eleanor's faith, but it is suggested that she was from a Catholic background and Hugh, according to Anne's biographer, Dr Edward Chitham, had no religious loyalty, although nearly all of the Prunty family are buried in the local Protestant churchyard. Interestingly, legend states that Hugh was a proficient storyteller, an attribute that appears to have been inherited by Patrick and his offspring.

Patrick, often a recognised Catholic name, after Ireland's patron saint who brought Christianity to the country, may be significant here, although it could have been chosen because of the coincidence of his birth on the saint's day. Rural County Down was an agricultural area and Hugh Prunty ran a kiln and laboured on the land. The couple went on to have nine more children and moved to a larger dwelling and farmed land of their own. Large families were not uncommon in Britain during this time, but not necessarily because of the poor infant mortality rate, as is often blamed. It was rather due to the lack of any form of reliable birth control. Also, the Christian Church viewed children as a gift from God and to inhibit their conception was to go against His will and blessing. This was especially maintained in the Catholic religion where birth control is often, even now, unacceptable.

Patrick showed all the signs of an intelligent and enthusiastic child who soon learnt to read and value education as a means of gaining work and status. He did not want to follow in his father's footsteps but hankered after teaching. He worked in various jobs, including blacksmithing and weaving whilst attending school. His love of learning and belief in education led to him running a small school of a few local children when he was only 16. This enthusiasm for education was matched only with Patrick's belief in God. He held Protestant leanings and whilst tutoring the children of local Anglican clergyman Thomas Tighe, his employer felt that Patrick had the potential to go to university and study to become a minister. Patrick was too poor to pay his way but managed to save enough money, over a number of years whilst studying incredibly hard, to pay for his entry fee of £10 into Cambridge University, England. He left Ireland in the autumn of 1802, aged 25, to become a sizer – a charity scholarship which Patrick complimented with various tutoring, awards and prizes for his studies. Whether by accident or design, he was registered as Patrick Brontë, possibly from a misunderstanding of his strong Irish accent. However, Patrick's admiration for Lord Nelson, who had been awarded the title Duke of Brontë, may have prompted Patrick to take this name, so similar to his own, in honour of his hero. Patrick had sponsorship from such notable figures as William Wilberforce and his associates.

After studying for four years at St John's College, Cambridge, Patrick left with a BA degree and as a novice minister in the Church of England. It is testimony to his dogged determination and natural intelligence that a poor boy from Ireland achieved such high honours. Patrick was impressed with, and drawn to, the Evangelical type of preaching advocated by the Wesley brothers, John and Charles. These men had been known to Thomas Tighe who had accommodated them in his home before they moved on to preach in Cornwall, where they were known and welcomed by the Branwell family. Evangelical preaching involves going out into the community to spread the word of God, and writing tracts for people to read and learn of religious beliefs and practices. Charles Wesley wrote over 6000 rousing hymns, which also helped people to enjoy the celebration of God and join in with their fellow man in a way that did not exclude those who could not read or write. Patrick was noted as a preacher who spoke '*extempore*', meaning that he had no written sermon to preach from but could '*ad lib*' as necessary. This allowed the preacher to link local and national events that his congregation could identify with. This impromptu method brings the minister closer to his people and means that anyone in the congregation is able to understand and relate to the sermon. It is a relaxed and more informal way of preaching that avoids set dogma and the obscure meanings in some religious teachings.

After his ordination as a priest by the Bishop of Salisbury at St James' Palace, London, in 1807, Patrick began taking up various curacies. By 1809 he had gradually made his way to Yorkshire, where he worked first in Dewsbury and later at Hartshead-cum-Clifton, near Liversedge in the West Riding. In true evangelical tradition, Patrick began to write poems and religious tracts to help spread his message, including *Winter-night Meditations* and, later, *Cottage Poems*.

Around 1811, in Apperley Bridge, near Yeadon, some twelve miles from Liversedge, Wesleyan Methodist leaders were looking for a place to house and train the sons of Methodist ministers into the Evangelical clergy. They chose the large and lovely Georgian house named Woodhouse Grove. Its newly elected governor would be John Fennell and his wife Jane Branwell, the uncle and aunt of Maria Branwell. By 1812 Patrick was invited to examine the boys in the classics at this new school.

The above is a very brief history of Patrick's life until the age of 35 when he finally met his future wife, in the summer of 1812. One can appreciate what an intelligent and driven man he was. Various reports during his first curacies describe him as tall, slender, very good with children, quick to defend the weak and often a little hot-tempered. He was also outspoken and devoted to his congregation with an absolute faith in God.

Patrick appears to have been rather reticent when speaking of his first twenty-five years in Ireland. He gave a very brief account to Mrs Gaskell when she was researching his family history for her book on Charlotte's life. Whether he was embarrassed by his lowly beginnings is hard to establish. Perhaps he was just eager to relish his status as the Reverend Patrick Brontë, a title he had fought so hard to obtain and a status far beyond his family's wildest expectations.

In these years between Patrick's birth and meeting his wife, the British Isles experienced enormous changes. The French Revolution and the war in America unnerved the British government and the rise of Napoleon was a constant threat to peace. However, the greatest effects came from within, with the huge impact of the Industrial Revolution. The move from an agricultural to an industrial state altered the way of life for the whole of England, the British Isles and eventually the world. Major discoveries in engineering, science and manufacturing changed the way of life of its citizens and altered the land for ever. Cottage industries became centralised in the factories and mills, which attracted thousands of people to the towns and destroyed a rural way of life that had existed for centuries. Invention of the steam engine was possibly the major advocate of change, introducing machinery that would overtake manpower.

It is hard to appreciate the changes that were taking place so rapidly. Perhaps comparison with our digital age is one analogy which helps us to recognise how one major invention can infiltrate lives and change habits over a very short space of time. Where there is change there is often political movement and upheaval. Wealth and poverty increases exponentially and the law has to change to accommodate new ideas and to legislate to control changes in lifestyle and the threat of social unrest. Religion had long been part of the way of life, but scientific discovery and later Darwin, helped to alter, if not remove belief in the Bible and to question man's faith in a higher being.

The aristocracy and royalty were very much leaders in all areas of social behaviour. Patrick and Maria were both born into the Georgian era, with George III on the throne from 1760 to 1820. Although England became a constitutional monarchy in 1689, the king was still held in high esteem and, as now, was responsible for opening Parliament, though he was not allowed to legislate. During the eighteenth century unrest in Ireland was engendered and continued after the Act of Union in 1801, which sought to dissolve the Irish Parliament and reassert and maintain British and Protestant control of Irish politics and reforms from Westminster. Britain was, of course, a male society in all areas of law and politics, education and business.

Whilst a man of the Church, Patrick could be roused to uphold what he saw as a just cause. His philanthropic and charitable nature brought him into the struggle over many issues where he encountered hardship, lack of education and poverty. He was also ready to fight for his country and trained with his fellow students at Cambridge as a soldier under the leadership of the future prime minister, Lord Palmerston. This was during the time of the Napoleonic wars when many were expecting an invasion of Britain. One can appreciate the turbulent times that Britain was facing in the late eighteenth and early nineteenth centuries.

Into all this upheaval, Maria Branwell was born in Penzance, Cornwall on 15 April 1783, the eleventh child of Thomas and Anne Branwell (nee Carne). Penzance was, at this time, a thriving coastal port of around 4000 inhabitants. It suffered stormy and cold winters beside the English Channel, but warm and sunny summers, especially missed by the Branwell sisters when they lived at Haworth. Maria was born into a wealthy and privileged lifestyle, totally opposite to that of her future husband. Wealth does not omit tragedy however, and the Branwell's suffered the loss of five of their offspring. Maria's nearest sibling, at almost seven years older, was Elizabeth, a girl who had inherited the name of a dead sister. Maria remained the youngest until an unexpected twelfth pregnancy brought Charlotte Branwell into the world, when her mother, Anne Branwell, was 46 years old.

Whilst wealth and prestige were enjoyed by the Branwells, this does not take away their grief at the loss of their children. It is often stated that death in infancy or childhood was a common phenomenon, especially in large families. This is true, at a time before the introduction of health reforms and the discovery of medicines like penicillin in the twentieth century. These medicines helped to minimise the losses by treating many lethal childhood diseases. However, there is a flippant attitude here that does not begin to explore and expose the suffering of both the parents and children in a household where death occurs. Children who witness the death and suffering of their siblings are also traumatised and today many disciplines may attempt to address this type of stress with counselling, or psychological and psychiatric input designed to help victims to deal with, and hopefully overcome, their trauma.

The Royal Manchester Children's Hospital publishes information on Adverse Childhood Experiences (ACE's) and Attachment, explaining that:

> *The experiences we have in our lives and particularly in our early childhood have a huge impact on how we grow and develop, our physical and mental health, and our thoughts, feelings and behaviour. Two important factors to think about when considering our mental well-being, are the quality of our attachments (i.e. parent and child relationships) and our experience of adverse childhood experiences.*[4]

I shall demonstrate this more in later chapters when discussing the Brontë family. Sufficient to highlight here is that Elizabeth Branwell, the elder sister who Maria came to rely on, was a victim of ACE, and would have recognised the signs and symptoms in her nieces and nephew years later. We now understand and acknowledge the behaviour and emotions expressed by children affected by trauma, but this is a relatively new branch of medical science. Post Traumatic Stress Disorder. (PTSD) was eventually recognised and treated following the harrowing experiences and behaviours of soldiers during and following the first World War.

Maria's birth, after her family's losses must have been a special blessing and for the next six years, she was the youngest, cosseted and much-loved daughter and sister. Her father, Thomas Branwell, was a merchant and a popular and notable figure in the town. The family moved to fashionable Chapel Street as his businesses expanded and they led an affluent lifestyle. They socialised within the community and Thomas was not averse to the sport of trying to outwit the local excise men! His import and export trade thrived and his only surviving son, Benjamin, was soon following in his father's footsteps, eventually becoming the town's mayor.

Sharon Wright, in her book *The Mother of the Brontës*, describes Penzance in the 1700s as:

> *Though often seen as remote and isolated by the rest of eighteenth-century Britain, Maria's prosperous home town was in reality a hub of regional and international trade.*[5]

The Branwell family were at the heart of this expansion in commercial growth with properties and businesses throughout the town. Maria and her sisters were elegant and fashionable young ladies who attended all the important social gatherings. The girls were well educated at home, in all the desired feminine attributes – reading, needlework, good manners, writing, music and the arts. Maria Branwell is reported as having musical ability and this may account for her children's skills, years later. The Branwell girls grew into prosperous and attractive women and the eldest two, Margaret and Jane, soon found husbands, After Benjamin married, only Elizabeth, Maria and Charlotte were left at home. By now, Thomas was a town councillor and a busy churchman. The Branwells were Anglicans who had leanings to Wesleyan Methodism and embraced the Wesley brothers and their evangelical method of preaching when they came to Cornwall. Methodism appealed to many who disliked the preachings of the high Church and preferred the simpler and more friendly methods employed by the Wesley brothers.

An important fact that Sharon Wright highlights in her book is that along with religious faith, the Cornish people had their own long held beliefs in myth and legends, the supernatural and pagan phenomena. I suggest that this also applied to the Irish and it is a particular area in which the Irish and Cornish were linked. Patrick was not averse to regaling his children with Celtic tales of their Irish ancestors and the myths surrounding folk tales and legends.

Tragedy struck the Branwell family in 1808 when Thomas died and his brother, Richard, inherited the house at 25 Chapel Street. Provision had been made in Thomas's will for his wife, and she and the three youngest girls moved to a house in Causewayhead, Penzance. They were joined by their elder sister, Jane, who had fled from her errant clergyman husband, John Kingston, in America. She had returned home with only Eliza, the youngest of her five children.

The Branwell's cousin, Jane, had left Penzance with her parents, John and Jane Fennell, in 1806 and moved to Shropshire. John Fennell was an ardent evangelical minister and when appointed to Woodhouse Grove School in 1811, he moved his family to the new Methodist establishment in West Yorkshire, where he and his wife would be responsible for the care and education of the sons of Methodist ministers. Despite their daughter's assistance, the task was overwhelming and Aunt Jane wrote to her niece, Maria Branwell, later that year, appealing for help with their huge task.

Maria's mother had died suddenly in 1809 leaving her four surviving daughters and little Eliza, at Causewayhead. A £50 annuity had been settled on each of the girls in their father's will, which was for life and allowed the young women to stay independently at home yet still have the funds to furnish a good social lifestyle. They were attractive, well-educated and pious. When the call came from Aunt Jane Fennell, Maria was 29 years old and happy to go and help out, not necessarily for the long term but certainly for a while. She looked forward to being with her aunt and uncle and cousin Jane and soon packed her belongings, sending them by ship before following overland on the long, 400-mile journey to Yorkshire.

The scene is now set, where generations of Irish and Cornish families meet, marry and interbreed to produce offspring with the genetics that have dominated and reproduced over centuries. Later in the nineteenth century, Charles Darwin, whilst referring to various animal species, introduced the idea of Convergence and Divergence which, I suggest, can be easily applied to humans. Darwin observed how species of different types or origins could converge to produce similar behaviours and characteristics. Similarly, animals of a common ancestor could diverge and develop as different types. Put simply into a human context, one can see here how parents converge and their offspring diverge, into similar but different characters.

Woodhouse Grove School was, therefore, the meeting place for Patrick and Maria and they married only six months later. After their marriage on 29 December 1812, Mr and Mrs Brontë went to live at Harsthead-cum-Clifton, near Dewsbury, where Patrick was now the incumbent of the local church, having received his own ministry in 1811. The newly-weds moved into Clough House in Hightown, about a mile from the church. The couple had a house, an income of £115, plus Maria's allowance, and were happy together with their small but engaging congregation and a recognised social status. Patrick was 35 and Maria 29 years old. They were comfortable rather than affluent and both had total faith in their God. They were old enough and wise enough to live sensibly and harmoniously together. Whilst Patrick saw to his new parish, Maria would entertain and aid its parishioners, carrying out the expected duties of a minister's wife.

Here we have a situation where two people from totally opposite backgrounds and experiences combine in mind and body in a strong and devoted partnership. It must be remembered however, that this was an age of patriarchal dominance. Patrick was the eldest child and a strong and intelligent man, living in a world where tradition, and the law, dictated that he was the leader and the decision maker. Maria was formerly the youngest child and had the position of the female who is loved and pampered by her older siblings, but who has always been subject to her father's dominance and her brother's influence. Although she had gained some independence after the deaths of her parents, marriage meant subservience and obedience to her husband. I do not suggest that Patrick was cruel or unkind to his wife, only that they both had a role to play and that wherever Patrick went in their lives and whatever decisions he made or whatever he chose to do, Maria would have to follow and support him. With regard to raising a family, Maria would submit naturally to her husband and if children arrived then that was God's will. For Maria, they arrived swiftly and repeatedly. Her first baby was born in April 1814 – a girl, christened Maria.

Maria Brontë was therefore the eldest, the first girl and the only child for the first year before her sister, Elizabeth, arrived on 8 February 1815. The family had outgrown Hartshead and Patrick sought a larger home and parish. Around this time, he was approached by the vicar of Thornton, the Reverend Thomas Atkinson, to exchange livings and Patrick welcomed the move. Thornton lay about four miles from Bradford and was familiar to Patrick, who had friends and dealings in and around the city. Patrick became the perpetual minister at Thornton and on 19 May 1815 the Brontës moved to the parsonage, a tied house that relieved the need to provide rent. Patrick's stipend increased to £140 per annum and the larger parish and freedom to socialise allowed the family to make friends and acquaintances in a wider, yet specific, social circle.

Patrick had now achieved the recognition and status of a minister with his own parish and home. The addition of a loving wife and a small family added to his happiness and he enjoyed preaching and writing for his parishioners. Patrick later commented that these years were some of the happiest of his life. Maria had help with the children following the employment of a nursemaid, Sarah Garrs, and continued to make friends and enjoy their acquaintance. This middle-class lifestyle was something Maria was used to and Patrick obviously enjoyed. Their friends were people of the professional classes and some became godparents and gave continuing support to the Brontë family for many years to come.

The year following the move, Maria gave birth to a third daughter, Charlotte, on 21 April 1816. The pattern of a baby each year continued and on June 26 1817 came the welcome arrival of the first boy, christened Patrick Branwell, but always known as Branwell. The following year saw the arrival of the fourth daughter, Emily Jane, on 30 July 1818. Even with extra help, the parsonage was becoming crowded and busy. Maria would have spent more and more time caring for her young family. On 17 January 1820, her fifth daughter, Anne was born. With six children under seven years of age one can only imagine the need for constant attention and organisation in the household. An extra nursemaid was employed, Sarah's sister, Nancy. Maria's sister, Elizabeth Branwell, had also travelled to Thornton to assist Maria in her pregnancies and births, strengthening their close bond and introducing and familiarising the children with their aunt Elizabeth.

Early in 1820, and after prolonged negotiations and setbacks, Patrick was able to accept another new post, that of the perpetual curacy of St Michael and All Saints Church at Haworth, around six miles to the west of Thornton, and here the family, servants, goods and chattels all relocated to the parsonage. Aunt

Elizabeth was able to return to Penzance, but it still meant accommodating ten people in the new dwelling.

Haworth parsonage, as I have often described, was a strange and unique Georgian house. It stands to this day on a rise above the village and is an attractive and solid four bedroomed accommodation with two front parlours, a kitchen, a back room and a small cellar. Built in 1778, the materials for its construction came almost exclusively from the wide moorlands that reached from the foot of the back door across a number of miles, into the neighbouring county of Lancashire. Stone and slate for the building came from the quarries on the moors and its peat was burnt in the fireplaces. The house stands four-square to the compass points and symbolises the meeting of the secular, the divine and the natural. I shall further explore the effects of the house on the Brontë siblings in later chapters but it is an integral part, along with its surroundings, of the Brontë psyche.

Like anyone born and brought up in the same house and place, they had fond and enduring memories, both good and bad. All of the Brontës loved their home and its surroundings. George Eliot describes this sense of place when speaking of Mr Tulliver in *The Mill on the Floss* who:

> *Couldn't bear to think of himself living in any other spot – where he knew the sound of every gate and door ... because his growing senses had fed on them.*[6]

Here we understand and appreciate Emily, Charlotte and Anne's homesickness both at school and at work. Their home held both sadness and happiness, but it was theirs and they needed its familiarity and protection. It is hard to see Branwell so much in this light as his enforced stay at home throughout his childhood and adolescence possibly turned him against its overshadowing presence in his life. However, he never settled well away from it and came home whenever his life was in turmoil, which was often. Despite its size and detached status, the parsonage was still a tight squeeze for ten people and offered no spare rooms or quiet spaces. Patrick needed, and automatically claimed, one of the front parlours as his exclusive study and the rest of the house was allocated according to the needs of everyone else at any given time.

We can now return to the focus of this study of the Brontë siblings – their birth order and sibling rivalry. Anne is my priority but to understand Anne, one needs to acknowledge her place in the pecking order. Anne was not yet the youngest child, only the fifth daughter. There is no reason not to believe that both of her parents would have expected more children to follow and this may well have been the case had not Maria fallen seriously ill in January 1821. Whether she had also suffered miscarriages during her marriage is unknown, but a possibility.

The Birth Order and Genetic Inheritance of the Brontë Siblings

Even with help, one can only imagine the ordered chaos that the parsonage household contained around this time. Six children between seven years and twelve months old, would produce an enormous amount of work for the three women in the house. The washing, dressing and feeding alone would have taken up most of the day. Each child was at a crucial stage of growth and needed as much attention as possible to nurture their development. The Garrs sisters were not educated young women and were there to help with the work load rather than as educators or governesses. Only their mother and their father, when able, could instruct the children in any meaningful way at a time when each child was rapidly developing their abilities and personalities.

Then suddenly, during all this melee, Mrs Brontë became seriously ill and was confined to bed for the next nine months until her death in September 1821. In my next chapter I will examine the effects of maternal depravation and loss and how it can interrupt the natural development of a child and actually inhibit, or even eradicate, stages in their physical and mental progress.

What is notable at this point in the family history is the practical dynamics that Patrick faced during his wife's illness. His stipend was barely £3.00 a week. He had six small children and two servants and an entire parish to manage. He needed help of every kind. The move from Thornton had isolated him from friends, godparents and neighbours who would have assisted him. Haworth parsonage stood above and detached from a village wrought with overcrowding and poverty. That had seemed beneficial at the time, but now Patrick's class and position in the community set the family apart, physically and psychologically. His meagre income inhibited his ability to spend on vital medicines, doctors and nurses for his wife and still provide for his family. In fact, Patrick got into debt in his frantic search for help and it was only when Elizabeth Branwell came back from Cornwall to help the stricken family and dismiss an unsuitable nurse, that Patrick got any relief during those dreadful months.

Meanwhile, his children – between Maria the eldest and Anne, the youngest – had to be looked after mainly by the Garrs sisters. Anne, and possibly Emily, were not likely to have been weaned when their mother became ill but the practice of wet nursing was a tradition used mainly by the upper classes at the time and was probably beyond Patrick's financial means. Interruption of weaning may also have affected Anne's health. Children were breastfed for a much longer time, partly for financial reasons and partly because it was acknowledged that breast milk not only gave all of the nutrients a child needed but also some protection from disease. It was also believed that whilst breastfeeding a woman was less likely to become pregnant. This is true to a point as it can inhibit ovulation but only for a limited time.

Maria, as the eldest child, and already noted for her intelligence and ability, was undoubtedly given responsibilities beyond her years as she, and possibly

Elizabeth, were commandeered into playing the roles of elder children in helping to take care of the younger ones. In later years, Charlotte would describe her eldest sister as being a 'little mother' to her siblings. Maria and Elizabeth would be acutely aware of their mother's suffering and probably understood what was happening around them. Whilst the younger children would have been less informed, their routines would be altered and upset and the need to stay relatively quiet during the day and asleep at night, would have put added pressure on them all.

If they had one huge advantage, it lay in the vast moorland playground lying outside of their back door, and this is where all of the children, with their nurse, would spend many hours in play and uninhibited freedom. This vast and natural landscape was the backdrop to their childhood and a major influence on their development both as children and later, as writers. Freed from the restrictions of age, gender and the need to stay quiet, they could do what all children love most – run, shout, play and express themselves without fear or reprimand. Without this asset, the Brontë children would have been solely dependent on life in the parsonage for almost every hour of their childhood and, especially during times of illness and death, it could have become a prison, rather than a home.

What we see in these trying months of 1821 are six children bereft of their mother's attention and yet all trying to grow and develop in a house of sadness, sickness and anxiety, which would only become worse. Patrick must have been overwhelmed by all the people needing his attention, not least his wife and children. He nursed his wife, day and night, throughout these long months and watched her suffer the agony of cancer, with no modern medicines or palliative remedies. Likewise, Elizabeth Branwell lived again through the trauma of the illness and death of a beloved sibling whilst simultaneously trying to comfort and organise her nephew and nieces. It was a terrible time for the family and it could only end in the tragedy of Maria's death.

There is nothing in writing by the children or their Aunt Elizabeth from this time. Patrick wrote of his wife's suffering and his heartache but it hardly conveys the full trauma of what he must have felt. He had only his faith and his duty to his family to keep him sane and able to function. His sister-in-law's help and support must have been a comfort to him, but he would have made a strong and valiant attempt to stay calm and positive in front of his offspring. This was a time when Patrick's faith in God would have been tested to the limit, but he had no choice but to strive daily to help and comfort his wife whilst knowing that there was no hope of her recovery.

When her mother died, Anne was twenty months old. She was probably walking, talking, but not in sentences, and possibly not yet toilet trained. As the youngest, she was kept closer to her aunt, probably seen as needing extra attention because of her age and lack of skills, but also as needing more love and affection from a female mother substitute. Anne was now officially the youngest child, unless her father re-married and had further offspring. She was at the stage in her development where she was learning a number of skills simultaneously, but there could only be a limited amount of time allotted to each child. Anne may have received more attention than her sisters, because of her dependency, but her brother would also, through his status as the only boy, receive extra notice. The remaining children would all be vying for whatever attention was left available.

The death of a loving parent removes half of a child's care, mentorship and security. If the child is one of many, there has to be rivalry for attention, whether consciously or unconsciously performed. Humans are animals who crave recognition, help and attention, especially when young, where there is a fight for survival and the need to establish a hierarchy. A child is soon acutely aware if a sibling is receiving more or better attention than they are. This imbalance and subsequent rivalry can last a lifetime.

In her article on adverse childhood experiences, Ciara Crummey writes about the effects of major trauma on children and their inability to cope with the added pressures of siblings all competing for attention. She says:

> *The potential consequences of these biological alterations following exposure to ACE (Adverse Childhood Experiences) include impaired social and cognitive development and compromised immune systems, increasing the risk of adverse adult health outcomes and early morbidity.*[7]

One can recognise that it was not just deaths that plagued the Brontë siblings, but also the girls' disastrous times at school and their constant rivalry for love and attention from an elderly aunt with little or no experience of motherhood and a father with a huge parish to organise and serve.

Modern research emphasises that prolonged and unremitting exposure to adverse conditions do not allow the child's stress levels to return to normal between traumas. Bucci *et al.* (2016) explain that:

> *With a normal stress response, the individual returns back to normal levels through self-regulation buffers, established through effective coping mechanisms and parental support. However, prolonged, repeated or chronic exposure to stressors such as ACE's, without effective returns to normal levels, can result in a prolonged or frequent activation of the stress response, known as toxic stress. When this stress response occurs during influential*

> *periods of brain development, without the effective buffers, this can become ingrained into the long-term biological processes and alter stress responses, resulting in adverse responses to any future stressors.*[8]

My suggestion is that the Brontë siblings were exposed to some extreme and ongoing pressures, tragedies and losses in childhood, adolescence and adulthood, which inhibited their development in certain areas and led to mental and physical disorders which affected their life long ability to adequately cope in socio-emotional situations. Furthermore, that it affected their interaction with each other and explains some aspects of their personalities and behaviour within the family circle.

Chapter Two

The Lasting Effects of Maternal Deprivation

During the long months of their mother's illness, Patrick took every advice and help that he could muster or afford. His wife's diagnosis was not readily available. It is only nowadays that we can analyse her symptoms and the presumption has been that she probably died of uterine cancer. However, an article in *Brontë Transactions* by the eminent Professor Philip Rhodes, stated in 1972, that in his opinion 'Maria could not have died of uterine cancer based upon the evidence we have'.[1] Instead, he hypothesised that she died of chronic pelvic sepsis and anaemia, brought on by the birth of her last child, Anne Brontë.

Untreated uterine pain, whether cancer or sepsis, is appalling and unremitting. Maria Brontë died after months of agony and her suffering must have made life for her and her family extremely traumatic. There was no cure and very little medication. Laudanum, a mixture of opium and alcohol, would have been only a palliative relief. Her suffering was almost too much for Patrick and Elizabeth to witness. One has to be aware that having to watch impotently whilst a loved one is suffering is almost as traumatic for the carer as the sufferer. When I recall my own mother's prolonged and agonising death, it is my helplessness that I recall and that is the hardest to bear. Even as a qualified nurse myself, there was nothing I could do to relieve her pain, and even modern medicine was only a temporary relief. Two hundred years earlier, Maria Brontë and her devoted husband and sister must have suffered tremendous torment. It is this emotional pain that would last the rest of their lives and they, as adults, would be no more able to cope with it than the children. At her death, her children would have probably been present and most certainly have seen and kissed their mother's dead body, as was custom and practice at the time.

The entire family were, naturally, devastated and Patrick wrote later of how hard it was for him to face each day – even the chattering of his children brought him heartache in his despair. It was most probably owing to his complete faith in God and that His will dictated life and death that Patrick managed to carry on. We are not told of how the children reacted. We can only speculate on their loss. What we do now know is that research done in the late twentieth century demonstrated profound effects on children deprived of their mothers. John Bowlby, in his famous treatise on this subject, stated that:

> *(Studies) make it plain that when deprived of maternal care, a child's development is almost always retarded, physically, intellectually and socially and that symptoms of physical and mental illness may appear. Such evidence is disquieting, but sceptics may question whether the check is permanent and whether the symptoms of illness may not be easily overcome. The retrospective and follow-up studies make it clear that such optimism is not always justified and that some children are gravely damaged for life.*[2]

Bowlby investigated many areas of maternal deprivation, including family homes, institutions, orphanages, refugees etc., anywhere where children were separated from their mothers, for whatever reason. He noted that even in tiny infants of only a few weeks old, deprivation had effects on the child's development. He noted that:

> *In the second and third years of life [Branwell, Emily and Anne] the emotional response to separation is not only just as severe, but substitute mothers are often rejected out of hand, a child becoming acutely and inconsolably distressed for a period of days, weeks or even longer, without a single break... Only exhaustion brings sleep, and comfort are alike refused.*[3]

We know that in childhood Anne was closest to her aunt, and that Branwell stated upon her death that she was the 'only mother I ever knew'. However, this does not mean that their aunt replaced their mother. I suggest that all of the children respected their aunt and were very fond of her and acknowledged her care, but she was not their mother and never could be. When researching the behaviour of Charlotte and Emily as adults, one suspects that they did not necessarily see eye to eye with their aunt. We can admire Elizabeth Branwell from the distance of time and laud her sacrifice, but we do not know how able she was to offer the love and comfort of their mother. She had strict ideas and old-fashioned and different experiences to their father and there was possibly friction at times between these two adults, which the children will have absorbed.

Realising that despite his loss his children needed a mother and he a companion, Patrick later began to make efforts to remarry. When these plans came to nothing, he had to resign himself to a life with no wife and six small children who needed him even more. To his relief, his sister-in-law agreed to stay on as a mother substitute until such time as circumstances changed and she could return home to Cornwall. As we know, this did not happen and Elizabeth never returned to her native home. For the next twenty years this amazing woman devoted her life to her nephew and nieces. She was 45 years old when her sister died, a spinster with a limited experience of child care. Her life was completely altered and her position in society permanently curtailed.

We know little about the Brontë children for definite during the years following their mother's death but certain patterns evolved and were noted, that one can rely on. There was now an established hierarchy and pecking order amongst the children. Maria, the 'little mother' fulfilled her role towards her siblings as she was promoted, possibly to perform and assist, beyond her years. She was remembered with love and deep affection by her siblings, years after her death. Patrick marvelled at Maria's ability to read and converse when still very small and obviously encouraged and promoted his eldest child and came to rely on her to help her aunt and care for her younger siblings.

There is a pattern here that tends to identify the eldest child. They are the only ones who have exclusive parental attention, even if only for the first year. They are gradually displaced by siblings but often retain their parents individual attention by behaving well and acting as the older and wiser sibling, who wishes to please. In Linda Blair's book, *Birth Order*, she describes a number of first-born attributes, stating that they:

> ... tend to be law-abiding and respectful of rules and regulations. They take up positions of leadership and may relish being in charge. Partly because of undivided attention in infancy, they tend to be academically successful and are organised and responsible but also may be highly self-critical and less likely to forgive themselves when they make mistakes... Another aspect of the first-born's tendency to anxiety and over-responsibility is that you find it hard to delegate responsibility, even when what you've been asked to do means you become overloaded, stressed and fatigued. You prefer to stay in control even when it wears you out, because you're so afraid that if you lose control, things might go wrong – and that if they do, you'll have only yourself to blame.[4]

I suggest that we see these traits, first in Maria and later in Charlotte when she is promoted to the eldest child. It is important to note that Patrick, an eldest child himself, appears to have been particularly close, proud and fond of first Maria and then, Charlotte.

A recent BBC Sounds programme (Dec 6 2022) focusing on how birth order may affect personality, noted that first-born children tend to hold the highest jobs and status in society. It focused on the high numbers of Nobel Prize winners, presidents and prime ministers, surgeons, airline pilots etc. They noted that these leaders in their field had five particular traits, which rose with age:

- Conscientiousness
- Agreeability according to life events
- Openness to new experiences
- Original ideas
- Honesty

However, these traits could also carry neuroticism. There appears a definite need to take control amongst eldest children.

Elizabeth, the second daughter, does not hold any special place, she is a spare child who was later schooled for housekeeping and domestic work rather than her academic abilities. As so often can be seen, a second child who is of the same gender as the older sibling does not carry a title and is not as noted as the eldest. Next came Charlotte, again a third daughter with no title, her intelligence and abilities not yet apparent. The fourth child is the precious and precocious son. Branwell was the first and only son and he was expected to shine in all areas and to excel beyond the other family members, including his father. Supported by the law and social convention, the male child had a special place in any family, and the first son was the one to inherit through primogeniture, and to uphold and extend the family name in perpetuity.

Branwell could not fail to be a favourite of his father and aunt and to become the adored and cosseted brother to his sisters. They would recognise him, at least in childhood, as superior by definition of his gender and the reactions of the adults towards him. His sisters would treat him accordingly, something he may well have exploited. Emily was the fourth daughter, and again, like Elizabeth and Charlotte, she had no special title or status. Anne, on the other hand, may be the fifth daughter but she is now the youngest and that carries with it a set of behaviours that only the youngest child can experience.

In her book, Linda Blair describes the last-born, or youngest child as often being low in self-esteem. She says that:

> *This characteristic makes sense if you look at life from a last-born's point of view. Everyone around you is bigger, stronger and*

> *more competent than you. You may even have seen yourself as 'behind' from the start... This is through no fault of your own; it's simply because the others have had a head start on life. None the less, this observation may cause you to feel even more helpless than you might have done because what gives your older siblings their advantage – age and experience – is something that you can't change or control in any way.*[5]

Turning to modern research on birth order, certain traits and patterns are explored and explained. Amongst the many books and papers on the subject, authors all tend to categorise children into areas of eldest or first-born, middle-borns, youngest and single child. Eldest children and singles are often described as having high expectations of themselves as encouraged by their primary carers. They have exclusive parental attention for some, if not all of their lives, a special attribute not experienced by younger siblings. Eldest children are most often encouraged to 'grow up' faster as other siblings arrive and are expected to have some responsibility for their younger brothers and sisters and take up positions of leadership. They have an exclusively adult-centred beginning rather than within the company of other children and tend to adopt adult speech and behaviours more readily. However, these traits can cause the eldest or single child pressures and feelings of failure if they cannot live up to the high expectations demanded of them by their primary carers.

Middle children are under far less pressure but may be caught in the battle between the eldest and the youngest, often acting as peacemakers. They are in the dilemma of attempting to attract parental attention whilst trying to avoid upsetting their older or younger rivals and creating various forms of jealousy. For these reasons they tend to give in more readily to peer pressure in order to maintain harmony. Rather than chasing academia, many middle children show more promise in the arts and music.

As we are aware, the human child is helpless and needy for a far longer time than any other mammals. Babies have to adopt ways in which to gain and keep the attention of the people who will provide their needs. As parents are limited in the amount of time they can spend with each child, the children, subconsciously or otherwise, have to find ways in which to engage them, above and beyond their rival siblings. Again, Darwin's observations are useful. He noted that in any family or environment there are limited resources. His survival of the fittest theories included this necessity for each animal, or human, to fight for their needs, often to the detriment of others. It is easy for middle children to feel that they are not getting enough attention and if, after numerous efforts, they fail to gain notice, they may well give up the fight and withdraw into themselves.

The youngest child has many advantages but also disadvantages which will affect their development. They will have carers who are now experienced in child care and the child is often over protected and over indulged by them. This may be partly due to the acknowledgement that this is their last child and the last time they can fulfil their parental role. There is a certain nostalgia attached which can make them subconsciously need to keep that child younger for longer. Unfortunately, this can have a bad side effect because the longer the child is kept in a baby or dependent stage, the more it will receive attention. This can result in it continuing, or indulging, childish ways that perpetuate that state. Older siblings may well copy their parents in this manner and also cosset and spoil the youngest by helping them too much and not allowing them to progress in an independent fashion.

I well remember watching my younger brother, the youngest child, unsuccessfully trying to tie his shoelaces. I couldn't bear to see him struggle and insisted on tying them for him. This continued for some time, until my mother told me off in no uncertain terms. She said, 'How can he learn if you keep doing things for him?' I remember this episode distinctly as he was my little brother and when he got things wrong or got upset, I was desperate to help and to make him feel better. This only lasted for his first few years but, I suggest that in hindsight, I may also have been demonstrating that I could do something better than he could!

The youngest can become the focus of the family and gain the most attention as they are, by virtue of being the youngest, less able, less experienced and, therefore, needing the most help and encouragement. The youngest is never threatened by having a rival younger child so is never pushed into taking second place or encouraged to develop in a way that their older siblings had to. This can also lead to a certain vulnerability, where everyone around you is older, wiser and more experienced. This may allow both the child and their family to see them as less competent and less intelligent.

The negatives of being the youngest can manifest as having an inferiority complex where one's opinions and ideas are not, or cannot be validated because of this presumption that they are less able in all areas. They can be viewed as weak and unable to take responsibility or perform any important tasks. Older siblings often complain that the youngest is 'spoilt' and I have heard and used this term myself when describing my youngest sibling. It is only now that I realise why not only me, but my older siblings also viewed him in this manner. It is a self-perpetuating dilemma that causes the older children to protect and indulge their inexperienced brother or sister, but then to criticise them for being the favourite. For reasons explained, the parents may help to foster this behaviour by expecting and encouraging their other children to assist and indulge their 'weaker' sibling whilst simultaneously doing the same themselves. In a family where the youngest is also a female and furthermore in any way disabled, this pampering can become even more pronounced.

Added to the advantages and pitfalls in the birth order, the Brontë siblings were now all reacting to their mother's death in their own personal ways. One supposes that the elder children were more affected because they understood more of life and death, but, as Bowlby and others since have explained, children's emotions differ from child to child and many children subvert their feelings when they are unable to express them or be fully aware of them, and this damping down or attempts by the brain to forget or hide the pain, can resurface in later years causing profound distress. Bowlby noted that any:

> ... prolonged break in the mother-child relationship, including death, leaves a characteristic impression on the child's personality. Such children appear emotionally withdrawn and isolated.[6]

He further maintains that maternal deprivation interrupts the psychological growth in the same way that a physical illness may retard physical growth and that both can be permanent. One cannot explain to a child under five that their mother is dead and has gone forever. A young child has little or no concept of time, whether it is an hour, a week or a year. People who believe in God may tell the child that their mother has gone to heaven and is living with the angels, in order to comfort them. Others tell the child that their mother is now a star in the sky or is in a place where she is watching over them. There are numerous ways of trying to explain whilst using euphemisms that may comfort. However, a young child does not have a notion of time and space. If a mother leaves a young child, even for a few minutes, it may well fret and cry because it has absolutely no way of knowing when, or if, the mother will ever return. Bowlby describes cases where when the mother has been away for days or weeks, despite returning, the child will reject her. This is part of the only power that the child has to demonstrate their hurt.

I remember vividly when my own mother was taken to hospital seriously ill when my siblings and I were aged between 13 and 9. My younger brother and I were sent, separately, to live with family friends, whilst my eldest brother and sister stayed at home with my father. Our lives were never the same, for any of us. It was a time, in the late 1950s, when children were not necessarily the confidantes of their parents and hospitals had very strict visiting regimes. I was not allowed to visit and I had no idea if mum would survive and no idea whether I would ever see her again or return home. No one told me how she was or if she was getting better. At the age of 9, I was traumatised and can only imagine how much worse it must be for a child who has even less knowledge about what is happening to their family. My mother did return, after six weeks, but she looked different and seemed different. I was a little scared to approach her and worried that she may become ill again and disappear. I don't think that I ever got over that fear of losing her or the irrational accompanying feeling of rejection. There was also guilt involved as I, along with my siblings, had been so busy squabbling the morning that the doctor visited, we were unaware of how ill she was until an ambulance arrived.

One consequence was that I insisted that my own children were kept informed on many matters that my own parents would never have discussed or explained. I introduced my children to the concept of death very early in their lives. We examined dead birds and animals; instead of shielding them from death I tried to show it as a possible consequence of illness and that it was the inevitable end of life, but not in a manner that would frighten or upset them. Not an easy task!

In the Brontë household, where absolute faith in God was instilled in the children, it may have made them confused and angry to realise that the loving God they believed in had taken their mother away when they needed her the most. There remains an ongoing argument about when and how to expose children to death. Unfortunately, in Britain, in the late twentieth and twenty-first centuries, there is an over-powering attitude to shelter children and young adults from the inevitable. We have not had a war on our own land for nearly eighty years and very few children ever see a dead body or attend a funeral. Parents worry that the child may be upset, but it means denying the child the chance to associate and possibly come to terms with dying. Separation can also encourage and create a mystery and fear around death.

We often view birth with similar, though different, reasoning. How many children witness a birth? It is the other most common and necessary part of life but we deny children the right to witness their own beginnings. It is part of modern western culture that has created a series of myths surrounding the two most common occurrences on earth. The proliferation of hospitals following the formation of the National Health Service in 1948 has played a huge role in hiding or disguising birth, suffering and death from the general community. Nowadays, we tend to be born and die in hospitals, separated from our families in a clinical and sterile environment which is alien and deprived of normal social interaction. Health and Safety regulations advise hospital births and the law, in Britain, (it is different in some American States) prevents a family taking a body home after a hospital death. In fact, as soon as death occurs, whenever and wherever, the body is not owned by anyone. There is a statutory duty on hospitals and undertakers to ensure that the body is disposed of correctly and this is usually done with the input of the executor for the deceased. The executor has a right to possession of the corpse for disposal only, but does not have possession as in ownership. Because a dead person's body is not property, under case law, it cannot therefore be owned. Our need to separate death and birth from the family, is so different from life even a hundred years ago and even further from the experience of the Brontë family.

Maternal deprivation is always traumatic where a child has formally had a loving and caring parent or guardian, but the trauma is intensified if that carer has a prolonged illness or suddenly 'disappears' into hospital where there is little or no contact. We assume that children cannot bear to see their mother suffering but at least they are with her and part of her experience. The mother needs the children as much as they need her. Maria Brontë was often heard by the family to cry out, 'my poor children, my poor children' (recorded by a nurse, Martha Wright, who tended to Mrs Brontë at the start of her illness, before her sister arrived). She was aware of the fact that she would not see them grow up and that she would not be there to guard and guide them or provide the love and comfort that they needed. Perhaps she knew better than anyone else in the household that she needed them with her as much as possible, both for their sakes and for hers.

Samantha Ellis, in her book, *Take Courage* highlights an important aspect of losing a parent that is not often acknowledged. She explains that:

> *If you lose your mother, you also lose the chance to argue with her. The danger is that instead, you spend your life trying to live up to a mother who is both dead and perfect.*[7]

One can see this following many deaths of parents and siblings. One only remembers and praises their good points, which become increasingly beatified. In the current news and media, one rarely hears of a nasty person being killed or the death of a horrible parent. Funeral services always find some characteristic to praise and the service is almost always positive and complimentary. In my role as the manager of various nursing homes, it was part of my job and privilege to attend many funerals over the years. I only ever once remember a widow stating during the wake that the deceased was a 'cheating, alcoholic liar'. It raised some eyebrows, but was quite an honest and refreshing change!

If a parent or sibling dies when one is young, there has been little or no time to have arguments or to criticise or fall out with them. What effect does a dead family member have on the living? I suggest that they become beyond who they were in life and gain a saintly personality. This is understandable and part of our reaction to death and loss, but it is a false perception and one is never able to live up to the image that one has concocted. For the child who never even knew or remembered their parent, there is a loss that is a void that cannot be filled by any remembered or rational image, possibly making that loss harder to cope with or understand. Elizabeth Branwell is often described as the Brontë siblings 'mother substitute' but, of course, she could not be, she could only be herself and give as much comfort and guidance to her nephew and nieces as her own experiences and beliefs would allow.

If there is a solace to be had following a death, it can be gained, at times, by indulgence in nature and the natural world. Grieving is natural and necessary but it can be a comfort to spend time out in the open air surrounded by trees, water, flowers, birds and all the affirmative representations of life. The Brontë children 'escaped' the house of death and wandered on the moors as often as they were allowed, as part of a process that must have comforted the children and freed them from the confines of their home, turned alien. These wanderings on the moorland amongst the natural elements had a profound effect on them all and are constantly represented in their writings and their art.

Around 1823, after their mother's death and before the eldest girls went away to school, Patrick played a game with his children which has always struck me as very pertinent as to how they were feeling and developing at that time. I quote it in full because of its significance and its insight into their gender, personalities, birth order and their understanding and expectations as children of a Protestant minister.

When my children were very young, when as far as I can remember, the eldest was about ten years of age and the youngest about four – thinking that they knew more, than I had yet discovered, in order to make them speak with less timidity – I deemed that if they were put under a sort of cover, I might gain my end – and happening to have a mask in the house, I told them all to stand and speak boldly from under cover of the mask. I began with the youngest (Anne). I asked what a child like her most wanted – she answered, age and experience. I asked the next [Emily] what I had best do with her brother Branwell, who was sometimes, a naughty boy. She answered, reason with him, and when he won't listen to reason whip him. I asked Branwell, what was the best way of knowing the intellects, of men and women – he answered, by considering the difference between them as to their bodies. I then asked Charlotte, what was the best book in the world, she answered, the Bible – and what was next best, she answered the Book of Nature. I then asked the next [Elizabeth], what was the best mode of education for a woman, she answered, that which would make her rule her house well. Lastly I asked the oldest

The Lasting Effects of Maternal Deprivation

> *[Maria] what was the best mode of spending time, she answered, by laying it out in preparation for a happy eternity. I may not have given precisely their words, but I have nearly done so as they made a deep and lasting impression on my memory.*[8]

How revealing this little episode appears and how telling of how these six precocious children demonstrated their thoughts and beliefs at this time. Knowing the adult lives of these children, one sees already the traits and personalities which grew to define and describe them. Anne wants what all youngest children want, 'age and experience'. Emily is bold and harsh in her reasoning; Branwell is the rebel who is naughty and noticing how the sexes differ, a typical cheeky answer. Charlotte studies religion and nature, Elizabeth is already domesticated in her outlook and Maria gives the perfect answer, one that she knows will please her father.

There appears something else here. Patrick is a father who is interested in his children and is already teaching them according to their abilities. They are all receiving religious instruction from him at family prayers and attending his church. The older ones are good readers and have insight into the Bible and an awareness of nature. Patrick knows that Branwell is rebellious and at an age when being surrounded by women has also made him aware of gender differences. Elizabeth has obviously been chosen as less academic and encouraged to housekeep, and his treasured eldest daughter demonstrates her intelligence and pious understanding. Patrick and Aunt Elizabeth, as their primary carers, have begun to fit the children into certain roles according to their gender, abilities and predispositions of birth order. These roles demonstrate the beliefs and biases of the two adults and reflect how they intend and hope that the children will develop.

This is normal behaviour in most households and at this time, in this setting, certain rules and ways of behaviour would have been followed. As the children of the minister, the Brontë siblings would have been well schooled in religious matters. Family prayers took place daily. Part of this Christian upbringing would involve the inherent rules of religious doctrine. They included the ten commandments, the belief in an afterlife in heaven and the expectation that avoiding evil and bad practice was necessary for a good and rewarding life. However, God was merciful and forgiving and would welcome sinners who truly repented. This was a very important part of the Christian doctrine. Regarded as universal salvation, it was the belief that true repentance of one's sins would foster forgiveness by God and the sinner could then be admitted to heaven. It is not the belief of all religions and that troubled the Brontë siblings a great deal at various times in their lives. Patrick and Aunt Elizabeth were both well versed in Christian matters and also understood and acknowledged

Wesleyan, Methodist and Evangelical teachings. This broad range of beliefs would have been part of the children's upbringing and education. With this grounding in religion the children would be taught to be mindful of others, courteous and polite, obedient and respectful.

When one reads many of the books and articles written about the Brontë children in their early years, the focus is almost always on their remarkable intelligence, their comradeship and their love and care for each other as they grew. Whilst that may have been the case for some of the time, I suggest that there are very few children who grow up with siblings who do not rebel, argue, fight and suffer jealousy and upset. By examining birth order with the Brontës in mind, one can note that the evidence shows a pattern of behaviour beyond and apart from their unique upbringing.

The tragic death of their mother, their father's grief and the new, permanent residence of their spinster, middle-aged aunt, helped to create in the children a special closeness and interdependence at times, separate from the adults as they sought to deal with their loss. However, I maintain that this was not without its problems and issues. Between the death of their mother in September 1821 and the elder girls going to school in July/August 1824, the children were all at various important stages in their development.

Branwell, Emily and Anne, the three youngest siblings, all under 5 years old, were experiencing highly important years of growth and progress. These are the years when a child learns to recognise and understand their surroundings and fully identify with their carers. They develop emotions and needs beyond just food, drink and sleep. They learn to walk, to talk and to develop their cognitive skills. These early formative years are essential times for children and many things can disrupt or alter these proceedings.

To focus on Anne, one sees a barely weaned child who is suddenly deprived of her mother and unable to understand where she has gone or why. Anne has not yet learnt to fully speak or possibly even to walk. She is carried around by a nursemaid or her aunt who are all simultaneously looking after five other bewildered children. It is likely that she would be put down to sleep as often as possible whilst the others had some attention.

Her development is, therefore, rudely interrupted and her physical and mental growth is impaired. She will develop slower and even lose some abilities for a time. A child learns to talk by listening to those around it but also by being spoken to. I suggest that it is notable that in a letter to Ellen Nussey in 1848, Anne writes that:

> ... *you must know there is a lamentable deficiency in my organ of language which makes me almost as bad a hand at writing as talking unless I have something particular to say.*[9]

The Lasting Effects of Maternal Deprivation

Charlotte, in a letter to Ellen Nussey, when Anne went to her first governess post in 1839, expressed her concern that:

> *I do seriously apprehend that her employer will sometimes conclude that she has a natural impediment in her speech.*[10]

If Anne had a speech impediment and these letters suggest this, then it could well have been due to her interruption in learning to talk as a child. I note that in Charlotte's portrait of Anne, her top front teeth could be judged as overlarge or overlapping her bottom ones. This possibly affected the way she spoke. Much of this would account for Anne's extreme shyness and reticence to speak. Whilst she may have suffered physical defects in her ability to pronounce her words, I suggest that Anne had, metaphorically, little or no voice. She is surrounded by older more experienced siblings, a busy father and a stressed aunt. It is very easy to dismiss Anne's ideas and questions as the annoying bleating of a youngest and irritating child, who has nothing relevant to say.

The adults in the parsonage did not have a great deal of time to concentrate on each child individually during these all-important early years. Even the practical events like washing, feeding and clothing would be mammoth tasks offering little time for individual care and attention. One can imagine the practicalities of toilet training possibly four youngsters at the same time, with an outside toilet and no hot water. The logistics speak for themselves.

Anne and her siblings would have suffered in various ways and areas according to their ages and abilities. Aunt Elizabeth was in her mid-forties with no children of her own. Whilst she may have helped to educate them later, one can appreciate that she had more than enough to do just organising and attending to their physical needs between 1821 and 1824.

I want to concentrate on Anne here as I suggest that she suffered especially because of her age and her position in the birth order. She could not make demands as she could barely speak, she was totally at the mercy of those around her to supply her needs. All children are at that age, but Anne was competing against five others. She would learn to be docile and undemanding by sheer lack of attention. Studies and research in the current area of child psychology highlight the behaviour of infants and children who fail to get individual and prolonged attention. They tend to withdraw and eventually give up trying. I believe that this may well have been Emily's fate. Branwell had, as the only boy, extra attention and the older children could vocalise their needs. Emily and Anne had no such skills and it is reasonable to suggest that Emily, with no official title or status, received even less attention accordingly.

Anne, however, as the youngest had other issues that possibly helped her to attract attention. She may have suffered from asthma *inter alia* and she was kept in Aunt Elizabeth's room to sleep for a number of years. This could have been to Anne's advantage or disadvantage. As stated, children resent a sibling who appears to have more than their fair share of the adults' attention even if it is not asked for or enjoyed. Anne may have been irritatingly slow at both speaking and walking and some resentment may have developed amongst her siblings. This is only conjecture but research into the development of siblings in large families highlights the competition amongst them, even if they are themselves unaware of it. It is natural and expected that each child will suffer in their own way from the rivalry and its consequences. I am sure that the Brontë children fought for attention and squabbled amongst themselves for very many reasons, not least to gain their place in the pecking order and for the attention of all of the adults.

Modern studies define the areas where children compete and the necessity of establishing their roles and dealing with their siblings and parents or carers. It is always important to remember that every child is unique no matter when or where they are born or at what place in the birth order they occupy, and all have different needs. However, so often adults treat the eldest and youngest differently than any middle children, so beginning the cycle of definitive birth order that establishes the child before it can walk or talk. In his seminal work, *The Birth Order Book*, Dr Kevin Leman states that:

> *Every time a child is born, the entire family environment changes. How parents interact with each child as he or she enters the family circle determines in great part that child's final destiny.*[11]

What he is advocating is that children copy parental behaviour and that parents cannot help treating each child in a certain way because they are of different ages and different abilities. Consequently, the first child is pushed out for the second and so on until the last child becomes the youngest and the one in most need. Dr Leman goes on to explain that:

> *From the time they are old enough to start figuring things out, 'last-borns' are acutely aware that they are the youngest, smallest, weakest and least equipped to compete in life.*[12]

However, it sometimes occurs that this youngest child rebels. Not all 'last-borns' are happy with their constant failure to impress. We see this in Anne Brontë when, as an adult, she decides to go it alone and prove that she can survive away from her family. She demonstrates, both to them and to herself, that she is a stoic who has an almost obsessive need to succeed as an individual. Anne's persistence against many odds can be viewed as a need to prove to her family that she was much more than the youngest, and far more able and capable than any of her siblings, and this she most definitely achieved. For years, she could not compete with her siblings, she lacked their 'age and experience' but finally, alone, she was able to break free and escape from the limiting home life and claustrophobic influences she had always known.

I view the children at this time in the following way. The intelligent and kind Maria was learning her lessons whilst under pressure to help out with her younger siblings and support her father and aunt. Elizabeth, already showing less academic flair, was helping out with housework and domestic chores alongside the two servants who also served as nursemaids, cooks and general help. Charlotte was studious and already showing an interest in religious matters and an affinity with nature, but had developed a serious short sightedness that inhibited her in many areas. Branwell, was doing what all boys still do, he was expressing his personality with naughtiness and demands and bullying his sisters whenever he had the opportunity. It is possible that he was epileptic, and if so, another reason to attract attention, albeit through no fault of his own. Branwell was surrounded by women and needed to assert himself as wiser and more important than his five sisters. He was 6½ when his sisters began going to school and he was aware of the difference in the sexes and of male domination over the female. It gave him a small measure of confidence and may have brought out a tendency to intimidate and take over their play. Emily is already withdrawn. She is the fifth of six children, the fourth daughter, and has little or no say in matters. She is just another girl and if she cannot gain attention then she will stay quiet and keep her thoughts and ideas to herself. Anne is now the permanent youngest child. She is small, shy and has trouble trying to keep up with her siblings. She has the disadvantage of asthma and is kept with her aunt, sharing her bedroom and separated from her siblings. Viewed as delicate and needing special attention alienates her from the others. I maintain that this separation endured throughout Anne's life and forced her into making her decisions to work and travel away from home for a large part of her adulthood. As I shall demonstrate in later chapters, Anne had an urgent need to outgrow her 'youngest' label and prove to herself and to her family that she had as much intelligence, ability and talent as her siblings.

Anne wrote a poem, amongst her many verses, that could be seen as a reference to her early years and how she viewed herself at that time. It was completed, though unpublished, in April 1848, a year before her death. It includes, perhaps, a more authentic description of her as a child than any other reported or assumed assessment. I have included here a small number of its lines. The poem takes the form of a dialogue possibly between Anne and one of her internal voices. If it is autobiographical, it examines herself and her relationship with Emily and with God, the two great loves and influences on her life. At times she loses one or both and the poem has an expression of her loneliness and her separation from her siblings. She says:

> *I see, far back, a helpless child,*
> *Feeble and full of causeless fears,*
> *Simple and easily beguiled*
> *To credit all it hears.*
> *More timid than the wild wood-dove,*
> *Yet trusting to another's care,*
> *And finding in protecting love*
> *Its only refuge from despair,-*
> *Its only balm for every woe,*
> *The only bliss its soul can know,-*
> *Still hiding in its breast.*
> *A tender heart too prone to weep,*
> *A love so earnest, strong and deep*
> *It could not be exprest.*
> *Poor helpless thing! What can it do*
> *Life's stormy cares and toils among;-*
> *How tread this weary desert through*
> *That awes the brave and tires the strong?*
> *What shall it do with all that trust*
> *Where truth maintains so little sway,*
> *Where seeming fruit is bitter dust,*
> *And kisses oft to death betray?*

> Lines from *Self-Communion*[13]

These lines are only part of this long and revealing poem and, if they are describing her own experience, they tell us a lot about Anne's view of her childhood, her struggles, her relationships with people who misunderstood and betrayed her, and of her belief in God as her only reliable hope. It is a poem worth a careful reading, and, written a year before her death, it is therefore unlikely to be related to the poetry that Emily and Anne wrote when they began their own imaginary kingdom of 'Gondal' separate from the writings of Branwell and Charlotte. I suggest that it is Anne's personal musing on how and why her childhood was difficult for her.

Edward Chitham describes here how Anne is describing herself in this intimate poem. He says:

> *Anne sees herself then as 'helpless'. She was the sixth child, with four larger sisters and a taunting brother. The eldest sister, Maria, has an impressive reputation for cleverness, unworldliness and untidiness. But she was certainly a leader, and even at a very young age, Anne will have learned from her. Elizabeth was calmer, with no great intellectual capacity (as the Cowan Bridge register shows) and destined to be a wife and housekeeper; like Anne she is never allowed to speak for herself. Charlotte, inventive, organising, short-sighted and directing, came into her own when the elder two died. Emily, assertive, tempersome and rude when she wished; these were the sisters who caused Anne to feel 'helpless,' though they often patronised her and certainly didn't act from ill will.*[14]

I would question Dr Chitham's final remark here, for I believe that, certainly as the children grew older, Anne was patronised by her siblings to a great extent and that patronisation, especially by Charlotte, was lifelong and deliberate.

Chapter Three

Death and the Family

It is interesting to examine the Prunty and Branwell families from the view of their large numbers and the birth order of the siblings. Patrick was the eldest of ten children, who all, but one, lived remarkably long lives. His sister Alice, the youngest of the five boys and five girls, was born in 1796 and lived until 1891. Only one of the Prunty children, Jane, died in infancy. The two eldest, Patrick and Hugh, both died in 1862, aged 84 and 83 respectively. Women produced their children repeatedly, and with little reference to wealth or status.

The Irish family, despite a comparably poor and working-class lifestyle, compared to the Branwells' affluent and middle-class upbringing, had more healthy babies and longevity than the Branwells. Before Maria was born, her parents had buried five of their children. Elizabeth Branwell, dying at Haworth in 1842 at the age of 65, lived the longest of her eleven siblings. What is comparable is the constant reproduction programme that gave no one control over the number and frequency of their offspring. Ireland in the eighteenth century was a predominantly Catholic country with strict laws against any form of birth control. No one in either country had any control over the mortality rate and the ensuing grief. Biographers who have condemned Patrick for keeping his wife constantly pregnant do not acknowledge this important fact or fail to recognise that this was 'normal' for the time and circumstances. As stated earlier, without birth control and with the unerring belief that children were conceived according to God's will, it is almost inevitable that his wife would have many pregnancies. Had Mrs Brontë lived it is very likely that she would have gone on to produce more children.

As mentioned, Elizabeth Branwell, the second of that name after the death of her sister Elizabeth, in 1776, had suffered the trauma of sibling loss. By the time she arrived permanently in Haworth, in 1821, she had suffered the deaths of five of her siblings as children and adults. Three of her siblings died when Elizabeth was under 5 years old, so one can assume that she well understood the trauma of her new charges, although it does not follow that people automatically empathise with those suffering similar losses. One has to remember that the joint religious backgrounds of the Branwells and Brontës offered a belief that death brought entry to heaven for the righteous, so there was, perhaps, a measure of solace. One wonders whether Elizabeth comforted her sister's children or sought to distract them or found it enough to emphasise that their mother was safe in heaven. Hopefully, she did all three.

Dwelling on loss is necessary, but unhealthy if it becomes overwhelming when, and if, people are unable to cope with their grief or come to terms with its effects. This applies especially to children, who have a greater lack of understanding of death and often appear to accept it and readily move on. Their inability to express their grief can drive it deep into the psyche and I suggest that this was the case with the Brontë siblings. They had no control over death and no means of coping with it. Not only had their mother died but they had witnessed some of the effects of her months of suffering. As stated, the helplessness that that engenders is particularly damaging and its effects long lasting.

By 1822, in the months following their mother's death, the children ranged in age from 2 to 8 years. Maria has to be the capable eldest. This is a trait of elder children, who under any circumstances can find themselves pushed forward into a more adult role when more children arrive. More is expected of them as they are, by virtue of being the eldest, more experienced and more knowledgeable, with all that that entails. In the Brontës' case, Maria had to stop being the baby when her sister Elizabeth arrived, when Maria was barely twelve months old. Each child that follows pushes the eldest up the ladder and they are expected to behave with less childish traits than their younger siblings. Anne was the 'baby' of the family all of her life, Maria for hardly a year. This puts a burden on the eldest child who has to become more responsible and less indulgent of their own troubles and needs. Her inexperienced aunt and her grieving father may have burdened Maria beyond her capabilities with their high expectations of her, both academically and as a 'little mother'. She may have felt under pressure to succeed in all areas. Meri Wallace notes that:

> *In an effort to win attention in the family, the oldest may try to be very good, drive themselves hard to be great at everything they do, or become super helpful to their parents ... with several children looking up to her, the oldest child of many siblings may experience even more pressure from her parents to 'set a good example'. Because she is the trailblazer for the rest, her parents may believe that if she does well ... and behaves correctly, everyone else will follow suit.*[1]

Unfortunately, Maria did not live long enough for her talents and personality to fully emerge, but I suggest she was a thoughtful and kind child who did her best to comfort her brother and sisters.

It is this inescapable birth order process that fascinates psychologists who use it to describe why and how parents treat their children differently and the ways in which this affects their development. Sigmund Freud believed that:

> ... the position of a child in the family order is a factor of extreme importance in determining the shape of his (her) later life.[2]

I hope to qualify this statement throughout this book by examining the way each child related to their carers and to each other.

During this awful time, there were three children in the middle of the birth order. Elizabeth, Charlotte and Emily were all struggling for recognition and attention and the need to establish their own identities. It is easy for parents to lump these middle children, who have no specific titles, together. Dr Leman states that:

> A number of middle-borns have told me they did not feel that special growing up. 'My older brother got all the glory. And my little sister got all the attention, and then there was me' is a very familiar assessment.[3]

He argues that each second or later child will always look to the immediate older sibling for influence and tries to copy. However, this can also have other effects. If they feel that they are strong enough to usurp the elder child then they may do so. When Charlotte becomes the eldest child she usurps her brother, who whilst younger, is the favoured male child. She usurps his prime male position and shows herself to be far stronger and superior. Other later born children may compete for a while and then give up and go their own way. This is what I shall discuss later when looking at the behaviour of Emily.

As a child, Branwell had his own role and attracted special attention as the only boy. He had status and was surrounded by a doting father and eight other females, including the two servants. He is cosseted and feted by a houseful of women. However, he also inherits part of the first-born syndrome and is under pressure to succeed and to mature into a leader and example to his family and a protector of, and possible provider for, his sisters. For a while he shares the lead role with his elder sister, but as they continue to work and play together, Charlotte gradually dominates him.

Anne, as the fifth daughter and only a 2-year-old toddler in 1822, is now the youngest, unless her father remarries and stepchildren arrive. For now, she is the youngest and possibly the most malleable of the siblings. She will receive attention as being the baby, a female and, if we are correct in her history, suffering from asthma and speech issues. She, like her other siblings, apart from Emily, is small, shy and is described by Ellen Nussey as 'the prettiest'. These are all attributes that attract attention and the need for others to help and protect them. Aunt Elizabeth would probably be extra attentive to Branwell, as the only boy, and Anne as the baby.

I emphasise here the background of Patrick and Elizabeth in their own birth order. Patrick is the strong eldest child who has flourished and outstripped his siblings and moved up in the world through his intelligence and his efforts. Elizabeth has not had to fight for all she has, but she was still a female child in a male world and, as such, has developed all the traits and attributes of a middle-class lady, subject to male dominance and influence. She had only one surviving brother, Benjamin, as she grew up, and he would have taken pride of place in the sibling hierarchy in a family that had already lost two other sons. There was the Branwell name and wealth, to pass on to the next generation and the onus was on Benjamin to ensure that this occurred. Elizabeth loved and respected her brother and when parted from him, for the next twenty years, it is likely that she held Branwell in very high esteem as a substitute for the male she had had to sacrifice.

Suddenly faced with the ordeal of raising six children it is likely that Elizabeth had more effect on the younger ones who had less memory of, and influence from, their mother. In adulthood, only Charlotte had any recollection of her mother, and that only a brief memory of her playing with Branwell in the parlour. It is likely that the two servant girls would be part of the children's world, apart from all of the heavy housework and cooking they would have been involved with. With Patrick overworked in his religious and parochial duties and Elizabeth struggling to cope with six youngsters, the Garrs sisters would have been involved with the children more than as servants, but as nursemaids, baby minders and friends as much as cooks and general dogsbodies. There was also a fondness for the children from these two household servants, who, when their work load offered a short break, were left to organise and entertain their charges. Most afternoons, weather permitting, Sarah usually took all of the children for walks on the moors.

These years between 1821 and 1824 saw the six children learning such skills as walking, speaking, toilet training, dressing, eating, playing, counting, exercising and early reading skills and more; all the stages of physical and mental growth that a child under 7 years old has to learn to emerge as a member of a family and community. Just getting them all up and all put to bed must have been a major operation. It would be difficult nowadays with all the advantages of modern gadgets like washing machines, fridges, cleaning tools and central heating, to keep the children warm, fed and clean. They had to be clothed and hours of sewing and mending would be spent refitting hand-me-downs as each child grew out of and into a garment. They would have slept two or three to a bed, each disturbing the others as illness and childhood nightmares upset and altered the dynamics. There was no electric light to comfort a frightened child and no candles at night, in a house where Patrick's job involved regularly burying children who had died in fires. Anne, the baby, slept from infancy in her aunt's bedroom, separate from her sisters and therefore apart from their developing closeness and nightly intimacy. This detachment continued for years and added to Anne and her aunt's special and shared relationship, and was probably different to her association with the other girls. Aunt Elizabeth was able to influence Anne in a way that did not occur with her sisters. Ellen Nussey described Anne as her 'Aunt's favourite'. She may well have been quoting Charlotte, but I suggest that it was more involved than that; that Anne was pliable and open to her aunt's attention and developed more of her habits and beliefs than her sisters did. Sharing a room with someone for a number of years provides an intimacy that is unique and, like all children who learn by watching and copying, Anne would grow up imitating her aunt's ways and ideas possibly to a greater extent than her siblings.

It is from Sarah Garrs that we know of the pattern of life at the parsonage during these years (see Juliet Barker, *The Brontës,* p.127). There was a routine that had to be followed each day in order to maintain control and to teach the children how to learn and behave in such a crowded space. After washing and dressing, the family and the servants met for prayers in Patrick's study before breakfast in the parlour. Apart from Anne, who was considered still a baby, the others returned to their father's study for lessons, according to their ages and abilities. Sarah dealt with the girls until dinner time, teaching them to sew, whilst Branwell would be involved in other tasks or play. Dinner was at two o'clock and following that the children could then go on to the moors for fun and exercise, with one or both of the Garrs sisters. Tea followed their afternoon exercise and later, if he was free, Patrick would spend time with his children, reciting stories and tales of history, geography and adventure, as part of their education. The children would say their prayers before bed, and on Sunday evenings everyone gathered in Patrick's study for Bible and catechism.

These three years of demanding and tireless work will have taken its toll on Sarah and Nancy and they left around the end of 1824, Nancy to be married and Sarah to a post travelling with a widow and her daughter, something that her mother disapproved of and Sarah had to return to Bradford. They spoke fondly of their young Brontë charges in their old age and always spoke well of Patrick.

Patrick was a very busy man, in demand from his many parishioners and his difficult and busy work. He did not ignore or chastise his children unduly, as far as can be ascertained, in fact he spoke of them tenderly and was very proud of them. William Dearden, a writer and poet and associate of Branwell's and well known to the Brontë family, writing in the Bradford Observer in June 1861, recorded that:

> *Branwell told me when accidentally alluding to this mournful period in the history of his family, that his father watched over his bereaved flock with truly paternal solicitude and affection – that he was their constant guardian and instructor – and that he took a lively interest in all their innocent amusements.*[4]

William Dearden was also known as the Bard of Calderdale and in 1842 challenged Branwell to a poetry competition. Dearden wrote a long obituary in the Bradford Observer on the death of Patrick Brontë and was one of those who challenged Mrs Gaskell's biography of Charlotte Brontë with its criticisms of Patrick. Dearden was a respected figure in the area and became an intimate acquaintance of the Brontë family. He held various important roles and died in 1889, after twenty-eight years as principal of Warley Grammar School at Sowerby Bridge in West Yorkshire.

It is from close friends, servants and observers of the family that we sometimes get a more reliable picture of them, especially at this time. It is easy to forget that although in comparative isolation, the Brontë family had a few important and interesting acquaintances, mainly through Patrick's work and status. Patrick is mostly shown as a benevolent and loving father. It was mainly in Mrs Gaskell's biography that he was described at times as harsh and heartless. Some of these accusations were endorsed by Charlotte's intimate friends, especially Ellen Nussey and Mary Taylor and it is sometimes difficult to know who gave accurate accounts. Perhaps they all did from their own personal experiences with Charlotte and Patrick, and later with Arthur Nicholls. Graham Watson, in his book, *The Invention of Charlotte Bronte* argues a very good case for examining Mrs Gaskell's biography of Charlotte from the multiple perspectives of those who knew Charlotte and her family. His book evokes a sympathy and empathy with Charlotte's position at odds with my interpretation, but I suggest that Charlotte can be viewed in many ways and all carry some insight into her life and character. There is no definitive version. Arthur was her staunch defender, and quite rightly so, and Patrick was the dominant male and behaved as a priest and a father according to his times and beliefs. As the patriarchal head of the household he would have had absolute jurisdiction over the house and its inhabitants. He would need to have order and demand good manners and a degree of peace in the house, if he was to fulfil his duties and uphold his position. He can, no doubt, be criticised in hindsight by modern readers of the Brontë saga, but this was a man under tremendous duress and, I suggest, that he did what he thought was best for his young family throughout their childhood.

Patrick spent a third of his life in Ireland with his growing siblings, and his status as the eldest and outwardly the most intelligent will have added to his confidence and self-belief. His brothers grew up to be labourers rather than professionals and, although the family acquired land of their own and moved to larger premises, Patrick never liked to explain his roots or expound on his upbringing. He described it very briefly to Mrs Gaskell when she was writing Charlotte's biography, but he had nothing special to say about it. He told Mrs Gaskell that:

> ... [his father] was left an orphan at an early age. It was said that he was of an ancient family. Whether this was or was not so I never gave myself the trouble to inquire, since his lot in life as well as mine depended, under providence, not on family descent but our own exertions. He came to the north of Ireland and made an early but suitable marriage. His pecuniary means were small but renting a few acres of land, he and my mother by dint of application and industry managed to bring up a family of ten children in a respectable manner. I shew'd an early fondness for books, and continued at school for several years. At the age of sixteen – knowing that my father could afford me no pecuniary aid – I began to think of doing something for myself. I therefore opened a public school and in this line I continued for five or six years. I was then a tutor in a gentleman's family – From which situation I removed to Cambridge and enter'd St John's College.[5]

One assumes that he was eager to detach himself from his lowly beginnings, although he never lost his Irish brogue and he often recited Irish tales and folklore to his children. He had a new life in England as far away from his old one as possible. In later life he still had written contact with some of his siblings and was occasionally able to send money to his mother, but he never visited Ireland again once he had his own family.

One can visualise the life of the family in Haworth parsonage in these early years following Mrs Brontë's death. There is a loving yet harassed and hard-working father, trying to come to terms with the loss of his wife and make room for his sister-in-law, whom he could only ever treat as a close family friend.

Even if he had thoughts of marrying her, it would not have been an acceptable state of affairs in the community or according to the Bible. Both adults would have been aware that in the book of Leviticus it suggests that such a union is incestuous. This was the argument used in 1835 in a Marriage Act that made such marriages illegal. We do not know just how well, or otherwise, these two adults lived together and whether they had differing ideas on child-rearing. We know that as they grew older, Patrick expected Elizabeth to teach the girls in all manner of female occupations, but he took total control of Branwell's education and the religious teachings of the family.

Meanwhile, Aunt Elizabeth was trying to establish her role as substitute mother, whilst already 46 years old and separated from all she had known and enjoyed. Marriage was now out of the question, even if it had been an option previously, and she could only look forward to life as a spinster, or 'old maid' as it was often cruelly referred to. She now had little if any social life. Haworth was a large and busy manufacturing area but mainly working class with a labouring poor and an unprecedented mortality rate. Neither Elizabeth, nor the children, ventured into the village very much or mixed with the local people as friends or acquaintances. The children were deliberately kept away from the diseases that were rife in the community and it is remarkable that all six children reached the age of 10 years old.

Perhaps the greatest asset for these growing Brontë children was the huge expanse of moorland that spread away to the west of their home. This was their playground, and as stated, they spent many happy afternoons there after lessons. This attachment to the moorland and all its diverse life was an education in itself for the children and nurtured a deep love of nature, especially in the three younger girls.

Over the next two years, the children developed their personalities and skills. All learnt to read well and enjoyed lessons and play. One wonders how much they echoed their mother's look and traits. It is both painful and a joy, when children express the familiar looks, gestures, colouring and expressions of their dead relatives.

George Eliot sums this up when describing genetic familiarity:

Family likeness has often a deep sadness in it.[6]

This is because the looks, gestures, expressions and voices of children often echo those of their relatives, dead or alive. This can have a disconcerting effect on the living causing them to recall their loss and grief. We note this in *Wuthering Heights* when the younger Cathy's eyes replicate her mother's and cause Heathcliff alarm and extra distress. One can imagine this constant reminder, that will never have ceased as the Bronte children grew. Their development will have sparked a constant echo of their mother, and caused exquisitely painful memories for her bereft husband and sister. Patrick remarked at this time how his grief weighed him down and even his children's innocent noise, upset him.

> *Do you ask how I felt under these circumstances? I would answer this, that tender sorrow was my daily portion; that oppressive grief sometimes lay heavy on me and that there were seasons when an affectionate, agonizing something sickened my whole frame, and which is I think of such a nature as cannot be described and must be felt in order to be understood. And when my dear wife was dead and buried and gone, and when I missed her at every corner, and when her memory was hourly revived by the innocent yet distressing prattle of my children. I do assure you, my dear sir, from what I felt, I was happy at the recollection that to sorrow, not as those without hope, was no sin; that our Lord himself had wept over his departed friend, and that he had promised us grace and strength sufficient for such a day.*[7]

One wonders whether this was also the case in the Branwell household. How did Thomas and Anne Branwell cope with the loss of their children and how did their remaining children react? Perhaps, where there is faith in God and in the afterlife, death is less final and less traumatic. If you believe that divine intervention is working within the family, there will be less questioning of why and how things occur. However, this cannot take away the grief and is hard for siblings to cope with when their own religious ideas are only just forming.

Children are helpless when there is illness or death in the family. These are events that are always controlled by adults. As stated, children are often neither kept informed nor given explanations. A read of any newspaper obituary section will show a long list of euphemisms that are used to comfort and conceal reality. Also, in the past few years, people have ceased to die! Nowadays, people 'pass', an Americanism that is becoming universal. What they 'pass' and where to, is not explained but it is seen as a less harsh and final word than 'death'.

One can see that the realities of illness and death were actually more understood and explained two hundred years ago than they are now. As a nurse for many years, the dead have ceased to hold any fear for me, which they most certainly did when I was a child. As a child I was terrified and fascinated by death and the thought of dead bodies. It wasn't until I was nearly 30 that I saw my first dead body. Whilst one can understand the trauma of children in the Brontë's time, seeing their dead relatives laid out in the bedroom, or in open coffins, it did at least dispel the myths and help them accept death as a part of life, something that I suggest we are failing nowadays to sufficiently acknowledge. When one actually sees a dead person, the realisation is that it is just a body, there is no life or spirit or enigma attached. No doubt there will be other new words that will seek to disguise ageing, disease, pain and death. There is, as Jane Eyre succinctly stated, a need for everyone to:

... keep in good health and not die.[8]

However, whilst Jane Eyre knew and experienced the death of her uncle, Mr Reed, and her friend Helen Burns, there is in Charlotte's story the ever-present Calvinist doctrine expounded by Mr Brocklehurst, attempting to frighten the children with threats that all naughty children go to hell and burn in a pit forever. Protestant beliefs relieved children of that fear whilst urging them to behave and not to take a road to sin, but with the caveat that if they did, they could truly repent and be saved. This difference in various religious beliefs became a worry to the Brontë girls when their schooling exposed them to diverse teachings. Anne, especially, was confused and concerned when her Protestant beliefs were challenged and temporarily overthrown by Calvinist ideas at Roe Head School.

Whilst nursing, I came to understand and feel the privilege of being with the dying and the dead. It was an honour to wash and dress and to cover the dead person in a simple shroud and clean sheets. We nurses would talk to them as we performed these important last tasks and felt that we had done the right thing and respected their status in both life and death. Unfortunately, death is now sanitised and hidden so that it is becoming more taboo and less acceptable. It is often, in Western countries, only medical staff who deal with the dead and dying. As soon as death occurs, families lose their loved ones. As stated, dead bodies immediately become under the care of the local authority and executor. One can no longer take one's dead relative home, or keep them at home if they died there. They are inevitably handed over to undertakers who know nothing of them and their families. I had the awful experience of seeing a dead relative who had been grotesquely made-up and had her hair in a totally different style, which made her look quite horrific. It brought it home to me about how little we know of what happens to our dead relatives and how much care and dignity is afforded to their bodies by strangers.

One can appreciate that for both health and safety reasons it may not be the best idea to keep a body in your lounge, certainly not for any length of time, but it seems as if there is no happy in-between state from a loved one being kept at home until their funeral or being sanitised and sterilised in a mortuary or funeral parlour in the hands of unfamiliar morticians. By removing death from our lives and hiding it from children, we can create a greater fear in them and an inability to cope when it does occur.

This is not to suggest that the Brontë children found it easier to accept their mother's death because they witnessed her painful and protracted illness and witnessed her dead body. Of course they were traumatised, but it was a natural trauma, produced by grief and loss, it was not the sudden disappearance that they mourned, or a fear that she had gone to hell. Maria Brontë died with and amongst her family and they were a part of that, not shielded from it but involved in the process. I suggest that, along with the suffering, this must produce a semblance of understanding and privilege.

However one views death or is involved with it, it is not an event that is easily set aside. Death of a close relative or friend can lead to a lifelong grief. That grief does not necessarily interfere with one's life, after the initial shock, but may always be there and always easily brought to mind. This is part of the grieving process and it affects different people in different ways. In 1969, the American/Swiss psychiatrist, Elisabeth Kübler-Ross,[9] devised a table of grief which she published as a guide to the stages one could expect to go through following a death. She listed Denial, Anger, Bargaining, Depression and Acceptance. Many people look to this model and it can be helpful. However, some people experience grief in a different order and some do not progress easily or even at all and never reach acceptance.

It is not enough to suggest that the younger a child experiences trauma, the more able they are to cope and move forward. Babies experience their lives from the moment of birth, and *in utero*, and everything that occurs has some effect on their development. The poet Tennyson had a beautiful way of describing the newborn child as it begins to appreciate the world around it. He describes that burgeoning of realisation as follows:

> *The baby new to earth and sky*
> *What time his tender palm is prest*
> *Against the circle of the breast,*
> *Has never thought that 'this is I'*
>
> *But as he grows he gathers much,*
> *And learns the use of 'I' and 'me'*
> *And finds 'I am not what I see',*
> *And other than the things I touch.*
>
> *So rounds he to a separate mind*
> *From whence clear memory may begin,*
> *As thro' the frame that binds him in*
> *His isolation grows defined.*[10]

Death and the Family

We all develop in this way, slowly learning to separate ourselves as individuals from the people and objects around us. As we come to label things, we learn to recognise difference and identify ourselves.

Even in the very young, trauma is an interruption of that development which upsets and disorientates the child's natural progression. It may be buried deep in the psyche, but it does not disappear. It may manifest itself in dreams, in depression, in anger and frustration; it may be a morbid fascination with death or a constant feeling of loss – of something missing. It can be any feeling or behaviour that is not consistent with a happy and carefree demeanour. During the twentieth century some psychotherapists decided that it may be beneficial to use methods to help people digress through and into their childhood in order to identify problematic issues; the idea being to revisit their traumas and deal with them as an adult. There has been some success with these methods, which often involve hypnotherapy and have been used in the far east for hundreds of years. We do not know how much of what we see, hear and feel as a child affects us for life because young children do not have the language or emotional capacity to recognise or describe their feelings. Regression and other methods of addressing these issues are now popular but it can be a dangerous area, especially where physical and sexual abuse are involved in a child's background. Reliving trauma is not necessarily the best way to deal with it, even if and when it is possible.

The Brontë children may have managed to see and feel death but acceptance suggests an overcoming of the trauma and there is no evidence to show that that ever occurred. Their writings, letters and poetry are, at times, testament to deep feelings of unrequited love and intense grief. The genius of all of the sisters for me, is their ability to put into words a grief that can barely be described. Again, Tennyson wrote in his wonderful poem to loss and grief, of the inadequacy of language to convey deep emotions. He writes that:

> *I sometimes hold it half a sin*
> *To put in words the grief I feel;*
> *For words, like Nature, half reveal*
> *And half conceal the soul within.*
>
> *But for the unquiet heart and brain,*
> *A use in measured language lies;*
> *The sad mechanic exercise,*
> *Like dull narcotics, numbing pain.*
>
> *In words, like weeds, I'll wrap me o'er,*
> *Like coarsest clothes against the cold;*
> *But that large grief which these enfold*
> *Is given in outline and no more.*[11]

The Brontë Family: Sibling Rivalry and a Burial in Paradise

It was during these intensive childhood years of enforced togetherness that the Brontë children learned to internalise their loss but it was always close by and erupted on to the pages of their writings, time and time again, both in their childhood and adult lives. Mourning, grief, loneliness, loss and sadness permeate their stories and especially their poetry. I quote here Emily's exquisite Gondal poem, written from her imaginary character, Rosina Alcona to Julius Brenzaida, as just one example of the Brontës' exceptional ability to use language to convey loss and its enduring heartbreak.

> *Cold in the earth, and the deep snow piled above thee!*
> *Far, far removed, cold in the dreary grave!*
> *Have I forgot, my Only Love, to love thee,*
> *Severed at last by Time's all-severing wave?*
>
> *Now, when alone, do my thoughts no longer hover*
> *Over the mountains on Angora's shore;*
> *Resting their wings where heath and fern-leaves cover*
> *That noble heart for ever, ever more?*
>
> *Cold in the earth, and fifteen wild Decembers*
> *From those brown hills have melted into spring-*
> *Faithful indeed is the spirit that remembers*
> *After such years of change and suffering!*
>
> *Sweet love of youth, forgive if I forget thee*
> *While the World's tide is bearing me along:*
> *Sterner desires and darker hopes beset me,*
> *Hopes which obscure but cannot do thee wrong.*
>
> *No other sun has lightened up my heaven;*
> *No other star has ever shone for me:*
> *All my life's bliss from thy dear life was given-*
> *All my life's bliss is in the grave with thee.*
>
> *But when the days of golden dreams had perished*
> *And even Despair was powerless to destroy,*
> *Then did I learn how existence could be cherished,*
> *Strengthened and fed without the aid of joy;*

Death and the Family

> *Then did I check the tears of useless passion,*
> *Weaned my young soul from yearning after thine;*
> *Sternly denied its burning wish to hasten*
> *Down to that tomb already more than mine!*
>
> *And even yet, I dare not let it languish,*
> *Dare not indulge in Memory's rapturous pain;*
> *Once drinking deep of that divinest anguish,*
> *How could I seek the empty world again?*[12]

The poignancy of these verses and their ability to transcend grief whilst acknowledging its everlasting effects, suggests to me that Emily and her siblings never recovered from death in their family and that it can be recognised within most of their behaviour and writing. Unlike many of us, they attained the ability to convey their innermost feelings and put into words what Tennyson later found unable to adequately explain. He was right, there is no adequate language to completely describe the pain and suffering of another person's grief, but some of the Brontës' poetry, including that of Branwell's, comes as close as our limited language allows. Poetry of this calibre is, I suggest, with its lyricism, its cadence and its choice of words, as close to music and the emotions as language can ever hope to achieve.

Chapter Four

The Return of Tragedy
A Vale of Tears

By the autumn of 1823, and after Patrick's unsuccessful attempts to find a new wife, he had to think long and hard about the future. No one wanted to marry a middle-aged clergyman with six young children and no money. In fact, the women he asked were deeply offended. On the death of his wife, Patrick had lost her £50 annuity and although Elizabeth helped out whenever she could, his stipend was still only £140 per annum. This was not enough to keep himself, Elizabeth, two servants and his six children. His sister-in-law had done her best to help him rear his children over the last few trying years, but she could not be expected to stay forever. Patrick realised that without Elizabeth, or a wife, he had no one on whom he could rely to educate his daughters.

The future of his children and their education was Patrick's main concern and he turned to his former friend, Elizabeth Firth, at Thornton for her advice. This may have helped to heal the two-year rift between them as she had been one of his marriage hopes, an offer she had firmly rejected. Both Miss Firth and Fanny Outhwaite, of Bradford, were godmothers to his daughters, and they had attended Crofton Hall school, near Wakefield, when growing up. On their recommendation, Patrick decided to send Maria and Elizabeth to the school and they did attend for a brief time. However, the fees were too high and he could not afford to send all five of his girls there.

The Brontë children had a wide, wild and unique genetic code and a nurturing pair of carers who had struggled for three difficult years to instil the children with both the skills necessary for development and an education befitting their age and gender. Simultaneously, the adults were trying to allow them the tools and information to form their own imaginations and ideas. The children may have looked like their parents, in colouring, height and manners, had their accents and their beliefs, but as they grew, Patrick, especially, realised the need for them to develop their own personalities and talents, and his belief was that education was always the way forward. In the rapidly changing world around them, he wanted his children to question and interpret all they saw, heard, read and experienced. He wanted them to grow into useful and successful adults, guided by Christian faith and a strong moral code. However, he knew also that his daughters would be limited in their options as adults. They may marry, or work as teachers, governesses or ladies' companions. One of them would stay at home in adulthood, to help with the housekeeping and look after their father, as was custom, but the other four girls needed an education to fit them for work as genteel ladies of middle-class backgrounds.

He was aware that his sister-in-law had not arrived with the intention of staying. She had been used to her independence, her circle of friends and social activities and enjoyed the pleasant climate and surroundings of her Cornish home. To find herself in Haworth in the cold winter of 1821 following Maria's death, and with six small, motherless children and their grieving father to care for, must have been very difficult for her and Patrick would have been acutely aware of the fact. As a Christian woman, she had bravely borne the burden to which she had been assigned, but Patrick could not expect her to spend even more years so far from her beloved home.

It was in December 1823 that Patrick saw an advertisement in the *Leeds Intelligencer* newspaper, that appeared to be an answer to many of his problems. A school, specifically catering for the education of clergymen's daughters, was opening at Cowan Bridge, a hamlet near Kirby Lonsdale in Lancashire. It was due to start taking pupils the following April, and at a fee of only £14 per child per annum, was half the cost of Crofton Hall.

During that spring of 1824, all six of his children fell ill with whooping cough and measles, both deadly diseases at that time, and yet each one, eventually, slowly recovered and by July, Maria and Elizabeth were enrolled at the new Clergy Daughters' School. Charlotte followed three weeks later and Emily joined her sisters there in November.

The purpose of the school and its curriculum was to produce young women with the education and skills to teach or work within the middle classes. There was a regimental approach which laid great emphasis on religious instruction. The school's benefactor, the Reverend William Carus Wilson, had Calvinistic leanings and it was this doctrine that was taught and firmly instilled into all that the girls did. The emphasis was on obedience, plain and simple food and dress, and a lack of home comforts that, it was believed, would distract the pupils from ideas of pride or self-indulgence. The reasoning was that the girls would become pious and humble. It is impossible to tell after all this time, just how strict the school was in its teachings and how much individual care and attention the girls received. They were there to learn and to abide by the rules without question or favour and it would appear that many found the regime harsh and even cruel.

Mixed reports from former pupils and teachers have been passed down through the years. Whilst some girls instantly recognised the school in Charlotte Brontë's description of Lowood in *Jane Eyre*, others were less accusing. There was talk of libel and a controversy arose which certainly showed that the cook had to be dismissed due to her dirty habits and the poor state of the food she prepared.

The removal to the school of the eldest two Brontë girls was the first of a series of dramatic events that would deeply affect the younger Brontë siblings. When Maria and Elizabeth were enrolled at the school on 21 July 1824 their close relationship and support were lost to their siblings and only three weeks later, on 10 August, Charlotte followed her elder sisters and was also enrolled.

When Charlotte travelled to Cowan Bridge, it was her first trip away from home and the shock of the school and its harsh regime caused her great unhappiness. Added to this, if we are to interpret her fictional Lowood and its pupils in *Jane Eyre* as the blueprint for life at school, she had to witness her own sisters being hurt and humiliated by the schoolmistresses. One wonders here if Charlotte blamed her aunt as the reason that the girls were being sent away to school. She must have heard that it was her aunt's intention to return to Cornwall when all five girls were at Cowan Bridge. This could, I suggest, have affected Charlotte's later view of her aunt and affected their relationship. Aunt Elizabeth, could have, and did, become the girls' educator and one could argue that it was perhaps her hankering to return home that led in part, to the girls being sent away. It is therefore possible that it was something that the girls, or even the family, blamed Elizabeth for, a circumstance that could not be forgotten or forgiven.

As stated, the regime at the school was one of discipline and obedience. The pupils were not expected to leave the school except for a five week break in the summer, and letter writing was only allowed once in every term. This meant that the Brontë girls had little or no means of seeing their family or home for nearly a year. Furthermore, they would be aware that their father was doing his best to have them educated for their future. To criticise the school, and ultimately his decision-making, would not be permissible. This placed the girls in a terrible dilemma; they could neither explain nor complain to their father for fear of seeming ungrateful and unworthy.

How much Patrick chose not to see or know of his daughters' school is difficult to assess. He badly needed the school to provide a home and an education for his daughters. The Garrs sisters would be leaving by the end of the year and he would employ a local woman, Tabitha Aykroyd (known as Tabby) as general housekeeper. Elizabeth was expected to return to Cornwall the following year, when Anne would be joining her sisters. This would greatly reduce Patrick's household and expenses. He would have only himself, Branwell and Tabby to cater for.

Patrick had taught at Woodhouse Grove and was aware that these types of schools had strict discipline with strong emphasis on religious teaching. At a time when many females remained uneducated, his girls had an exceptional opportunity. If the regime seemed difficult, after the leisure and security of home, then so be it, in many ways it was to be expected. The girls were there to learn not to be pampered or privileged.

Patrick accompanied each of his daughters to school in 1824. In the July, Maria and Elizabeth, in August, Charlotte and in November, Emily. He had the opportunity to meet the staff and view the surroundings. If the school was suitable and efficient, then it was the perfect opportunity for his girls and his family to settle into order and economic sufficiency. Having intimate knowledge of the male equivalent of his daughters' school at Woodhouse Grove, he would be aware that in comparison, the Clergy Daughters' School was, in fact, smaller and better equipped. The children had more clothing and better facilities in some areas. Patrick would also have been impressed by the list of patrons which included William Wilberforce, one of Patrick's own educational benefactors, and the Reverend Charles Simeon, who had inspired Patrick at university. There was also Miss Currer, a philanthropic lady who had sent Patrick money after the death of his wife. Such eminent people, among others, would help to assure Patrick that the school was to be held in high esteem. We can perhaps criticise Patrick in hindsight but it would appear that he sent his girls there in absolute faith that he was doing the right thing by them and by the rest of his household.

Back at Haworth, after Charlotte had left for school, the three youngest, aged 7, 6 and 4 had a strange experience which could have cost them their lives. On the afternoon of 2 September 1824, whilst out walking on the moors with their nurses, a sudden and dramatic storm occurred. This was accompanied by a massive upheaval of earth as the local bog burst at Crow Hill, about four miles from Haworth. It caused a landslide of mud and water that rolled down the moors killing livestock and sweeping aside all vegetation and stone walling in its path. Patrick heard the explosion from the parsonage and was fearful for his children's safety as he had no idea if they had reached shelter in the ensuing deluge. It is thought that they probably took refuge at either Top Withens Farm or Ponden Hall; both survive today – one as a ruin and the other as a beautiful private home. They all returned safely though thoroughly drenched and frightened. To Patrick this was a sign from God and he preached a sermon on this apocalyptical event the following Sunday. He believed that the explosion or earthquake and its ensuing destruction was a reminder to people that the end was always near and that they should always be prepared for the final judgement. Had his children been closer to the eruption and its fallout, they could easily have died or been seriously injured. This was another traumatic and dangerous situation that these very young children experienced.

Towards the end of November, when Patrick took Emily to join her older sisters, it left just Branwell and Anne at home. Their aunt was still looking after them but the Garrs sisters were preparing to leave. Branwell was now 7 years old and Anne would be 5 in January. However, before arrangements could be made for Anne's turn to go to school, tragedy struck. In February 1825, Maria was sent home from school fatally ill with Tuberculosis.

Branwell and Anne saw and heard the return of their eldest sister and experienced the effects of her painful and drawn out death. Once again, the bedroom turned into a sick room as Maria suffered for many days and nights with pain, shortness of breath and loss of appetite and weight. Her suffering would overtake all other household demands as her father and aunt fought tirelessly for her recovery. In a scene echoing that of Mrs Brontë's death, the adults did their best to save another member of the family and yet, on 6 May Maria died and within a couple of weeks, Elizabeth also came home with the same fatal illness and took her sister's place in the sickroom.

Tuberculosis, possibly caught and exacerbated by the lack of physical care at the school, had taken hold and on seeing his second daughter dangerously ill, Patrick rushed over to the school to bring Charlotte and Emily home and found them already removed to Reverend Wilson's home at Silverdale, near Morecambe. There was an obvious crisis at the school and girls had been ill for some time with various ailments and a 'low fever'. It was reported that:

> *Of the fifty-three pupils there at the same time as the Brontës, one died at Cowan Bridge and eleven left school in ill health; six of them died soon after reaching home. There clearly was a particular problem in the first nine months of 1825 ... the school lost a third of its pupils in only the second year of its existence.*[1]

With the four youngest now all at home during Elizabeth's last weeks, the children must all have felt that some dreadful ongoing cycle was claiming their family, one by one.

It is interesting to note at this point that Tuberculosis is still a killer, 200 years after the deaths of the Brontë girls. Statistics for the disease worldwide show it as thirteenth in the table of twenty highest causes of death in humans. Approximately ten million people contracted the disease in 2021 and 1.6 million died. The chances of recovery for the sisters were nil. They would have died from an accumulation of symptoms that could include any or some of the following: Pneumonia, sepsis, gastrointestinal bleeding, suffocation, cardiac arrest, renal failure, meningitis, pleurisy, and haemoptysis (vomiting blood). The main symptoms of the disease in its early stages are a persistent cough, shortness of breath and chest pain, each caused by the effusions from the pleura that coat the membranes of the lungs. There are three stages of the disease:

1. Exposure. A person comes into contact with someone coughing or sneezing and the droplet infection is passed on to them.
2. Latent. This is where the infected person harbours the disease and may spread it to others. They may die within a short time or suffer repeated symptoms and flare ups, which eventually cause death over a period of time.
3. Active. The end stage of the disease when it takes full and permanent hold and causes death.

Once the active stage occurs there is little chance of survival. It is an awful way to die, and I will argue later that Anne's death may not have been the quiet fading away described by Charlotte.

Branwell, especially, revered his older sisters and wrote long poems about the deaths of young girls and his losses. The others also recalled, time and again, the effects of these deaths on their young lives. Glad to be home once more and together, the children were surrounded with the memories of their sisters and living in a house that had become both familiar and unfamiliar, happy and sad, with adults who were helpless to make things better. Life resembled a, *Vallis Lacrimarum* the Christian 'vale of tears' that is left to those on earth when a loved one dies.

There was no question of the children going back to school and Aunt Elizabeth's remaining hopes of returning to Cornwall were now gone. She was needed even more to help the children deal with their grief and to support their broken father. Elizabeth Branwell had lived through the loss of her own siblings and now she was vitally needed to help her charges to come to terms with theirs. Those months of 1825 must have been some of the saddest for all of the family and the children were all so much more aware of what was happening in the sick room. The remaining family must have noted how rooms, objects, clothes and dreams would all serve as constant reminders to them, as they did to Heathcliff, that:

> *The entire world is a dreadful collection of memoranda that she did exist, and that I have lost her.*[2]

If there was one consolation, it was the firm belief, instilled by their father's faith, that their mother and sisters were together in heaven, where there was no more suffering. One cannot question why or how others choose to embrace religious beliefs. Indoctrinated from birth one can understand how children develop their faith, when their parents or carers believe absolutely and rear their children within that same mindset. Belief in the afterlife may not seem viable in modern day science-based ideology, but Christian belief is, and always was, based on the resurrection and of Christ as the son of God, who prepares the way for believers to enter the kingdom of heaven. It is not my place to argue religious beliefs, all I can comment is that the young Brontës, Patrick and Elizabeth all clung to these Christian principles and that they must have been some comfort to them all.

What had happened at the Clergy Daughters' School to bring about this appalling result? As we know, Charlotte described her experience of the school in *Jane Eyre* where she names it, appropriately, 'Lowood'. She gave her personal account of the regime and included the abuse and degradation of some of the girls, which suggested that she was also describing Maria's treatment. As stated, there is evidence to support Charlotte's description and her complaints, and also against them, from pupils and teachers who attended at the same time. The school, like many other similar establishments, was rigorous and demanding of the pupils. They were there to learn and to be disciplined and meticulous in their habits and their behaviour. They were poor children and were expected to recognise that fact and not expect anything fancy or frivolous.

It is interesting to note that Patrick had arranged for Maria to have extra coaching as she was deemed intelligent and academic, whereas Elizabeth would receive only a grounding which would prepare her for domesticity. Woodhouse Grove school offered a very similar education and regime for boys of Methodist ministers, but with the view of the boys entering the Church or some other respectable profession. Criticism of many schools occurred at this time and Woodhouse Grove had its fair share. Dickens later satirised schools like them by describing Dotheboys Hall in *Nicholas Nickleby* and, even today, some of the most prestigious private schools still carry an air of strong religious faith and strict discipline. Patrick could not expect his children to enjoy their schooling so much as appreciate their opportunity to be educated, according to their needs. A low fever, probably Typhus, pervaded the school but was either unrecognised or ignored by the staff. Maria and Elizabeth's recent recovery from whooping cough and measles and lowered resistance to disease, may have attracted the Tuberculosis bacteria, a disease spread by droplet infection through coughs and sneezing.

We know now that the housekeeper was totally inefficient and often ruined whatever decent food the children were given. We also know that the positioning of the school in a low, damp valley, was not conducive to healthy fresh air. The four mile round walk to Tunstall church and a full day spent in the unheated building every Sunday did little to improve the health of underfed and weak children who were often cold and wet. This Sunday ritual was at the insistence of Reverend Wilson. His Calvinistic beliefs meant that he preached to the girls more about sin than salvation. His religious scripts highlight this attitude and could further confuse and upset many of the Anglican pupils. In one of his tracts, he wrote about a little girl who died a horrible death and went to hell for her sins. He wrote that this child:

> ... *would have her own way. Oh! How cross she looks. And oh! What a sad tale have I to tell you of her. She was in such a rage, that all at once God struck her dead. She fell down on the floor, and died. No time to pray. No time to call on God to save her poor soul. She left this world in the midst of her sin. And oh! Where do you think she is now? I do not like to think of it. But we know that bad girls go to hell when they die...*[3]

It was this type of terrifying story that the girls at the school had to listen to and to live with and try to come to terms with. The Brontë girls had been reared to believe in a loving and merciful God and these horrible tales must have both frightened and confused them. It would appear that the staff also believed in the doctrines of sin and hell and therefore treated the girls as sinners rather than as children who had been blessed and needed to be coaxed into abiding by Christian morals and principles, through example and guidance.

Calvinism is a type of reformed Christianity and a major branch of Protestantism. It was founded by John Calvin, one of the Reformation theologians and it centres on three main doctrines. Firstly, God as the centre and creator of all things; secondly, the human species as depraved and in need of constant attention to God and the Bible for guidance and belief. Thirdly, and in this they differ from most other Protestant religions, they believe in predestination. This is the idea that God decided a long time ago who could attain heaven and who could not. He selected a number of souls on which to grant salvation and it was seen as impossible to join this select group. These people were 'the elect' and nothing one could do could alter what God had preordained. However, no-one but God knew who 'the elect' were and therefore, all people had to behave as if they might be one of the chosen. This suggested that one had to remain free of all the sins known to mankind!

One can imagine how challenging this could be for children brought up to believe in the concept of universal salvation, where anyone who had faith in Christ and atoned their sins could enter heaven. Both at the Clergy Daughters' School and later at Roe Head School, the Brontë girls were all exposed to Calvinist beliefs which questioned and contradicted their father's teachings. It is difficult, even now, to fully explain and understand all of the different religious beliefs prevalent in this country at this time. I have offered a list of the most common ones and some of the terms used at the beginning of this book, for that very reason. Many ideas had infiltrated from Europe and the more people became educated and travelled, the more aware they became of the multiple belief systems. Haworth itself had various religious churches which all preached slightly different beliefs and ideas. Patrick had issues with some of them but was wise enough to accept difference and the need to educate people in all areas of their spiritual requirements. I shall refer to Calvinism often in this book and I support Stevie Davies's bold statement that:

> ... the greatest predator on the Brontë family was not consumption but Calvinism.[4]

Dr Davies describes how Anne was fearful that she would not be allowed into heaven because of her sinfulness. One also questions whether Anne ever dared wonder if her mother and sisters had been allowed into that hallowed place. A religious morbidity appears to have surrounded Anne for most of her life and its many conflicting doctrines and dictates upset and troubled her. Anne wrote an amazing poem which she entitled *A Word to the Calvinists*. The title was later changed, by Charlotte, to *A Word to the Elect*. It was written long after Anne's religious crises and at a time when she was more sure in her faith and her God. She appears to have been able, by May 1843, to challenge the religious doctrine which had caused her so much heartache.

There is a very interesting breakdown of this poem by Emmeline Burdett in her 2023 essay, 'An Erring Spirit? Anne Brontë's Words to the "elect" and the Question of Universal Salvation'. Dr Burdett describes Anne's poem as:

> ... a passionate defence of Universal Salvation – the idea that there is no Hell... In many ways it represents a final victory over a doctrine which plagued Anne for much of her short life.[5]

The essay links the poem to events in both *Agnes Grey* and *Wildfell Hall* and it also highlights Anne's preoccupation with sin, something that may have been influenced by her aunt's strict dictates. One is reminded of the scene in *Agnes Grey* where the Reverend Hatfield has no care or empathy for Nancy Brown, an elderly parishioner who is unable, due to rheumatism, to walk to the church. He tells her that if she cannot derive comfort from the church and her Bible then 'it is all up' and she will not be able to enter heaven. Sin is shown here as having no ending; Nancy is doomed because she cannot get to the church. This scene, which Nancy describes to Agnes, is very telling of the idea that religion can be difficult and confusing to grasp, especially if the preacher has little or no commitment to his job or to his flock and no patience or understanding of their needs. Going to church was seen as a necessary part of one's faith, so to fail to attend was a sin in itself. One had to be seen to believe and church attendance was part of that.

Anne appears to have worked through her doubts and fears by the time this poem was published in the sisters' book of poems in 1846. It is an impassioned statement that denies predestination and challenges its concepts. Anne had now the strength and surety to admonish the doctrine after years of her religious torment. The first two stanzas set out Anne's argument.

A Word to the Elect

> *You may rejoice to think yourselves secure,*
> *You may be grateful for the gift divine,*
> *That grace unsought, which made your black hearts pure*
> *And fits your earth – born souls in Heaven to shine*
>
> *But is it sweet to look around and view*
> *Thousands excluded from that happiness,*
> *Which they deserve at least as much as you.*
> *Their faults not greater nor their virtues less?*[6]

The poem is well worth a close reading and shows Anne with a renewed strength where she can challenge the doctrine that blighted her early faith.

In 1825, Anne had the comfort of believing that her mother and sisters were together in God's safe keeping, long before Calvinism brought her doubt and worry. The devastation to the Brontë family following the deaths of the eldest two girls is hard to imagine. Patrick must have felt some responsibility for their deaths and this could only have added to his grief. The weeks and weeks of sickness and long nights of suffering permanently affected the adults and children. Juliet Barker recalls these losses on the remaining children, in the following:

> *It was not simply that they lost two of their sisters, but that they lost their two eldest sisters. The younger children had naturally looked to them for the leadership and support which elder children provide. In their case this role had taken on even greater importance because Maria, and to a lesser extent Elizabeth, had helped to fill the void caused by their mother's death so early in their lives. Once again they had been deprived of a maternal figure in the family.*[7]

Knowing that other people are suffering in a similar way does nothing to relieve one's grief, and it is still important to recognise that life in Haworth in the early years of the nineteenth century was extremely difficult. Poverty and poor housing added to the problem and with no health care to speak of everyone was vulnerable. Juliet Barker reminds us that:

> *Typhus fever was virulent in the neighbourhood; one of Patrick's parishioners, Benjamin Burwin of Far Oxenhope, lost his wife, four daughters, three sons and a grandson in under three months.*[8]

These stark statistics are appalling but not uncommon. A walk around the graveyard surrounding St Michael's church in Haworth presents dozens of gravestones listing children who have died in infancy and childhood. They are buried here in their thousands as testament to the conditions and hardships in Haworth and the surrounding areas. These deaths may have been common, excessive and repetitive, but the grief that they engendered was surely enduring.

In an earlier chapter I referenced what is now known as ACE. or Adverse Childhood Experiences. These are:

> ... *highly stressful, and potentially traumatic, events or situations that occur during childhood and/or adolescence. They can be a single event, or prolonged threats to, and breaches of, the young person's safety, security, trust or bodily integrity.*[9]

A look at the lives of the young Brontës presents a horrible example of trauma and stress, and to fail to acknowledge this is to misunderstand them all. Their home had become a place of death and there was no escaping from it, except to leave it behind on the only journey they could achieve, which was long walks into the natural habitat of the moors. The moors offered solace, it had life and energy and all the cacophony of nature and the smells and beauty of flowers and heather. There are lonely and quiet areas, hills and sheer rocks and the sound of water and waterfalls. It is the opposite of the sickroom and the coffin. It has light and fresh, breathable air, sun and rain, warmth and wide and distant aspects. There is little wonder that it was, and remained, a place of escape and comfort for these harassed children.

But something else had changed when Maria and Elizabeth died, something that would also affect these children for the rest of their lives. With the death of their two siblings, the natural hierarchy within the family had been upset and altered. The third daughter, the untitled and less important girl, Charlotte, *suddenly became the eldest child.*

Charlotte was just 9 years old when her elder sisters died, but old enough to take on their mantle. I suggest that she did so completely and absolutely, becoming the lead child in the household, a challenge to her brother and a superior to her two younger sisters. Whether this happened consciously is difficult to assess, but Charlotte moved up in position and remained there permanently. I will show how this move gave her dominance and authority which she never failed to express. Charlotte became the loudest voice, the dominating and domineering eldest child who became the decision-maker, the leader and eventually, through her belief that she had to be seen to be doing her best for everyone, turned into someone who may have caused more suffering by her interference and repeated tyranny than most researchers are willing to acknowledge.

The Return of Tragedy

Many people hold a belief throughout life that they know what is best for everyone around them. They try to help others and may have their best interests at heart, but can become so blind to their own behaviour that they fail to recognise that how they interpret others, even those they love, is not necessarily the correct version. Had Charlotte remained the third daughter, I believe that she would have developed a far more generous and loving relationship with her siblings. She would have had no need to direct them and dictate how they behaved. Charlotte also appears, as she matured, to have overtaken the adults in the family. She took her father as her confidante and used his 'illnesses' as a constant excuse not to do anything that she did not want to do. She pampered and protected him more and more as she grew older and he seems to have relished it. Similarly, her aunt also appears to have succumbed and become subject to Charlotte's demands and persuasions, possibly following Patrick's lead and not wishing to cause upset.

Charlotte was the only one who gained anything by the death of her siblings. I am not suggesting that it was something that she wanted at the time, and it was unavoidable that she became the eldest, but I do believe that once she realised the power that it gave, she clung on to it and it dictated the way she lived and communicated with her family and friends throughout her life.

Charlotte had had no identity; she was very small, short-sighted and unattractive. In other words, she had almost no attributes, nothing to make her predisposed to others, and she was very aware of that fact. Suddenly, after nine years of being just the third daughter she was the eldest, with all the control and prestige that this new status gave her. There are many people who are challenged in height who try to make up for it by drawing attention to themselves in other ways. Charlotte was exceptionally tiny, probably well under five feet and had little to attract attention or praise. Being the eldest brought a privilege and recognition that she had never previously known. As we move through the next chapters, I hope to show how this renewed family structure affected all of the remaining children and how their new roles in the hierarchy altered their behaviour and personalities in many subtle and often detrimental ways.

Emily was now the only one without a title. She was neither the eldest, the youngest nor the first of her gender. She was just the second daughter. This put her in an unenviable position. She had no particular status and her ideas and opinions could be smothered by her titled siblings. I suggest that Emily did what many children in her position end up doing; she withdraws into herself and disengages with much of the communication between her siblings. She may not do this physically and she may still communicate with them, but she is emotionally isolated within herself and does not willingly yield to the demands of others. Consequently, she may be viewed as stubborn, stoic and distant. Very often, a middle child will turn to other ways of gaining attention – art, music, or writing, for example. If a female, she may become placid, a peacemaker between her siblings rather than demanding or attention seeking.

We see these traits in Emily Brontë – the withdrawal, the lack of communication, the reserve and the need to be left alone at home, where she feels safe and yet permanently on watch in case another family member succumbs to illness. Emily's height, as opposed to her siblings' short stature, is often remarked on as her particular distinguishing feature. Again, a child who is taller than those around her of similar age may well stoop or try to minimise their distinguishing feature. It makes them too noticeable and standing out from the crowd. Branwell, the male, needs to be the tall one, not one of his sisters.

This is another way that parents often signify their children. 'Look how tall he/she is' / 'Hasn't she got lovely hair' / 'Is your child the one with the lovely singing voice?' / 'He is so naughty, isn't he?' Parents and others often pick an outstanding physical feature and label the child accordingly and these labels often remain. They can be harmful and very difficult to lose. Branwell is short in stature, has red hair and a long nose, Charlotte is tiny, stunted even, and short-sighted, Emily is tall and withdrawn, Anne is shy and delicate. These attributes separate and define children in ways that objectify them rather than enhance their personalities and characters. As so with the Brontë siblings where we define Branwell as the 'Black Sheep', no matter how talented and intelligent he was. He is defined by his behaviour in his last few years, not by his childhood abilities or contribution to the Brontë canon. It is dangerous to continue to label anyone by a single and detrimental, or attractive, attribute. It blinds one to their true abilities and qualities. How often are we told that Charlotte was a 'genius', Emily was a 'mystic' and Anne, 'dear gentle Anne', was a 'lesser writer' in the shadow of her talented sisters. These labels stick and they wrongly define these people. Language can be a very dangerous tool and one throw-away remark can label a person for life. I will argue again, later how Ellen Nussey's description of Emily and Anne as 'like twins' has become a defining phrase that has carried this anomaly throughout two centuries.

I wonder about another label that we all give our children ... their names. I am especially interested in the names that Patrick gave his children. Names are the particular label that defines each person and is their signature. We are labelled at birth and it is done without our knowledge or consent and I suggest it can affect people both positively and negatively, especially if one dislikes their given name. It must be noted that the name Anne begins with a soft vowel and has only one syllable, unlike those of her siblings. It is difficult to bawl the name Anne across a room, or even a moor! (One cannot imagine Heathcliff hollering Anne across miles of heathland.) There are not enough consonants in the word to strike a significant noise. The very name is quiet, almost silent. One almost expects it to continue to the next syllable (e.g. Annabelle). Anne on its own carries little weight, it is light and soft. It suggests gentleness. The definition of the name comes from the Hebrew, Hannah, and means 'Grace'. A very apt description of Anne Brontë. It also means 'God has favoured me'. *AN* was also the name of the mythical Sumerian sky god, with its Babylonian counterpart, *ANU*. I am sure that Anne would be aware of the meaning and interpretations of her name and that it may also have influenced her dilemmas around 'salvation' and 'predestination'. Feeling that her name meant something special and that she was 'favoured' by God may have helped Anne to believe in herself and her salvation in Christ.

Most British names have derived from Hebrew, Greek, Italian, French and Aramaic. Patrick means 'Nobleman', though most names have more than one meaning, and in Patrick's case it was of course the name of Ireland's patron saint, and is a common Catholic Christian name. Maria is from the Aramaic meaning 'Beloved' but the Biblical meaning is 'Meek', 'Merciful', 'Pure in Heart or Blessed'. Elizabeth is derived from the Hebrew, Elisheva and means 'God's promise' and was the name of the mother of John the Baptist. Charlotte is the French or Italian derivative of Charles, meaning, 'Freeman or Industrious'. Emily is from the Roman name Aemilius meaning, 'Rival', 'Industrious', 'Eager' or 'to Emulate'. Furthermore, at this time names were seen as a way of bringing the child into the extended family. Children, as in the Brontës' case, were named after close relatives and carried both mother and father references. For example, Patrick Branwell Brontë. Nowadays this happens far less often. Research has shown that children with unusual names are often separated from their peers and that adolescents with names they dislike are more likely to become deviant, or certainly adopt nicknames to hide their embarrassment.

The Brontë children took a great deal of trouble over the names of their characters. Many in their various sagas were made up from foreign and strange sounding words with alliteration or forceful syllables or romantic connotations. Sometimes they were a caricature of local people, for example Mr Sudbury Figgs (Abraham Sunderland, their early music teacher); others were strong like Alexander Rogue, or noble like Arthur Augustus Adrian Wellesley, the Duke of Zamorna and Marquis of Douro. In the 'Gondal Saga' there is the romantic and beautiful Rosobelle Eraldon. The children put a lot of thought and imagination into naming their characters. One wonders how much Anne's name affected her siblings view of her.

Anne could also be the butt of internal jokes by the others that were cruel and hurtful. After Anne's death, Charlotte appears to blame Anne for being her own worst enemy. Charlotte recalls Anne as:

> *Long-suffering, self-denying, reflective, and intelligent, a constitutional reserve and taciturnity placed and kept her in the shade.*[10]

It sounds to me far more as though Charlotte is trying to abnegate any responsibility for Anne's quiet reserve and self-deprecating manner; as if she had no harmful effect on Anne's personality.

Like birth order, our names are also significant as to how we see ourselves and are seen by others. My husband and I argued for the best part of nine months as to what to name our first child. After he was born this continued until we had to compromise with a name that neither of us were truly happy with. I still regret not being able to name my child from my choices and feel that he now has a name that is rarely used anymore and does not suit his personality as an adult. Ironically, he has recently altered it by deed poll. Naming your child is a difficult and important decision that could deeply affect them, especially as nowadays names are often fashionable and even linked to celebrities or completely made up.

Charlotte and Branwell had strong family names and as highest in the new pecking order, they naturally fought for dominance. Emily had only Anne for comfort and partnership and Anne was the youngest and least valued in the group. Dr Edward Chitham, distinguished academic and renowned biographer of Anne, drew my attention to an article in the *International Handbook of Research of Giftedness and Talent*, in which Joan Freeman (University of London) states that:

> There are ... recognised personality characteristics for each child's position in the family. First-born and only children are more likely to be more concerned with the effects they have on adults and to be more responsible; the second-born is more easy-going and has more friends; the third-born is often more difficult to live with; while the fourth is often babied and so learns to be more dependent.[11]

I suggest that we can see some of these traits in the remaining four Brontë siblings and wherever there is more than one child in a family of mixed or single gender. The eldest leads and the others follow. They may challenge the eldest and argue and battle with them, but their position is subservient and always will be so. Branwell challenged Charlotte until she left home to go to Roe Head School when she was 15 years old. Emily had no status and withdrew physically and emotionally into herself, and Anne was dominated and even bullied by her elder siblings, especially Charlotte, and this was a life-long relationship.

In her book *Sisters*, Brigid McConville says that:

> Researchers have found that the oldest child ... tends to assume responsibility for other children, and it is a sense of responsibility that is rarely shaken off ... the glow of self-satisfaction, of being useful, of being needed ... and of being in control... (are the rewards).[12]

Charlotte's control of the Brontë family slowly emerges throughout her life and in her letters and behaviour. Charlotte is the narrator of the Brontës' lives and I maintain that it is her beliefs and opinions that have dictated how we have come to see and understand the rest of her family.

Edward Chitham, in his latest biography of Anne Brontë, makes a most valid point about Charlotte's influence on the Brontë Story. He states that:

> *I regard Charlotte as a stage-producer of the Brontë drama, and Elizabeth Gaskell as an interpreter of the play.*[13]

I totally agree but would go a step further. To me, Charlotte is a 'Nelly Dean' figure who often misunderstands and misinterprets life around her and whose interference and belief in her position is sadly misguided. Nelly Dean states in *Wuthering Heights*:

> *I went about my household duties, convinced that The Grange had but one sensible soul in its walls, and that lodged in my body.*[14]

She has been described as the true villain in the book because she manipulates the characters and is the root cause of some of their unhappiness. The main characters trust her and go to her for advice, like they would an older sister. However, her advice is often unreliable and subjective. Like Charlotte, she wants to do her best for others but doesn't understand them or appreciate them enough to know what is best, and causes them grief by interfering. Charlotte was an extremely talented writer but, I suggest, often a rather poor sister.

Charlotte is the family mouthpiece, the organiser, the controller and the censor. She is a person who needs to be in control. Most of what is known about the Brontë family comes via Charlotte and she only related what she wanted people to know. Later in this work, I will demonstrate how Charlotte manipulated family members and how much she dictated and organised events. She is the 'unreliable narrator' whose observations and recordings cannot always be presumed as authentic. Charlotte only allows us a version of her family that she has sanitised and approved. Being the last surviving sibling, she can say and do whatever she likes about her brother and sisters, with no-one to contradict or challenge her.

After Anne's death, almost nothing of her remained – a couple of letters and diary papers and a handful of effects. Most of the 'Gondal Saga' and her many letters have not survived. If Anne had never written her books, poetry and hymns, and had them published, there would be almost nothing to show that she had ever existed.

Chapter Five

Confined and Contained
1825–1831

When Maria and Elizabeth died the remaining children ranged in age between Charlotte at 9 years old and Anne at 5. Branwell was nearly 8 and Emily was coming up to 7. They were lively, healthy and intelligent children all saddened and deeply affected by the deaths, but with the exuberance and resilience of childhood. They wanted to play, to learn, to run about and to investigate life within the confines of the parsonage and the church, and in the freedom of the moors. Home, religion and nature were their options and they had the enthusiasm of their young lives to explore all three.

Their father and aunt would keep them at home together for the next five years, rarely mixing with other children and turned in on themselves for all their childhood needs and companionship. They would have laughed, cried, played, washed, ate and slept together, in what was initially a harmony that they probably expected to last throughout their lives. Charlotte later described them in these years as like 'mushrooms growing in a cellar'. Their enforced, enclosed and restricted home life kept them in the dark as regards social interaction and their growth was confined and forced rather than a natural development.

This confinement and inter-dependency fostered the burgeoning of vivid imaginations. Each child read widely from books, journals and newspapers and listened to tales from their father about his rogue Irish ancestors. Their aunt related tales from her gay life in Cornwall, with all of its sea stories and smuggling adventures, and their housekeeper Tabby became a friend and confidante who repeated all the old tales of Haworth, at a time when 'fairies' lived in the valley bottom and the mills had not been invented.

The necessity to keep them occupied and educated meant a strict regime of lessons and play that would help them to overcome their losses and keep them focused and amused. Drawing and music took their interests and writing their own stories and verse began to take over their leisure time.

They established a number of plays over the next two years involving a varied list of characters, places and events, often using their toys as the impetus. They would act out their dramas all over the house, including the cellar or away on the moors. Their boisterous playing once had Tabby run away to her sister's house describing the children as all 'gooin mad'.

They were children and had to express themselves as all children want to. The elder ones would push and boss the younger and tell them what to do and when and where to do it. This would cause all the inevitable fallouts and tears and aunt or Tabby, or even their father, would have to step in and sort out their little problems. This was natural childhood behaviour and has always been so. Anne would not be the leader or the role model, and Emily would probably stand back and let her enthusiastic brother and bossy sister take charge. It is the unwritten law of childhood, to learn one's place in the pecking order.

Charlotte and Emily shared a bed and they created their own secret 'bed plays' which were never written down as Charlotte noted that she would '… always remember them'.[1]

Anne was excluded as she was still sharing a room with her aunt. This separation helped to reinforce her isolation from her siblings' stories and emphasised her as the youngest, the baby and least able or notable.

The children had plenty of toys and Branwell received at least three sets of toy soldiers. However, one particular set was bought by Patrick, along with toys for the girls, in June of 1826. We still reward unhappy children with gifts to cheer them up and Patrick chose carefully and well. His choices reflected his observations made during the mask incident. For his lively and naughty son, he brought a box of soldiers – a typical, 'boys' toy' – perhaps in the hope that he would one day embark on a military career; a disciplined and ordered life which would calm and focus Branwell and build his confidence and self-esteem.

When Branwell came to Charlotte's room to show the girls his gift, Charlotte immediately rushed to claim hers before Emily. Charlotte described the scene and it completely echoes how each child behaved and their characteristics at this time:

> *Branwell came to our door with a box of soldiers. Emily and I jumped out of bed and I snatched up one and exclaimed this is the Duke of Wellington it shall be mine!*
>
> *Emily likewise took one and said it should be hers. When Anne came down she took one also. Mine was the prettiest of the whole and perfect in every part, Emily's was a grave looking fellow, we called him Gravey. Anne's was a queer little thing very much like herself. He was called Waiting Boy. Branwell chose Bonaparte.*[2]

How telling! What an insight into the children's personalities and Charlotte's role. She 'snatches' hers before Emily can touch them and names it proudly after her hero, The Duke of Wellington. Branwell has already taken Napoleon Bonaparte, he is the manly soldier who is ready to fight and conquer his sisters. Emily and Anne are left with less choice. Emily's soldier is grave and solemn, far less excited or excitable than the others, and Anne's is small and always waiting in the wings for her cue to act. These toys represent the children's temperaments and how Charlotte saw them and described them. The pecking order is being established with Charlotte and Branwell vying for first place and Emily and Anne background characters; Anne, hardly a character at all.

Another play, 'The Play of the Islanders', came about one night in December 1827 when the children were bored and tired but resisted going to bed. Gathered around the kitchen fire, Charlotte suggested that they each choose an island and a famous person to be their 'Chief of Men'. Predictably Branwell and Charlotte chose first, taking the two main British Islands. Branwell took the Isle of Man and Charlotte the Isle of Wight. Emily looks to the remote north and chooses the wild Isle of Arran, whilst Anne's choice is the warm but less notable Isle of Guernsey. Again, Charlotte wants the military leader, politician and soon to be prime minister, The Duke of Wellington as her chief, whilst Branwell choses Lord George Herries, the politician and financier, who is currently the Lord Chancellor. Emily champions the Scottish Baird, Sir Walter Scott and Anne promotes Lord George Bentinck, former British army officer and Tory politician. At this point the clock strikes 7 p.m. and they are shuffled off to bed.

These choices show again the dominance of the elder siblings but also one observes children completely conversant with British politics. They can name Tory politicians and know their military history. Reading and appreciation of literature was also emerging; Walter Scott became their favourite author. The children were still all under 12 years of age and obviously gaining more and more political awareness. This was partly due to the high level of education that their father was supervising and his encouragement and discussion of important events. Added to this was their free rein to read whatever books they chose.

One of the major sources of information came from the children's reading of *Blackwood's Edinburgh Magazine.* Founded in 1817 by William Blackwood, this Tory journal, published to rival the Whigg supported *Edinburgh Review,* was edited by John Wilson, writing under the pseudonym of Christopher North. There were major contributions from John Lockhart and William Maginn. The magazine offered a range of political and social essays, humour, stories, criticism, romances, satire, reviews and poetry and later included horror stories. The poets included Byron, Shelley, Keats, Wordsworth and James Hogg, the 'Ettrick Shepherd'. Their poems were often published for review and criticism – a skill which the Brontës all adopted so that they learnt to be self-critical and to be careful and exact in their later writings. William Maginn went on to edit *Fraser's Magazine* in London, another journal popular with the Brontës which was subscribed for them by Aunt Elizabeth in 1831.

I have my own two volumes of bound copies of *Blackwood's Edinburgh Magazine* running from July to December 1825 and January to June 1827. They contain everything that the Brontës would have read in them between those dates and the contents are fascinating. I often read them and find myself linking some of the poetry and articles to Brontë literature. The following few headings give an idea of the range and variation of the subjects:

The Catholic Question. (July 1825)
Parry's Last Days of Lord Byron. (August 1825)
The New German School of Tragedy. (September 1825)
Letters on the present state of India. (October 1825)
The Orphan Maid's Lament. (November 1825)
On the Use of Metaphors. (December 1825)

Letter on Ricardo's Theory of Rent. (January 1827)
On Murder, Considered as One of the Fine Arts. (February 1827)
The Corn Laws. No 2. (March 1827)
The Shepherd's Calendar. (April 1827)
Sierra Leone – Civilization of Africa. (May 1827)
Dr Phillpotts Letters to Mr Canning. (June 1827)[3]

There cannot be a more eclectic list of titles and each magazine averaged a dozen of these features. The poetry and prose were music to the Brontës and were reflected in many of their literary endeavours. The magazines were a wealth of information to their readers and useful sources of political, geographical and literary events from around the world. Blackwood's did not cease publication until 1981!

On The Death of a Daughter in the February 1827 edition is a poem that reads like an ode to Maria and Elizabeth. Part of the verses are as follows:

> *Tis o'er-in that long sigh she past-*
> *Th' enfranchised spirit soars at last!*
>
> *And now I gaze with tearless eye*
> *On what to view was agony.*
> *That panting heart is tranquil now,*
> *And heav'nly calm that ruffles brow.*

The Brontë Family: Sibling Rivalry and a Burial in Paradise

And those pale lips which feebly strove
To force one parting smile of love,
Retain it yet-soft, placid, mild,
As when it graced my living child!

And I have sat the long, long night,
And mark'd that tender flower decay,
Not torn abruptly from the sight,
But slowly, sadly waste away!

The poem ends with the lines:

But the sad conflict's past- 'tis o'er,
That gentle bosom throbs no more!
The spirit's freed-through realms of light
Faith's eagle-glance pursues her flight

To other worlds, to happier skies;
Hope dries the tear that sorrow weepeth.
No mortal sound the voice which cries,
'The damsel is not dead, but sleepeth!' [4]

Blackwood's must have comforted, excited and informed its readers in so many ways and reading it today gives a wonderful insight into the world 200 years ago; a world studied and embraced by the Brontë siblings. Its information added enormously to their knowledge of home and abroad and helped to furnish their ideas. It also demonstrated how to write articles, to punctuate, arrange and focus.

The urge to write and to explore myths and fables, love and relationships, death and horror, peacetime and battles, peasants and nobility, all became a passion and their lively and enquiring minds began to devise a whole new world for themselves. This world was theirs and no-one else could enter it or know of it. It was populated by fantasy figures who lived in exotic places and remote islands where conflict was ever present. It also gave these stricken children an exceptional power – that over life and death itself. They could resurrect the dead whenever they wished, they were answerable to no-one but themselves and they could create anything that they chose.

Their writings and musings became the 'Great Glasstown Saga' and was initially the work of all four children, with Branwell and Charlotte, as always, taking the lead roles. One can imagine the arguments and rivalry as four equally intelligent and enthusiastic children fought to have their individual views and ideas accepted by the others. Branwell's enthusiasm for soldiers and his indulgence in battles and warfare was perhaps less acceptable to his sisters, over time. One wonders whether anyone was listening to Anne's ideas. It is doubtful that her input was exceptional but more an indulgence by the others to include her. She did not have the 'age and experience' of her siblings, so her views would not carry the same weight.

It was inevitable that the two eldest and the two youngest would eventually separate. Children often pair off when there is an even number. Charlotte and Branwell were very close during these five years that they all spent at home. They may well have rivalled each other and encouraged each other's literary output. Closest in age and with similar drive and enthusiasm, they were more of a pair than Emily and Anne during this time. Charlotte and Emily would still be sleeping together though and were able to bond over stories and ideas, separate from Anne.

One feels that Emily and Anne had little option but to eventually turn to each other, not because they were similar in ideas and personalities, but more because they were, at times, abandoned by their elder siblings and excluded from their writings and their ideas. Charlotte's school friend, Ellen Nussey, described the family when she visited the Parsonage in 1833 recording that the two youngest girls were 'like twins. Inseparable companions and in the closest sympathy which never had any interruption'.[5]

This labelling has blinded Brontë scholars ever since and bound Emily and Anne together. I suggest that the personalities of the two girls were widely different and that twinning them has, again, suggested that neither of them could stand alone, but always had to be attached to the other. Whilst there is no doubt that the girls were close, I feel that they had little option but to join together in their writing because as they grew older, Charlotte and Branwell drifted away and set up their separate tales of 'Angria'. Eventually that partnership perished as Charlotte left for Roe Head School and met new friends who were outside of the close family circle. Whilst their sagas continued, Branwell eventually lost his writing partner and he and Charlotte were never as close again.

However, between the years of 1825 and 1831 all four children were inseparable whilst developing their own personalities and ideas. Their imaginations were prolific, but much of the writing down of their plays, poetry, sagas and letters was completed by Charlotte and Branwell, especially as they were the most proficient writers. Some writings were recorded in their 'little books' using whatever paper they could find. In order to keep their fiction from the eyes of the adults, they wrote in miniscule letters. There are other reasons for this. Both Charlotte and Branwell were very short sighted and both had to wear glasses. Charlotte suffered especially and both her writing and her drawings show the minutiae of letters and detail. Although there is not very much extant writing remaining from Emily or Anne, it is clear to see that Emily, especially, had atrocious spelling to the point where one wonders if she was possibly dyslexic.

Writing with a quill pen is not easy and is a skill that not everyone can master. I have tried it lately and am hopelessly inept. It must have taken a great deal of time and effort for a child to master. Whilst the manuscript of *Jane Eyre* proves that as an adult, Charlotte had beautiful and easily read hand writing, we do not have the manuscripts of Emily or Anne's novels to compare. The scraps of 'diary papers', written by Emily and Anne, are messy, blotched and the grammar and spelling is poor, even when they were writing as adults. This would all help to explain the frustration of Charlotte and Branwell if and when the younger two wanted to be the scribes. Neither of the two eldest were noted for their patience and one suspects that they would have imagined, directed and recorded 'Glasstown' themselves, rather than wait to indulge the younger girls. This must have caused conflict. Branwell tended to have an idea, run with it for a while and then pass it over to Charlotte to complete. This happened with his 'Branwell's Blackwoods Magazine' and his history of the 'Young Men'. It shows Branwell's excitable and mercurial nature; his enthusiasm and drive followed by a period of disillusionment and then abandonment of his venture. This echoed throughout Branwell's adult life where his initial eagerness is lost and he hasn't the patience or stamina to continue.

Charlotte had a great deal more stoicism in her writing and the ability to stick to a task. She was as hard on herself as she was on others and tended to hold on to the bitter end rather than give up. However, both she and Branwell were not averse to ridiculing the younger girls and sometimes used their fictional characters as mouth pieces for what they wanted to say, without causing direct offence. This indirect form of insult continued well into and beyond their childhood years. Whilst it can be viewed as harmless fun and banter, I find an undercurrent of direct humiliation. In 1834, when Charlotte was 18 and Anne 14 years old, Charlotte, in the guise of Branwell's character, 'Benjamin Wiggins', wrote a sarcastic tale in which Wiggins describes his sister as: 'Anne is nothing, absolutely nothing ... What! Is she an idiot?' he is asked and he replies, 'Next door to it'.[6]

This is not small children bickering at each other, but Charlotte continuing to belittle her sister under cover of a character, under cover of Branwell. It is insidious and one feels that it rather expresses Charlotte's view of her youngest sibling.

There is a very important fact to consider here. The Brontë children had no friends, only each other, for all of their childhood. Their social position, plus the separation of the parsonage from the townsfolk, and also the poverty and disease lower down in the valley amongst the overcrowding and appalling sanitary conditions, meant that the children were isolated from children of their own ages. This has benefits and drawbacks. Although they did suffer a variety of childhood diseases, as stated, all six children lived to the age of 10, almost unheard of in this age and area. They had each other and an intense and shared education that had no distractions from outside of the family. They had to learn to share and live with each other despite differences and birth order. How successful they were in this is debatable. Their upbringing will have instilled in them good manners and respect, but they were children. Often described as shy and withdrawn by people visiting their home, they will have had the need to argue and fight as part of the natural cycle of growing up and into adulthood. They were very lucky to have two 'parents' who cared about them, protected them and were also highly intelligent and able to converse with the children and direct their studies and behaviour.

I suggest, however, that there is a danger here. Normally, children in whatever size family go out and meet other children of similar age and circumstances. This helps a child to stay grounded and rational. If there is conflict or upset at home, a chat with friends or a trip outside can de-escalate fears and worries that may build up in a confined area where there is no external relief or comparison. When Charlotte described them as 'mushrooms growing in a cellar', she was accurately describing their forced growth. However, it is an unnatural growth that affects their emotional development by allowing them to grow without the steadying hand of rational and realistic understanding of the real world of colour, noise, conflict, harmony, hustle and bustle.

One can argue that the four Brontë children, between 1825 and 1831, where imprisoned in the parsonage, albeit for their own physical safety, but that this was a limiting experience that denied natural external influences of everyday social life in the community. The substitution of realism by a massive amount of reading and study negates the necessity of the everyday that keeps the human mind cogent and sane. The siblings could only argue and rationalise within their own family, there was no major physical outside influence to disturb or question their behaviour and whilst they developed in many ways as siblings do, this lack of local and differing lifestyles must have inhibited their social development and would certainly account for their extreme shyness. It was not until their mid-teens that they ventured into any sort of external friendships or schooling. Of the girls, only Charlotte acquired firm friendships outside of the family and this upset and altered the Brontë family dynamics, ever after.

To be so confined restricts children in the art of social communication and appreciation of others. They were very limited in this respect and all had great trouble and fear of social intercourse as young adults. Branwell, unlike his sisters, was never sent to school and in hindsight this was perhaps a major mistake by his father. One can understand that Patrick believed that he was better able to teach his son than most, and quite rightly so. However, whilst he could regale Branwell in Latin and Greek and many other important subjects for his future, Patrick could not be a substitute for the social interaction that Branwell needed to develop into a confident and well-rounded young man. He had no confidante and no role models when growing up, and it inhibited his social progress. When Branwell did try to make friends and acquaintances as an adult, he appears to have used drink as a palliative to his shyness and as a confidence booster. He often appeared loud and boastful, as though trying to over compensate for his lack of social skills, in nervous and false bonhomie. One is constantly aware that this young man had no mother, brother, male friend or lover and must have found life particularly difficult and lonely.

Charlotte was luckier in that she made two lifelong friends after she went to Roe Head School. These two friends were almost the two sides of Charlotte's personality. Ellen Nussey was a shy and traditional daughter who was the youngest of ten children, easily lead by others and put upon by her family. Mary Taylor was a brash, brave and outspoken young lady and Charlotte envied her self-confidence and independence of thought and behaviour. Ellen stayed at home and never married. Mary departed to New Zealand and opened up a shop. She also never married but one feels that that was her choice. She travelled on the Continent, taught at a boy's school and wrote a book. She was a busy, independent woman who spoke her mind, once telling Charlotte that she was ugly!

Having these two friends made a huge difference to Charlotte's life; she didn't have to depend on her brother any more for company and she had something that her sisters had not, and never would have. Her corroboration with Branwell gradually dissipated and her external friendships possibly contributed to their later complete separation.

Branwell is tragically lonely in many ways with no male companion until he is in his late teens. This is unnatural and sad. One wonders at Branwell's difficulties in life but this lack of a friend and confidante shaped his character and, it would seem, affected his later actions and behaviour. Branwell develops as a sad individual who has talent but no confidence and ambition that is without the backing of money or connections. He is under tremendous pressure to succeed but lacks the commitment or strength to expand his talents or deal with the people who could possibly have helped him to progress. He did what many people in his situations did and still do, they turn to alternatives that relieve the pressures and help them to endure life with all its hazards. For a while this works, until the very remedy becomes the cause of their final downfall. Freud described people who found life too difficult and their search for alternative relief and it sums up Branwell perfectly:

> *Life as we find it, is too hard for us; it entails too much pain; too many disappointments; impossible tasks. We cannot do without palliative remedies ... powerful diversions of interest, which leads us to care little about our misery; substitutive gratifications, which lessen it; and intoxicating substances, which make us insensitive to it. Something of the kind is indispensable.*[7]

Unlike Branwell, the sisters did not have his options and turned instead to other palliative comforts; for Anne especially, it was God, nature and poetry. In *Agnes Grey* Anne states through Agnes that:

> *When we are harassed by sorrows or anxieties, or long oppressed by any powerful feelings which we must keep to ourselves, for which we can obtain and seek no sympathy from any living creature, and which yet we cannot or will not wholly crush, we often naturally seek relief in poetry – and often find it, too – whether in the infusions of others, which seem to harmonise with our existing case, or in our own attempts to give utterance to those thoughts and feelings in strains less musical perchance, but more appropriate, and therefore more penetrating and sympathetic, and, for the time, more soothing. Or more powerful to rouse and to unburden the oppressed and swollen heart.*[8]

Emily, we are frequently informed, was a shy and withdrawn person, who shied away from others and preferred her own company. This has made her seem another isolated and rather tragic figure. Emily certainly made no friendships and it is inevitable that she and Anne were close ... there was no-one else! As Charlotte gradually gained in social confidence, Emily appears to have wanted nothing but to remain quietly at home following a domestic routine that allowed her freedom to explore the moors and look after her pets. Nowadays, medics might label her as Autistic, a symptom of which is that one finds it hard to make friends or prefers to be alone, seeming blunt, rude or disinterested in others, whilst not necessarily meaning to, or having Asperger's Syndrome, a form of Autism Spectrum Disorder which can make it hard to relate to others socially. Perhaps that was the case, or maybe she had a genetic trait similar to one of her Cornwall cousins; naturally self-absorbed and unable to mix well with others. We know from Charlotte's letters that Emily suffered horrendously from homesickness when she went as a pupil to Roe Head School at 17 years old, her first venture away from home, apart from a few short weeks at the Clergy Daughters' school. We see Emily as a recluse, unable or unwilling to waste her time on the everyday lives and issues of others. Happy in her own company or her immediate family.

Anne stayed at home until she was 15 years old, when she left to take Emily's place at Roe Head School. Even when visiting the church or helping in the Sunday School, Anne was shy and retiring and, like Emily, had no friends. Anne had only Emily and as we have seen, Emily was not answerable to anyone. She seems not so much to argue with her siblings as choose to ignore controversy or upset. This would make life even more difficult for Anne who had no ally unless one of her siblings chose to befriend her. Anne had little presence or say in the household and was at the mercy in many ways, of all of the other people in her family. They all dominated her childhood and youth, chronologically, physically and academically, until she herself was able, as an adult, to prove that she had just as much intelligence, stoicism and creativity as the others, in some areas, even more so.

One important and creative influence on the siblings who is often overlooked by Brontë writers, is Tabby Aykroyd, the housekeeper who took over after the Garrs sisters had moved on. Tabby was 53 years old when Patrick employed her at the parsonage. There is a debate as to whether she was a widow or not, but she was local to Haworth and had family living in the village. Tabby had all the experience of small-town living and gossip and she had a kind and sensible approach to life and to the Brontë family. Her local knowledge and no-nonsense attitude would differ greatly from the stern Aunt Elizabeth and their busy father. Tabby became a loyal friend to the family for the next thirty years. She and Aunt Elizabeth may not have always agreed, but Tabby offered the warmth and the homeliness of a trusted mother figure who was less of a servant and more of a maternal friend. She was old and wise and had a great influence on, and a loving and close relationship with, the children. It was Tabby to whom the children often turned for help and advice and she could regale them with all of the local gossip and history of Haworth, for their amusement and information. Tabby was very different from the other two adults in the house, with her Yorkshire dialect and her amusing tales; she was perhaps a foil to her employer and wanting the formality and discipline of Aunt Elizabeth. She may have lacked the knowledge and education of the other adults but appears to have made up for that with her open and good-hearted care and affection.

Tabby outlived all but Charlotte and Patrick and remained with the Brontës until the leg that she had broken three years previously reduced her ability to walk and work. In November 1839, she moved into a house with her sister in Haworth. However, she returned in 1843, as much as company for Emily, who was now running the household, than of any great practical use and stayed until a few months before her death, six weeks before that of Charlotte in 1855. Martha Brown, a daughter of the sexton, John Brown, had arrived in 1839, aged only 11, to help out and stayed until 1861, after the deaths of all of the remaining family, even visiting and corresponding with Arthur Nicholls in Ireland after he left Haworth.

The loyalty and affection given and received by the Brontë servants is notable and cannot be dismissed from the Brontë story. These two women, Tabby and Martha, became friends with all of the family and there grew mutual respect and trust between them. They were much more than servants and, I suggest, appear in the sisters' novels in various guises. The family knew Tabby and Martha intimately and lived with them for most of their adult lives. It would be naive to disregard the effect that they must have had on all of them.

If, as I believe, Emily and Anne had very different experiences and personalities to their two elder siblings, I find it likely that it would be to Tabby or Martha that they would turn rather than their aunt. Whilst we are told that Anne was her aunt's favourite, and she probably was, I feel that Tabby and Martha would have been far more approachable, down to earth and sympathetic. Emily chose, as an adult, to become the family housekeeper and probably spent as much time with Tabby as anyone else in the house. The domesticity of the warm parsonage kitchen and its bustling and kindly cook, was, I suggest, the most welcoming and safe refuge in the whole of the house.

Some years later, when the girls are in their teens, the kitchen is the setting of Emily and Anne's charming 'diary paper' of November 1834 and offers a wonderful clip of domestic life in a split second of time:

> ... *Anne and I have been peeling apples for Charlotte to make an apple pudding ... Tabby said just now, come Anne pillopatate (i.e. pill a potato) Aunt has come into the kitchen just now and said where are your feet Anne? Anne answered, 'on the floor Aunt'.*[9]

It is interesting to recognise here that it is the three girls who are occupied in the kitchen. Where is Branwell? In our enlightened times we see nothing wrong with a male in the kitchen but it was completely unheard of at this time.

I am reminded of an incident in my own family. My father arrived unexpectedly one day at my house when my two children were washing up together. My son was washing and my daughter was drying the pots. They were 8 and 7 years old respectively, so it was the late 1970s. My father scowled at them and then at me, 'You will make that lad soft', he growled and walked out. I don't think that he had ever seen a male child do the washing up and never wanted to be in a world where such abominations took place. I smiled and let him go, safe in the knowledge that I was right in my child-rearing philosophy and that he was wrong. It was a small incident but it demonstrated so much to me and re-affirmed my belief in the need to let my children share responsibility and for neither to over dominate the other by using gender as a weapon.

Whilst many biographers concentrate on the parlour as the room where the Brontës wrote and ate, studied and conversed, and where Emily may have died, I suggest that, like in almost any home, the kitchen lies at its heart and is the room of warmth and cosy familiarity to all of the family. The parsonage kitchen was not large but it was comfortable and comforting and a room that could be used by all of the family at any given time, day or night. This was a home where tragedy had struck three times and the familiar rooms had turned unfamiliar and full of sadness and distress. The kitchen would remain a communal area of normality, of domestic comfort and a settled daily order. One is reminded of Goethe's quote, 'All comfort in life is based upon a regular occurrence of external phenomena'.[10]

This is an important quote, and it especially applies to the way in which the Brontës needed the comfort of home and the normal, everyday experiences to encapsulate their sanity. In important plays such as *'Gas light'*,[11] one sees the phenomenon of what can happen to the brain if things suddenly appear different to how one expects them to be. It only takes a few shifts in the normal to upset our reason. I suggest that the death of a family member is one of the shifts in the normal that can cause a stress on the brain that is difficult to overcome. It is very easy for the irrational and uncanny to take over if our *'status quo'* is upset.

Only familiar things concern kitchen domesticity at a time when it offers the working machinery of the home. This, I believe, was very important at Haworth parsonage. All the tragic events in the house happened away from the kitchen. The kitchen did not change. It was the room that had warmth and the smells and production of food and drink and the comforting fire and the atmosphere of conviviality, overseen by a kind and friendly housekeeper. This was at a time when servants were part of middle-class life, though not always happy and appreciated in their domestic role. However, Tabby and Martha were friends and companions who worked well together and were deeply appreciated by the Brontë family.

Ironically, as many twentieth-century novels began to explore that domestic world, that realm of female occupation was changing and the kitchen later became a symbol for domestic drudgery where the female spent her life cooking and cleaning and serving her husband and children with their sustenance. Two hundred years later what the Brontës valued and accepted as the female domain, has come to be seen as a flagship of female restraint and an unacceptable example of male dominance. In my own childhood, no male in the house ever cooked, washed up or did the washing and cleaning; a trend that is only now beginning to change. During the Brontës' lives, this domestic hearth was a welcome abode in a house turned strange and often cold, dark and echoing of the dead.

I find this snippet of life at the parsonage and in the kitchen to be so real and so normal. The girls are united in their efforts to produce the pudding and Anne is obviously sitting on her feet. This unladylike gesture meets the disapproval of her aunt and Anne instantly places them back on to the floor. It brings the sisters to life in a way that second-hand descriptions by visitors and acquaintances can never produce. One can 'see' the scene and hear Aunt Elizabeth's tone of voice and Anne's chastened response. One can trust this scene as being authentic and, even in so few words, it describes the interaction between the girls and between the girls and their aunt. To me, it is a treasured moment in time that brings the Brontës to life in a unique and vital way. We so rarely witness events as they occurred in all their household actuality for the sisters and it is a privileged glimpse into their domesticity.

Between 1825 and 1831 the Brontë children matured in isolation in a house where religion and education were the priority, but also where the introduction of music, art and writing were beginning to lighten the atmosphere and allowed some distractions to the remaining four siblings who had already suffered death and grief as a major part of their development. As they all moved into their teenage years, things were changing and their father's fears for their futures had to be addressed.

Chapter Six

Anne Brontë
Learning to Be the Youngest

Anne spent the first almost sixteen years of her life at home, rarely venturing out except onto the moors. During those years she learnt to be the youngest, she learnt to be subservient and to be intimidated by her older siblings. She learnt that they were older, stronger and wiser and she had little say in what happened around her. She and Emily teamed up eventually, as there was no-one else to befriend them and they did not begin their 'Gondal Saga' until after Charlotte left to attend Roe Head School. Charlotte and Branwell spent years competing with each other, both trying to rule their siblings and directing both their writing and their play. It is in many ways a natural state of affairs, but, unfortunately, there was no outsider, no friend or school mate who could counteract or challenge the elder children and little control over how the younger ones were treated by them.

Patrick was a busy priest with an enormous parish of over 4000 people, including outlying areas. Whilst he directed his children's formal studies, he did not necessarily sit in with them whilst they did their lessons or supervise their play, especially when they were on the moors. Outside, the Garrs sisters, and later Tabby, were usually the ones to accompany the children, until such time as they were deemed old enough to take themselves. In many ways these children were not just a self-absorbed group, they were a self-controlling group with leaders and followers. Until the disaster of the Clergy Daughters' School, Maria was the leader, the much loved big sister to all of her siblings. After her death, there was a leadership battle between Charlotte and Branwell which continued into their teenage years. Charlotte finally stepped to the fore after her sojourns at Roe Head School, away from Branwell and growing in confidence and knowledge. Charlotte finally had friends beyond her siblings and this was the start of a new and different life for her which left Branwell behind.

Anne did not only follow her older siblings, she also followed her aunt's beliefs and instructions. Sharing her aunt's room for many years and possibly being her favourite amongst the girls, her aunt was able to have greater sway over Anne's development and especially her religious understanding. Elizabeth Branwell was a Protestant, the same as Patrick, but had more Methodist leanings and beliefs. Anne was given her first Bible by her godmother, Elizabeth Firth, when she was not even 3 years old. Another of her godmothers, Fanny Outhwaite, gave Anne a Book of Common Prayer when she was just 7. Each sibling possessed these two books as the core of their father's faith, but Anne appears to have developed a far more intense relationship with these two tomes and appeared especially affected by them. Anne read the Bible cover to cover whilst working as a governess at Thorp Green and also, later, wrote hymns. Religion was an important factor in her life and it was her family's belief in universal salvation that had sustained her following the deaths of her two sisters. When this idea was questioned at Roe Head School, with its Calvinistic teachings, Anne went into crisis and it took a Moravian Priest, the Reverend James La Trobe, to calm her and to revalidate her beliefs. Also at this time, Anne probably had a 'low fever' or possibly a flare up of latent tuberculosis which would eventually cause her death. Added to this, Anne was away from home for the first time in her life and unsettled despite the good reputation and education at the school, offered by mainly friendly teaching staff. Charlotte who was now there as a teacher, did not necessarily mix with Anne or attend to the needs of her youngest sibling. In fact, Charlotte hated teaching and had no empathy or affection for her pupils. Samantha Ellis states that: 'For Anne, Roe Head was a crash course in the dark side of sisterhood'.[1]

As the children of a Protestant minister the children were of course well-schooled in the Bible but Anne, especially, appears to be the only one who clung to that faith throughout her life and tried to live by its teachings. Her belief in God was unshakeable and once she reasserted the knowledge that all sinners could be forgiven and enter heaven, she was able to live a happier and more settled existence. One sees in Anne, a child who has possibly a religious fervour that is, at times, overwhelming and helps only to make her anxious and troubled. She sees her quiet and ordered life not as a perfectly ordinary and acceptable one, but as one full of sin in which she has to strive every moment to do her very best in order to gain that goal of a heavenly afterlife.

In these years of childhood, one finds in Anne a girl who worries about herself and her family and who mourns her mother and sisters and needs constant reassurance that they will meet up again in heaven. It is too difficult to bear if that is not the case and that is what worried her so much at Roe Head School when she realised that other religions focused on sin and the sinner's banishment to hell. No wonder that she became so ill and broken down, she was in a religious torment, a crisis of faith that brought about a mental and physical breakdown.

The Brontë children were not robust, physically or mentally and this confined and protected childhood may have kept them safe from some of the life-threatening diseases of the town but, it inhibited their mental growth and limited their social development.

So, what is happening to Anne during her childhood years before her removal to Roe Head School in October 1835? She has always stayed at home so she could well have viewed her home as both a place of safety and/or somewhere that enveloped her in a claustrophobic atmosphere that allowed only a very restricted view of life and her immediate society. She had no friends and no knowledge of other girls her age outside of the family or any interaction with boys, apart from her brother. Anne was sheltered and protected from life to an extent that we would perhaps recognise today as both unnatural and unnecessary. She carried the label of 'youngest' and was treated as such, throughout her life. It is a label, like all other sibling birth orders, that is inescapable.

Anne does not appear to have stood up in any way to the teasing, bullying or dismissiveness of her siblings. We are told that she was quiet, docile, eager to please and a peacemaker. Did she argue back and fight for her rights and opinions? I rather think not. She seems to have been overwhelmed by the intelligence, the requirements and the demands of her older siblings. I suggest that she clung to Emily as her defender but, as stated, their collaboration on 'Gondal' did not occur until after Charlotte was out of the way. Emily lost her bed partner and her closest sister at this time. It is far more likely that she would identify with Charlotte, rather than Anne. One tends in childhood and adolescence to drift towards older children, rather than younger. There is a more defined concept of an age gap in children, and it is much more obvious than in adulthood. One remembers one's own experience at school, trying to emulate and admire the older children, but having little or nothing to do with the younger ones. It is natural and part of the striving to be grown up.

Ellen Nussey, I suggest, has created a false impression by describing Emily and Anne as 'like twins'. Emily was of a very different character and was more aligned with Charlotte for many years. Charlotte had to cope with Branwell, with his male status and excitable personality, and also with the tall and demur Emily, with her acid tongue and superior charisma. There seems to have been little effort made to acknowledge or even notice Anne.

Anne must have been lonely in many ways. She had no-one on her side who understood her position or fought her corner. This appears to have continued throughout her life. There was both love and rivalry amongst the children, but Anne had far less to offer during their childhood and far less impression on the others. Anne only becomes a noticeable part of the Brontë story after her sojourn at Roe Head School and the crises she developed there.

The Brontë Family: Sibling Rivalry and a Burial in Paradise

For almost sixteen years Anne followed a predictable daily, weekly and monthly routine that hardly differed. She had lessons from her father and aunt, she spent hours sewing, hours on domestic chores, and many hours studying the Christian faith. Anne presents as the most religiously affected of the four siblings and the one who worried the most about the afterlife. Her faith was instilled from birth and as her aunt's 'favourite' and sharing her room, that faith would be manifest in all she saw and heard. Elizabeth Branwell had been brought up with Methodist and Wesleyan influences and, like traditional Protestantism, this faith included the belief that everyone could get into heaven if they acknowledged and asked for forgiveness for their sins. This was especially important to Anne, who naively believed that she was a sinner in God's eyes and needed the reassurance that she and her family would all eventually be reunited.

Like Emily, Anne appears to have kept her own counsel on many issues. The youngest child does not carry much weight in arguments or ideas and I suggest that, whereas the older children questioned religion as they grew older, and even lost their faith, Anne accepted and welcomed it until the teachings at Roe Head offered an alternative view, one which mortified her.

There is almost no evidence of Anne's day to day existence at Haworth parsonage during her first fifteen years. We know of her through the other people in the house. She is a background figure, always there but rarely referred to. It is as though she is living an apprenticeship for her life as a governess. There, but unseen, a part of the furniture and fabric, necessary but unacknowledged. Samantha Ellis sums this up perfectly, describing her as follows:

> *Anne turned into a character in someone else's 'story', especially a minor character who doesn't have many lines and makes an early exit.*[2]

Charlotte and Branwell are the leaders, the two movers and shakers who decide what the children do. The two eldest decide that they will collaborate on writing songs, poetry, and stories and building up fabulous imaginative countries and people. It is Branwell who insists on the battles and the political fallouts. It is Charlotte who counteracts with a more feminine and romantic view, whilst still including battles, but between people rather than armies. There is little evidence of input from Emily and Anne.

As stated, it is notable to look at the children's handwriting as another reason for the predominance of the elder authors. Emily and Anne wrote in a barely legible hand with major grammatical errors, even into adulthood. Dyslexia may have been a reason, left-handedness, lack of written language guidance or merely the fact that they were younger and never able to reach the dexterity of their elder siblings. As mentioned, writing with a quill pen is notoriously difficult, especially for children and Branwell and Charlotte are not likely to have wanted to wait for their sisters to struggle through reams of dialogue that was not only grammatically indecipherable, but in the minute lettering that made it extremely difficult to write and almost impossible to read.

Early writings by Branwell and Charlotte show all the blots, crossings out and mistakes but their writing develops and by the time Charlotte, at least, was in her twenties she wrote with a proficient and steady, clear hand. In the 'diary papers' of Emily and Anne, begun in November 1834, when Emily was 16 and Anne 14 years of age, the writing is by Emily and is a wonderful vignette of daily life in the Parsonage. However, as Juliet barker notes:

> *While the diary paper is a lively evocation of the hustle and bustle of a wash-day Monday at the parsonage, the dreadful handwriting and spelling are scarcely credible as the work of a highly intelligent sixteen-year-old.*[3]

We do not have evidence of their script in their later years, except one or two letters by Anne. Anne's last letter, to Ellen Nussey, is cross written, which makes it harder to decipher, but she writes in a neat sloping hand, despite being gravely ill at the time. When Branwell boasted that he had written *Wuthering Heights*, allegedly reciting parts of it by rote, I have often wondered whether he did, in fact, assist in the actual copying down of the manuscript, which may have been otherwise unreadable.

It would certainly appear that Charlotte and Branwell did not have the patience or the inclination to allow the two younger girls to write down the 'Glasstown' adventures, or to inscribe the series of little books and magazines that the elder two produced. Here, I suggest, is one of the great divisions between the two eldest and the two youngest. There is a speed and enthusiasm between Branwell and Charlotte where each are competing against the other to gain the upper hand. Emily and Anne, the two quieter and less demanding younger sisters are not part of the competition and their personalities are more insular. Whilst they may not be happy to step back and remain in the background, they do so. This helps to keep the peace but it also suggests that they did not have the drive or the need to prove their abilities against the squabbling of their siblings. Their detachment led to the forming of their own saga of 'Gondal', but not until after the insistent and bullying Charlotte had departed and Branwell had lost his writing and sparring partner.

Again, I have issue with Ellen Nussey's description of Emily and Anne as 'like twins'. They were not like twins at all, except in their shared withdrawal from the antics of their brother and elder sister. Emily was tall and physically strong with dark hair and hazel eyes. Anne was small and had fair hair and 'violet eyes'. Emily did not like or mix well with other people. Anne was shy but had a determination to go out to work with strangers. Emily was sharp tongued with a mind of her own, whereas Anne was compliant and rarely spoke out of turn. Emily gradually withdrew into herself and her parsonage world, whereas Anne blossomed and became a strong and stoical governess in two very trying families. If the girls were in anyway twin-like, it was because they needed to join forces because there was no-one else to be friends and companions with. Emily and Anne were different, but had a shared place at the bottom of the birth order. The fierce and passionate sibling rivalry between Branwell and Charlotte helped to keep Emily and Anne firmly in place as the younger siblings.

There were some areas however, where the younger children could excel. During these years at the parsonage, Anne and Emily both learnt to play the piano and to study music. Emily was especially proficient as a pianist and Anne had a sweet singing voice. Branwell learnt to play the flute and the organ but Charlotte's very poor eyesight inhibited her in many areas and reading music was one of them.

By the early 1830s, Anne was learning to play the piano, to read music and to learn songs and psalms, to which she could accompany Emily's piano playing. The ability to play an instrument was yet another expected talent for a middle-class female and an aspiring governess. In their 'diary paper' of 1834, Emily remarks that:

> *It is past Twelve o'clock Anne and I have not tided ourselves, done our bed work (or) done our lessons and we want to go out to play...the kitchin is in a very untidy state Anne and I have not Done our music exercise which consists of b major...Mr Sunderland is expected.*[4]

This suggests that piano practice was part of their daily routine. It also suggests a very disorganised and somewhat childish attitude and highlights Emily's poor spelling and grammar. Neither their father, aunt or servants are controlling the girls, although Emily states that her father and aunt are both present. Perhaps the chaos of the Monday washing day has upset the smooth running of the household or was it always like this?

Perhaps the parsonage did not run very well with four teenage children at home. However, Patrick Brontë's love of education, art and music meant that he found money in his limited stipend to provide both a music and an art teacher for his children, perhaps choosing the importance of their artistic development over that of an ordered and placid household.

Music was an important part of life, not just in Haworth but throughout the country. Music was a pastime, a hobby and an important way of relaxing and of keeping a community together. In his highly informed book, *Emily Jane Brontë and her Music*, John Hennessy explains that:

> *For the middle, as well as the upper, classes in the first half of the nineteenth century, music in the home was an important element of family life, and not just for the purpose of enjoyment. Girls were expected to sing and play a musical instrument, most often the pianoforte, as an 'accomplishment', particularly if they were to pursue employment as governesses ... one of the outcomes of the technological advances brought about by the Industrial Revolution had been a great increase in the publishing of music scores.*[5]

As he goes on to catalogue, the Brontës had numerous musical scores covering many different types of music and composers. The late eighteenth century had produced the works of Beethoven and Schubert, Haydn and Mozart, all centred around Vienna. Hennessey tells us that these four composers, in what became known as the Classical Period, produced 'symphonies, piano sonatas, concertos, chamber music, songs, sacred music and operas'.[6]

They were followed in the Romantic Period by Chopin, Berlioz, Schumann, Liszt and Mendelssohn, with Rossini spanning both eras. There was then a wealth of music at this time and the sheet music to accompany it. It saw the formation of orchestras, choral societies, concerts and recitals, in homes, halls and churches throughout the country.

In West Yorkshire there was the formation of the Halifax Choral Society in 1817 and it is currently the longest continuing choral society in the country. Brass bands also flourished with the now famous Black Dyke Mills Band having its forerunner formed in 1818. Philharmonic orchestras were gathered together and many choirs. Nearly every town and village had a group of musicians of some kind and Haworth was no exception. Even Mrs Gaskell acknowledged this, saying that:

> *I have gone to Haworth and found an orchestra to meet me, filled with local performers, vocal and instrumental, to whom the best works of Handel, Haydn, Mozart and Marcello etc. were as familiar as household words.*[7]

One feels that this author, who so often misled and misguided her readers about Haworth and its population, was fairly shocked to find a cultural aspect in evidence. Famous singers and musicians regularly played and sang in many places in and around Haworth and would have been seen and appreciated by members of the Brontë family. St Michael's Church had its first organ installed in 1834, but had had a number of musicians for accompanying the hymns and psalms for many years. Branwell learnt to play this church organ; a complicated and difficult instrument to master.

Music was, therefore, a part of the daily life of Haworth and of the Brontës. They knew and studied the great composers of the time and their music, in many different forms. The musicality of their verse and even their novels has been noted. My friend, fellow Brontë trustee and former musician, Virginia Rushton, herself an accomplished soprano, had, before her untimely death, begun to research *Wuthering Heights* in the form of a musical score, with each word representing a musical note, suggesting a mystical song hidden inside the story. This is not a fantastic proposition as words and sounds and pictures blend inextricably in Brontë verse and writings.

Ellen Nussey records listening to Emily and Anne playing the piano and singing within the family home. Patrick had acquired a Cabinet Piano around 1834. An advertisement for a similar one in the *Leeds Intelligencer* in 1831 was priced at ninety guineas but was selling for less than half that amount. Patrick's stipend never reached more than 200 pounds, so such a purchase, even at half price, would have been beyond his means. However, as suggested by Hennessy, Aunt Elizabeth or the children's godparents may well have all collaborated towards the purchase of a piano to fulfil a need in the children's education and future employment. It was sold at auction after Patrick's death for only 10 pounds but was donated back to the Brontë Society in 1917. In his book, Hennessy describes the history and restoration of the piano and the amount of time, effort and money it needed to return it to its original condition. Virginia Rushton was involved in this and arranged for Ken Forrest to undertake the two-and-a-half-year restoration programme. The newly restored piano returned to the parsonage and into Patrick's study in June 2010. There have been a few selected recordings made by outstanding musicians, such as Belarusian pianist, Maya Irgalina and the French pianist, Isabelle Oehmichen. The piano is still financially supported and maintained by John Hennessy and Ken Forrest.

Patrick somehow found the money for both art and music teachers for his children, again, possibly with the aid of family and godparents, but it shows his commitment and recognition of their artistic talents and his determination that cost would not inhibit them. Abraham Sunderland gave musical tuition to all of the Brontë children but the dates are uncertain. Branwell began playing the flute in 1828 and it was probably Mr Sunderland who later taught him to play the organ.

Both Anne and Branwell copied songs and musical pieces into notebooks. Anne's 'Songbook', as it has come to be known, was written whilst she was a governess for the Robinson family at Thorp Green. Having purchased a music manuscript book for three shillings and six pence in June 1843, possibly whilst on holiday in Scarborough, she transcribed musical pieces over the next year and a half. John Hennessy states that:

> ... she copied into it, not with complete accuracy and often with simplified harmonies, a total of thirty-four hymns, sacred pieces, songs and melodies ... the purpose of the book was probably twofold – firstly as a teaching aid, and secondly to be just for her own enjoyment.[8]

Hennessy suggests that Anne began playing the piano somewhere between 1832 and 1834. This would mean that the children went to Sunderland for lessons, at a time before their own piano was installed. He says that in the six years before she became a governess she could probably play tolerably well, but not in the same category as the gifted, Emily. Hennessy quotes Ellen Nussey's description of the two sisters' musical abilities:

> ... whereas Emily played with 'precision and brilliancy, which was not often if other than the family circle were within hearing' Anne also played, 'but she preferred soft harmonies and vocal music. She sang a little; her voice was weak, but very sweet in tone'.[9]

Branwell also transcribed his own copy of a book of flute music, an instrument he learnt to play in his late teens. The flute itself was not the modern metal version we see today, but a wooden instrument with a thumb hole and only eight finger holes. Hennessy remarks that, like Anne's song book, Branwell's flute book is not highly technical. He wrote it in 1831 and it contains the same poor spelling, grammar and notational errors. Hennessy quotes a passage written by Francis Leyland, the brother of Branwell's friend, the sculptor, John Bentley Leyland:

> [Branwell] was acquainted with the works of the great composers, and although he could not perform their elaborate compositions well, he was always so excited when they were played for him by his friends that he would walk about the room with measured footsteps, his eyes raised to the ceiling, accompanying the music with his voice in an impassioned manner, and beating time with his hand on the chairs as he passed to and fro.[10]

This lovely glimpse of Branwell, behaving just as we have come to expect, allows us to see the passion and enthusiasm Branwell, and all of his sisters, gained from playing and listening to music. Like the moorland, music is a universal phenomenon which can be appreciated by anyone according to their own interpretation and understanding. The Brontës exposure to the arts is sometimes overlooked by biographers who concentrate specifically on their writing. I suggest that they cannot be separated. The cumulative effect of all of the arts inspired their writing and enhanced their lives to an enormous effect.

Despite sight issues, Charlotte and the others all studied and became proficient in art and drawing. In their excellent book, *The Art of the Brontës,* Christine Alexander and Jane Sellars described as many of the Brontë paintings and drawings, sketches and oils as could be found extant at the time (1995) and they numbered nearly 400. There are still many in private hands that keep appearing in salerooms and catalogues throughout the world. Very recently, I inspected part of the Blavatnik Honresfield Library collection, on display at The Brotherton Gallery, University of Leeds. This incredible collection of manuscripts and art of many famous authors including the Brontës, Jane Austen, Walter Scott and Lord Byron, include sketches by Emily and Branwell that were thought to have perished many years ago. There exist many pictures by the Brontë children and they are, especially in Charlotte's case, minutely detailed and expertly drawn. Branwell failed in his ambition to become a portrait painter, but some of his oil paintings remain, including his famous *pillar portrait* housed in The National Portrait Gallery in London. Alexander and Sellars state that:

> ... *pictures enabled the four surviving Brontë children, Charlotte, Branwell, Emily and Anne, to visualize other worlds, to escape the sorrow of their mother's and two older sisters' deaths, and to combat both the boredom of life in an isolated moorland village and the later loneliness of the life of a governess.*[11]

Pictures abounded in the Brontë household, not just in their books, especially, *Bewick's Book of British Birds,* the wood engravings of which they often copied, but in the pictures in their father's study, especially those reproductions of John Martin who specialised in biblical scenes. There were also two oil paintings of Bolton and Kirkstall Abbey. The art of drawing and painting was seen at this time as another important accomplishment for a middle-class female, and especially for an aspiring teacher or governess. Once again, Patrick found the money to engage a tutor, or it may have been as a favour, according to Alexander and Sellars (page 23) and John Bradley, a fellow member of Keighley Mechanics Institute gave the children art lessons for a short time between 1829 and 1831.

The Brontë sisters mainly copied prints and engravings from pictures in books and magazines before beginning to draw from life. Branwell and Emily were especially talented in drawing from nature. Barker reminds us that:

> *The presence of so many pictures in a financially hard-pressed household is an indication of the importance the Brontës attached to art.*[12]

In 1834 the family were treated to a visit to The Royal Northern Society for the Encouragement of Fine Arts. This was an annual event and took place in Leeds. It was here that they encountered William Robinson, a notable artist who later became Branwell's art master. This exhibition was a major event, not least because Charlotte:

> *... had submitted two of her detailed pencil copies of engravings for exhibition, 'Bolton Abbey' and 'Kirkstall Abbey', famous views of two local landmarks.*[13]

There was a wealth of art at this exhibition, not least works by William Turner, portraits by William Bewick and sculptures by Joseph Leyland. William Robinson gave only a few lessons at the parsonage as at two guineas each, it was a costly venture. However, in 1835 it was arranged for Branwell to receive lessons at Robinson's studio in Leeds. The lessons ended in September of the same year but Branwell's bright hopes of following in Robinson's footsteps did not transpire.

Music and the visual arts, books and conversation, all combined to influence the siblings and enhance and increase their writing talents by widening and informing their imaginations. They were all not just talented writers, but became accomplished in many areas of art and music. So Anne is not just following a daily routine of lessons and chores, she is also studying music and art along with her siblings.

Furthermore, and perhaps to an even greater extent and influence, the children were all going out on to the moors and observing nature. They were experiencing it in all of its vast range of animals, birds, flora and fauna, the streams and waterfalls, the light and the dark, the sun and the rain and the almost ever-present wind. This was their huge picture, their artistic canvas of nature that was a special and exclusive area of learning and enjoyment for all of the children. They each interpreted and loved this vast moorland behind their home and it fed their understanding of life and death and influenced their artistic talents as much, if not more, than any human artist.

This for me, is the root of all of the Brontës' inspiration and emotions. They are taught to worship God, but it is in the manifestation of God in nature that they learn about life and about themselves. Haworth moor stretches across wide swathes of heath and bog, streams and hills and it is an ever-changing landscape sculptured by both man and nature. Some people find it empty and barren, for me it is exquisite; the sights, smells and sounds are so in harmony. Unfortunately modern life encroaches on it ever more each year and there are currently plans to erect a huge windfarm in the area with turbines overlooking Top Withins. However, up to now it still offers a fresh and fragrant air and a place to commune with the natural world and one's own thoughts and feelings.

These moors change with the seasons and can also alter from hour to hour. At night it can host a panorama of stars or be as black as pitch. In fog it is an alien landscape, in sunshine it is bright and welcoming. It is a dangerous place at times, where people have been lost and died of exposure. At others it appears friendly and warm; an escape from modern stresses. It can be freezing cold and insufferably hot. The wind can literally blow you over or waft soft breezes on to your face. These moors are the essence of unpredictability and yet hold a deep and meaningful anchor to those who appreciate and love its wilderness. Sit for a few moments in one of the small hollows or dells and you will quite literally hear silence.

Its landscape, dotted with the old ruins of ancient farmhouses and broken stone walls is evocative of a time and people long gone who have left their mark but not their fascinating stories. It is why I return year after year and why the Brontës never left it or escaped its captivating effects on them. When the Brontës talk of home, I believe that they see the moors as a major part of it. It is as much a part of the background to their lives as the parsonage, the church, the graveyard and the tolling of the sexton's hammer, the weather and the family that they grew up with and amongst. The moorland is simply profound.

However, I leave it to Emily, the writer who knew and loved this land as much, if not more than anyone else, to describe the depth of feeling that the moors can evoke.

Stanzas

Often rebuked, yet always back returning
To those first feelings that were born in me,
And leaving busy chase of wealth and learning
For idle dreams of things which cannot be:

To-day, I will not seek the shadowy region;
Its unsustaining vastness waxes drear;
And visions rising, legion after legion,
Bring the unreal world too strangely near.

Anne Brontë

I'll walk, but not in old heroic traces,
And not in paths of high morality,
And not among the half-distinguished faces,
The clouded forms of long-past history.

I'll walk where my own nature would be leading:
It vexes me to choose another guide:
Where the gray flocks in ferny glens are feeding;
Where the wild wind blows down the mountain side.

What have those lonely mountains worth revealing?
More glory and more grief than I can tell:
The earth that wakes one human heart to feeling
Can centre both the worlds of Heaven and Hell.[14]

This was also Anne Brontë's world and included the parsonage, the moors and her life of education, art and music. It should have been idyllic but it was constantly interrupted by tragedy, by the squabbling of her siblings, the control of her aunt, the anxiety of religion and her role as the youngest child.

Chapter Seven

The Brontës and Mental Health

By examining research on children's behaviour during the last fifty years, and there has been a deluge of it, one sees a growing attention to psychological and emotional issues as almost more important than physical development. An abusive or deprived childhood is now seen as the root of many mental health issues in later life. When I managed a Care Home for adults with enduring mental health issues during the 1990s, I discovered that fifteen of the sixteen residents had suffered childhood trauma of varying degrees, much of it physical and sexual abuse. I maintain that child-rearing is one of the most difficult and important jobs in the world. If you do not look after children well, you produce failed adults, not just mentally and physically scarred, but unable to function on recognised levels and that affects the future of the whole of society.

Whilst I am not suggesting sexual or physical abuse in the Brontë family, even though that could of course have been the case, as it is the potential in any family, I am concerned that their childhood limited their mental development in a number of ways. As adults, they all found it difficult to cope at different times and in different environments. Charlotte writes repeatedly of depression, headaches, sickness, pain, anxiety and an inability to cope. We see Emily as the withdrawn, strange and obsessive young woman who lives, at times, in a fantasy world. Branwell becomes an adult unable to cope in a man's world; trying and failing at every venture and turning to palliative remedies to try and get through each day. Anne is stronger than the others in her determination but can only express her ideas and emotions in her writing. Her religious mania and her worry over her family make her reclusive and timid and, like Emily, she succumbs to Tuberculosis before she can fulfil her potential.

Anxiety appears the dominant emotion. Patrick worries over his health, his family, his finances and his flock. Aunt Elizabeth frets over the children who become beyond her control and she longs to return home to Cornwall. Charlotte is a bundle of nerves and depression, constantly ill and fretful. Emily is awkward, stubborn, withdrawn and highly unsociable. Branwell is unable to cope with adulthood or responsibility and has illusions of grandeur which he can never realise. Anne is nervous, unable to speak up for herself and forever the youngest and least noticeable. They all have mental health traits that we would label nowadays amongst such diagnoses as autism, hypochondria, mania, depression, attention deficit hyperactivity disorder (ADHD,) neuroses, compulsive disorders and, in Branwell's case, possibly schizophrenia. In *The Brontës in Context,* edited by Marianne Thormahlen, there is an essay by Janis McLarren Caldwell on the Brontës and mental health. She describes the times when Emily and Anne are unable to continue at Roe Head School because of severe homesickness and or/religious melancholy. She describes Branwell's daily decline as he partook of addictive substances at a suicidal rate. She writes of Charlotte's constant low spirits and hypochondria, identified as pain in the chest.

She is not talking of inherited madness like we see displayed in Bertha Rochester, but of a constant underlying morbidity. She says:

> *The whole family, then, experienced mental suffering; but like most in their culture, they drew no clear line between physical and mental health, often experiencing a specific somatic correlate for a particular kind of mental ailment.*[1]

I recognise a darkness in the adult Brontës that overshadows them all. It may be the effects of early deaths or a lack of social interaction, an unrequited love, or a constant longing for a lost childhood when they were happy and healthy. Part of Charlotte's poem, 'Retrospection' sums up distinctly the lives of all four of the children She describes in these three stanzas how:

> *We wove a web in childhood,*
> *A web of sunny air;*
> *We dug a spring in infancy*
> *Of water pure and fair;*
>
> *We sowed in youth a mustard seed,*
> *We cut an almond rod;*
> *We are now grown up to riper age;*
> *Are they withered in the sod?*
>
> *Are they blighted, failed and faded,*
> *Are they mouldered back to clay?*
> *For life is darkly shaded,*
> *And its joys fleet fast away!*[2]

There is a longing in this poem that carries the nostalgia of childhood; that craving for a lost world that we believe that we once inhabited. It is summed up in the words of the French writer, Marcel Proust (1871–1922) in his *A la recherché du temps perdu*, or his search for or 'remembrance of things past'.[3] This idea runs through a great deal of Brontë poetry. It is the profoundly emotional nostalgia of childhood. However, Proust suggested that memory is a past that is triggered by senses linked to emotional centres in the brain and that when we remember it, we alter it, thereby creating our own reality. It is a medical fact that our sense of smell goes immediately to the olfactory bulb in front of the brain, leading directly to the limbic system which relates to memory and emotion, and bypasses the synapses that filter other senses. There is, therefore, an instant reaction to a smell from childhood, for example a flower or warm loaf of bread. Similarly, a bad smell, blood or rotting food, can likewise promote a response. What is being suggested here, is the idea that the idyllic memories of childhood are not necessarily as they actually occurred, but are remembered with a dream like quality; illusions that leave some memories untarnished and deeply attractive, whilst others may reveal the opposite. There is a longing to return to a time and place that we think we once inhabited. This is also manifest in homesickness when we crave a return to a place where we felt safe and comfortable, without acknowledging that it may also have had many drawbacks. Known as 'The Proustian Moment', a sudden sensory experience triggers a rush of memories that instantly recall a time or place unprompted and undesigned. The sense of smell is particularly acute in children and diminishes as one grows older and sight becomes the major sense. The scents of childhood are therefore particularly evocative.

I recently found reference to nostalgia in a book on theology which likened religion as a form of nostalgic melancholy that especially affects displaced people or immigrants longing for their homeland. I suggest that it applies to any 'exiled and harassed' person. It noted in the abstract that:

> *Religion comforts people under stress and in transition by providing nostalgia for a lost paradise (or former country); and nostalgia, while fraught with melancholy, generates imagery of a paradise to be regained in a new and improved form.*[4]

It is difficult to view any of the Brontë siblings without recognising that nostalgia and remembrance of things past was a major part of their psyche and referred to time and again in their writings. It is as much a modern day phenomenon as it has been throughout the centuries. Anyone displaced from the familiar will become disorientated for a while and look to the past for comfort. One of my granddaughters happily and willingly took a two-year contract to teach in New Zealand, a week later the Covid pandemic struck. The New Zealand government acted immediately and banned all arrivals and departures. Despite loving the country and her job, my granddaughter found it difficult because she knew that she could not get home, even had she wanted to. It is the difference between choice and restriction and it is this duty bound and inability to return that affected all of the Brontë sisters at various times in their lives, starting with the horrors of the Clergy Daughters' School.

Furthermore, all of the Brontës were very familiar with John Milton's poem, *Paradise Lost*, a favourite of Patrick Brontë. This epic poem, first published in 1667, is a retelling of the fall of Satan and the creation of heaven and hell, with the exclusion of Adam and Eve from the Garden of Eden. It again explores the idea of man's free will and predestination, that constant worry to Anne Brontë, in particular. Can humans make their own choices or are they fated from their beginnings? It is an age old dilemma and one which both religion and philosophy try to answer. The message is that sin leads to hell whilst obedience to God is the road to redemption. *Paradise Regained*, written four years later, explores Christ's baptism and his temptation in the desert. Again demonstrating that despite evil, mankind can gain paradise/heaven by faith in God and Christ as his son. These poems would have been familiar to the children and along with their Bibles, constant reminders of how easily sin could tempt them from the 'narrow way'. There is little wonder, that imbued with all of this stress, children, then, as ever, worried over their future afterlife.

This is not to say that the Brontës did not have some very happy times, but, as Charlotte asks, why and how did everything they had hoped for in childhood and enjoyed, slip away from them? Did they all suffer a melancholia that, when attacked with Tuberculosis, caused each to die. There is such an air of sadness surrounding the family and it is not just the early deaths. There appears an almost death wish, a longing to join their lost mother and sisters. Charlotte tells us that, 'Anne, from her childhood seemed preparing for an early death'.[5]

In fact Charlotte experienced a 'vision' as a child where she was convinced that she 'saw' an angel standing beside Anne's crib. What does this mean? Was this a joint hysteria; a level of insanity that drove them all eventually to their deaths. Why did Emily deny the help of a doctor when she was dying from Tuberculosis? How much did their losses affect their sanity, because none of them, in the light of our modern society, appear totally sane or in control of their own destiny.

There was, especially in Victorian times, an emphasis on 'madness' as almost self-induced, as well as inherited. There was even a suggestion that if madness could be cured then it must be self-inflicted. There was also an element of choice involved, especially in women where madness was sometimes viewed as a form of punishment for their immorality. Hysteria, based on the Greek word for the female reproductive system, suggested that too much passion in a woman could overtake her reason, as it affected her mental and emotional behaviour. This produced episodes of madness including seizures, incoherence, raging and a complete lack of control.

Patrick Brontë had an interest in medicine, illness and modern cures. He kept a copy of *Modern Domestic Medicine*, published in 1826 by Thomas John Graham. Patrick annotated much of the texts including those pertaining to insanity, both hereditary and acquired. It is likely that he saw in his children's repeated illnesses, melancholia and morbidity, the stirrings of mental illness and this would have added to his fears. Jane McLarren Caldwell states that:

> *The Brontës, however, wrote not so much about hysteria as about religious melancholy, monomania and hypochondria. While lovesickness may be a precipitating cause for both male and female characters, isolation from any human companionship seems most important; and desires are not repressed into the unconscious mind, but are rather fiercely debated in the conscious mind and amplified in the body.*[6]

It is not hard to see this applied to both the Brontës and their fictitious characters. Loneliness, isolation and separation caused by death, or any other trauma, affected them all and they wrote about it repeatedly. One only has to look at Lucy Snowe, confined and alone, gradually sinking into depression and breakdown, or Heathcliff's blind and aggressive behaviour after the death of Catherine. Both these characters 'see' apparitions; hallucinations that identify the tumult in their brains. Some of the most poignant lines in *Wuthering Heights* have, for me, always echoed life in the parsonage where the loss of the three females was a constant companion to the living. Heathcliff cries:

> *Be with me always – take any form – drive me mad! Only do not leave me in this abyss where I cannot find you.*[7]

This is the loss and grief that was ever present in a house where it was impossible to move away from the memories and the associations with the dead. I suggest that grief is a type of mental illness. It consumes the body and the mind and interferes with the normal functioning of the brain. Not only the house and its contents were reminders, but, especially for Patrick and Elizabeth, the recognition of Maria in the looks, gestures and talents of her children. As mentioned, George Eliot describes this process in a way that is particularly relevant to the Brontës:

> *Nature, that great tragic dramatist, knits us together by bone and muscle, and divides us by the subtler web of our brains; blends yearning and repulsion; and ties us by our heart-strings to the beings that jar us at every movement. We hear a voice with the very cadence of our own... We see eyes – Ah! So like our mother's ... and our last darling child startles us with the air and gesture of the sister we parted from in bitterness long years ago ... the long lost mother, whose face we begin to see in the glass as our own wrinkles come, once fretted our young souls with her anxious humours and irrational persistence.*[8]

There is a terrible nostalgia here and one that, I suggest, Emily Brontë especially dwelt upon. When Catherine states in *Wuthering Heights* that she and Heathcliff are the same, it is a recognition by the author, that in families or close attachments, we are the same person. Stevie Davies takes this a step further claiming that:

> *When we crack the code of individual names, labels, clothing, behaviours – the file of eccentricity upon the surface – there is an identity, so fundamental, that we 'are' one another.*[9]

There is a deep philosophy here that is not the subject of this book but helps to explain some of the behaviour and writing of the Brontë siblings. They could not get away from their losses, which constantly haunted them and had to be confronted in their writing in order to help them cope. There is a subtle insanity here that is relentless and is far different and beyond what was acknowledged as 'madness' at the time.

I suggest that Charlotte's description of Bertha Mason (Mrs Rochester) in *Jane Eyre* is almost deliberately a piece of writing that emphasises all the worst traits of an unbalanced mind, as if she is pointing out that it does not apply to her! Madness to Charlotte is the ranting and raving of a severely damaged brain, not the depression and melancholia of her own experience. Her description of Bertha is that of a wild animal completely out of control. It displays all of the commonly held beliefs of the time about mental illness. Bertha is the mad woman in the attic who represents the link between female passion and insanity. Charlotte describes her as follows:

> *In the deep shade, at the further end of the room, a figure ran backwards and forwards. What it was, whether beast or human being, one could not, at first sight, tell: it grovelled, seemingly, on all fours; it snatched and growled like some strange wild animal: but it was covered with clothing; and a quantity of dark, grizzled*

> *hair, wild as a mane, hid its head and face ... the clothed hyena rose up, and stood tall on its hind feet ... The maniac bellowed: she parted her shaggy locks from her visage, and gazed wildly at her visitors. I recognised well that purple face, those bloated features ... Mr Rochester flung me behind him: the lunatic sprang and grappled his throat viciously, and laid her teeth to his cheek: they struggled. She was a big woman, in stature almost equalling her husband, and corpulent besides: she showed virile force in the contest – more than once she almost throttled him ... at last he mastered her arms ... and he pinioned them behind her: with more rope he bound her to a chair. The operation was performed amidst the fiercest yells, and the most convulsive plunges.*[10]

One could analyse the innuendo and metaphors in this description as a perfect Victorian model of insanity and of the female loss of rationality, if separated from male dominance and control. Charlotte is desperately trying to show that Bertha, with her animalistic looks and behaviour, her size and her ferocity, is the opposite of feminine, she is a wild, uncontrollable animal; a species all of her own.

We do not see this level of behaviour nowadays in people with mental health issues, partly because it is more often diagnosed and treated before it becomes overwhelming. Modern research and medicine have highlighted the cause and effects of much mental illness and padded cells and straitjackets are rarely in use in our enlightened times. We have, to some extent, mainly obliterated the old psychiatric hospitals, or asylums, and substituted short term mental health facilities which treat and control, and try to cure. However, as a nurse, I have experienced mental health wards where there is still fear and upset on the side of both health carers and patients. Our modern understanding and research explains much of how and why emotional and psychological illness and disease cause mental upset, but it is still an area of life that is attached to alarm and worry. No one wants to be labelled as mentally ill and it still carries a stigma. It is fair to say that almost no child is born mentally ill, it is a state that occurs through various adverse experiences. Brain injury, at birth or otherwise, is a totally different handicap.

It is also important to realise that mental health is recognised differently in different cultures at different times. We are able to recognise dementia as opposed to calling people witches, we understand schizophrenia and medicate rather than placing someone in a straitjacket because they are having hallucinations and acting outside of the norm. We recognise how and why an abused child will not function as well as a happy and protected one. We know that violence initiates violence and that children need a safe and secure environment. Furthermore, the effects of alcohol and drugs are far more understood and there is more understanding, if not control, of their ill-effects.

It is the acting outside of the norm that usually defines mental illness, but it changes constantly. An example is the cultural upheaval of society in Britain during the 1960s and 1970s. This social revolution saw, and came to accept that, young people could grow their hair long, wear strange clothing, produce their own music and change the moral norms and mores of the time. A teenager with a Mohican haircut, safety pins hanging from his trousers and make up on his face, would probably have been sectioned during the 1930s. My future husband and I, during the late 1960s, were once ordered off a bus because he had long blonde hair and the conductor did not want 'your hippie sort' on his bus. Time and circumstances alter our definitions of mental illness and its accompanying behaviour. When I was a child there was an asylum in a neighbouring village a few miles away. As I found out years later when my daughter did some of her training there and I joined the Friends of the Hospital group, there were women confined for life for having an illegitimate child. In fact, one poor boy was institutionalised there at 8 years old, for stealing apples. The asylums were as much for deviant behaviour as genuine mental illness.

The changes brought about in the last sixty years have made change and difference far more acceptable, to the point where difference is now not only accepted but encouraged. We now live in a society where institutions such as marriage and the legitimacy of children has entirely altered. My father, with his Victorian views and experience of war, remarked on first seeing a punk rocker, 'They should all be put in the army, or shot!' If a punk rocker walked down Haworth Main Street in 1825, they would very likely be institutionalised for the rest of their lives, or be on the receiving end of my father's solution!

There are enormous changes between Haworth in 1820 and Haworth in 2020, and the human condition has changed alongside. However, it is still possible to see that the Brontës, even for their own times and circumstances, were not ordinary or traditional in some areas. I suggest that their confinement and their traumas as children affected their mental health and whilst their art flourished their health suffered in equal measures.

A paper published by BMC Public Health in 2016 and written by Hughes, Lowey, Quigg and Bellis, described their research into the effects of Adverse Childhood Experiences (ACE) on adult mental wellbeing. They noted that research into long-term impacts of ACE's were associated with increasing risks of conditions including depression, anxiety, panic reactions, hallucinations, psychosis and suicide attempts. Their research took them further into taking nine ACE's and looking at the various ways in which they affected people in the long-term in areas such as feeling optimistic, useful, relaxed, close to others, able to make up one's own mind, dealing with problems and thinking clearly.

There was a high reaction to physical and sexual abuse but also to exposure to such adversity as parental stress or disrupted care patterns, both relevant to the Brontë children. The authors found that:

> ... exposure to such adversity can trigger epigenetic modifications (i.e. the way the brain functions) to gene expressions, altering brain structure, stress reactivity and consequently vulnerability to both mental and physical ill health.[11]

One can read the volumes of research on the links between adversity in childhood and mental and physical illnesses in adulthood, and there is, I suggest, a definite and proven inter-relationship. The Brontës did not just suffer the effects of three deaths but ongoing and subsequent losses, adversities and unhappiness at various times throughout their lives. They may all have suffered from that sad and deeply distressing state of unrequited love. Also, their circumstances left them all with an inability to work through their ordeals and resolve their problems due to a lack of personal insight and the times in which they were living.

I also wish to refer back to the Clergy Daughters' School as being another trauma in the lives of Charlotte and Emily that has not been fully recognised. The anger and frustration experienced by children when they are impotent to change or unable to avoid bad experiences is often internalised. Charlotte was able to eventually display her anger in her novel but Emily did not. Whilst Emily was once described by her teachers as 'the pet of the nursery', we have no evidence to prove this and no reason to believe that Emily was given special treatment as the youngest pupil. The regime was hard and it was the opposite of the Brontës home life and environment. Emily was only 6 years old and I suggest that it was this move to the school, with all of its defects and tyranny, that probably caused or propounded Emily's withdrawal and her inability to cope socially and emotionally with outsiders. Charlotte and Emily were severely damaged at this school and unable for years to vent their anger and hurt, if at all.

The school had its defenders and after the publication of *Jane Eyre* there was talk of a libel case. Even if Charlotte exaggerated, one has to appreciate how a child sees the world around them and interprets the events. The secure and protective environment of home had been taken away and a monstrous alternative had to be endured. I return to our modern recognition of Adverse Childhood Experiences and Attachment and quote again from the paper produced by the Royal Manchester Hospital:

> *Two important factors to think about when considering our mental well-being, are the quality of our attachment relationships and our experience of adverse childhood experiences.*[12]

The same paper quotes from *Young Minds*, 2018:

> *ACE's are highly stressful and potentially traumatic events or situations that occur during childhood and/or adolescence. They can be a single event, or prolonged threats to, and breaches of, the young person's safety, security, trust or bodily integrity.*[13]

Examples of ACE include some or all of the following and are generally referred to under the umbrella heading 'abuse'. They can be physical, emotional, sexual, abandonment, withdrawal of life necessities, violence, divorce or death, neglect, living with someone with severe mental or terminal illness, drug addiction and alcoholism.

Mental illness is not about ranting and raving, it is about being unable to cope with life at various times and in various ways. It is about the disturbance of one's equilibrium and for some people, it is about that equilibrium never having been established. The mental illnesses we see today are not necessarily new, although lifestyle and diet can be attributed to changes in behaviour over the years. For example, Attention Deficit Hyperactivity Disorder (ADHD) has only recently been given a name. This neuro-development disorder manifests in children as difficulty in concentrating and focusing and impulsive and often inappropriate behaviour. It has always been present, although it may have been mislabelled as 'naughtiness' years ago. It is just that we now have the science to analyse and label the disorders that have always affected people. When people say that 'no-one had ADHD when I was a child, you just got a clip round the ear for misbehaving', that is not strictly true, it is just that scientists now understand much more about the brain, the environment and behaviour, and can diagnose and try to treat mental instability. However, one can wonder at the amount of chemicals, exhaust fumes, artificial flavourings and monosodium glutamate that ends up in the food chain and in the air that we breath, as having a part to play. Factors that were, mostly, mercifully absent from the Brontës era, although industrial pollution was becoming a major issue.

I maintain that the surviving Brontë siblings had some of the most severe adverse childhood experiences and that they continued in various forms into their adulthood and that these permanently affected them all. However, I am the first to acknowledge that all children have adverse experiences of some kind and at some level; it is part of our make-up and turns us into the characters and personalities that we become. In the case of the Brontë siblings, I suggest that there is evidence to show that whilst they had some happy and interesting times, the adverse traumas had to be internalised. There was nothing and no-one to explain and subdue the effects on their lives of traumatic events. Religion did not comfort them; in Anne's case it only further traumatised her.

They had a mother substitute who could not offer the love and devotion of their actual mother, no matter how she tried, and they had a loving, but extremely occupied father who did his best but unwittingly made some major errors in their upbringing. This was not an era of counselling or media information on illness. Mental issues were feared and hidden; in fact so little was understood about its cause and treatment that children, especially, were hardly seen as victims of it. It was an adult affliction. Children who displayed symptoms of trauma would not be viewed as mentally ill but described in such words as delicate, difficult, disposed, withdrawn or excitable, words that could be used to describe all of the Brontë siblings.

This containment of suffering is what David Daiches describes when he wrote in his introduction to the 1965 edition of *Wuthering Heights* that:

> *One of Emily Brontës most extraordinary achievements in this novel is the domiciling of the monstrous in the ordinary rhythms of life and work, thereby making it at the same time less monstrous and more disturbing.*[14]

I suggest that when you carry grief and trauma in your head and yet have to function in the everyday, you do suffer the 'monstrous in the ordinary' and it is both disturbing and extremely wearing on the nerves and the ability to function.

It is important here to reiterate that there is no such thing as 'normal' behaviour in any era, place or culture. People behave and react according to their experiences and circumstances, but it is important for a society to try and keep its population on a certain level on which it can be controlled. This is monitored by the government, the law, employers, teachers and parents, in order to avoid seeds of anarchy and revolution, either in the family or the society at large. In the centuries before the advent of mental health research and medication, no-one wanted, then or now, to be labelled as 'mad'; it was seen as a sign of weakness, a deficiency of the faculties and a lack of self-control. I suggest that at various times in their lives, each Brontë sibling recognised that they had moderate to severe mental health issues, but that there was very little that they could do about it. The worry and stress involved would only exacerbate their trauma.

I also believe that both Emily and Anne struggled especially with God and nature. The 'Gondal Saga', and later, 'Gaaldine' were forerunners to their novels and demonstrated the forming and organising of their ideas and beliefs. Their three novels explore the inescapable dilemma of being trapped both as a person and as a woman. The books explore the 'madness' of domesticity, with its deception, cruelty and terror, but to escape from it can lead one to encounter the insanity of nature with its random and inhumane forces. Therefore, one is trapped completely and absolutely for sanity equals insanity whichever route is chosen. The claustrophobia of being shut in or the agoraphobia of being shut out, inevitably become one and the same thing. As previously quoted, Emily looks to nature for questions and answers only to find that:

> *What have these lonely mountains worth revealing?*
> *More glory and more grief than I can tell:*
> *The earth that wakes one human heart to feeling*
> *Can centre both the worlds of Heaven and Hell.*[15]

Being indoctrinated with Christianity, did not help the Brontës mental health so much as confuse and baffle them. Charlotte, aligned to her father, appears to have accepted his beliefs. Branwell behaved as if Satan was more of a known entity and he lost any faith he may have had until forced to confess and ask for forgiveness, literally on his death bed. Emily sought her answers in nature and appears to have seen the afterlife in the mountains, trees and rivers rather than a Christian heaven. Anne clung to her father's and aunt's beliefs and the hope of universal salvation, but it harmed and affected her life and spoilt her enjoyment of it. Their preoccupations with sin and the afterlife were part of their consciousness and affected each one in a different way, but all suffered from the religious dogma that haunted their lives and, I believe, it added to their mental distress and inability to be truly content.

Chapter Eight

'Mushrooms Growing in a Cellar'

It is important to remember that in Georgian and pre-Victorian times there was no equality of rights and responsibilities. Children were told what to do, what to think, where to go and how to behave. They were not seen as individuals who could think and function without instruction. Children were to be seen, not heard, and many children were not even seen or recognised as important. In her essay on Anne Brontë, Professor Marion Shaw makes an interesting point about the religious view of children in the 1830s. She reminds the reader that this decade:

> ... *was marked by a powerful confluence of ideas from both Evangelical and the Romantic movements, particularly in relation to the nature and nurture of children.*[1]

In her essay, she contrasts the teachings of Rousseau with that of the Calvinists, stating that for Rousseau:

> ... *there is no original sin in the human heart; the how and the why of the entrance of every vice can be traced.*[2]

Using Charlotte's character of Mr Brocklehurst in *Jane Eyre* as a representative of the Evangelical Calvinist doctrine, she describes how this opposing religious idea fixed original sin as the basis of its treatment of children. Children were seen as having innate evil which must be purged. She says that:

> *Mr Brocklehurst's whole endeavour is to subdue the evil which is innate in the children in his school.*[3]

These two opposing beliefs defined how children were treated. Professor Shaw goes on to say that:

> *The history of the nineteenth century in relation to the upbringing and education of children is that of the struggle between these two approaches to childhood, with the eventual triumph of Rousseau-esque or Romantic over the Puritan or Augustinian.*[4]

We see here the notion that a child can no more be branded as bad than of being good. As I have previously stated, children are not born with these notions of good and evil. They are acquired throughout childhood and it is the circumstances and experiences that the child is born to, and the beliefs of its carers, that will, to a great extent, decide its morals and behaviour.

It was the Romantics who helped to raise the status of children by dealing with this issue, especially William Wordsworth. Hugh Cunningham states that:

> *Wordsworth shared with Locke the view that the mind was at birth a 'tabula rasa', but whereas Locke wanted it imprinted from the outset with habits that would go to the making of a gentleman, Wordsworth urged that it should be wide open to feelings and sensations, above all those from nature. In this he seems close to Rousseau, but for Rousseau what the child would learn from nature would be experience – the fire burns – whereas for Wordsworth nature would implant the foundations of moral virtue and of beauty; and these in turn would shape the adult life.*[5]

('*Tabula rasa*', literally a scraped tablet, or empty plate, emphasising that it was empty of notions of good or evil.)

As I will show in later chapters, Anne Brontë was particularly concerned with these issues and not only with how infants and children were recognised and reared, but especially the difference between the upbringing of the male and female. In her essay, Professor Shaw maintains that:

> *What constitutes true manliness and womanliness in the formation of Christian character during childhood, and what mistakenly passes for these attributes, bring forth Anne's most heartfelt and independent views in her novels.*[6]

We see in the Brontë siblings how children develop when forced into close and intense relationships. Between 1825 and 1831 they are in an encapsulated environment, overseen by their aunt and father who have Georgian norms and mores, but both have intelligence and experience to share with the children. They are being taught the Protestant belief that children are born pure and unsullied with evil. The onus is then on the child to avoid sin, an almost impossible burden. Added to this stress on the child are all the gender and birth order anomalies that pin them into a position they cannot alter.

There evolves in all human and animal families a hierarchy of position and power. In the nineteenth century a family of more than one child would tend to see the eldest, or first boy, take on the lead role. This is also based on the centuries old state of primogeniture, where the first-born boy inherits the family wealth and titles. In a male dominated world, women were not seen as able or capable of managing this important role. Their gender had, for centuries, been allotted the status of home-maker and mother.

Much of these ideas and behaviours continue and are still accepted as the norm in many cultures. The recent removal of primogeniture in the British royal family may well help to abolish this notion eventually, but for now and certainly in the Brontës day, the eldest boy was that special person; the inheritor of his father's estate, wealth and title, and he was schooled and raised with that goal in mind.

Patrick Brontë followed in some aspects of this in so far as he believed that Branwell was his heir and expected him to do well in his career so that he could, if necessary, take full responsibility for his sisters, should they not marry or be unable to work. Patrick's position was always precarious in his 'tied house'. Had Patrick died at any time whilst his children were still living there, they would have had to leave and make way for the next incumbent. This had been the case when Patrick's predecessor, the Reverend James Charnock, died after a long illness in May 1819, and his wife and four children were obliged to vacate their home. This must have been an overshadowing anxiety for Patrick. However, he also knew the power of education and sought to arm his daughters with almost as much knowledge and artistic opportunities as his son. As Branwell developed into a teenager his father must have been proud of his son's abilities; it was only when he repeatedly tried and failed various ventures that Patrick would have begun to worry.

Because of the lack of status of children in the early nineteenth century, there is not much research or serious consideration of their role or their importance. The proverb 'Children should be seen but not heard'[7] dates back to the fourteenth century where it is attributed to an Augustinian Monk, John Mirk, and recorded in his collection of homilies known as *Mirk's Festial*. Unfortunately, its effects have continued throughout the following 800 years. His ideas became almost a rule by which the population treated children as lesser human beings who had no knowledge to impart and therefore nothing to say of importance, so should stay silent. This spread to the notion that children should not speak in front of adults unless specifically requested. It enforces the idea that children are subservient and their views and opinions are worthless. By this token, children are ignorant, disposable and of little use. They are seen as the domain of women/mothers and as women had little or no say, rights or education, so their children were hardly worthy of attention. Unfortunately, this old adage has, I suggest, caused countless harm over the centuries and still exists today. In my own family in the 1950s and 1960s, my father (born in 1913) and raised by Victorian parents and grandparents, stuck to this proverb rigidly. As children we were not allowed to talk at the table, not allowed to question anything he did or said and would be met with a strong and stern 'Do not answer back', which instantly silenced us.

The treatment of children is reflected in various religious doctrines. As stated, one has only to consider the extreme Calvinistic teachings issued to the poor pupils of the Clergy Daughters' School to realise the depth of antagonism and even hatred towards children who did not conform to its dictates. The Reverend William Carus Wilson may have thought that by instilling fear of God rather than love of God in his charges, he would promote obedience and acceptance but, as has been shown time and time again, most children, and adults, respond far better to care and encouragement rather than threat and aggression.

My research into the lives and descriptions of various British children in the early nineteenth century shows a variety of standards and expectations, according to class and status. As is the case today, children are raised according to the class and financial state of their parents. Wealth can be seen today as the over-riding factor in status whereas class was at least as important in Britain 200 years ago. The two often, though not always, tend to go hand in hand.

In a democratic society, and in a country where rights and equality are acknowledged, one expects class to be less of an issue. In Haworth in the early nineteenth century people were very much defined by their position in society according to their wealth, their accommodation, their profession, their ancestry and their intellectual abilities. These attributes would define the class structure. Haworth was a working town in the midst of the Industrial Revolution. The vast majority of its inhabitants were working class and employed in heavy industry such as textiles, quarrying, farming and labouring. The population was high and accommodation at a premium. Wages were low and many people had to share living accommodation and all the problems associated with poor and overcrowded homes. Disease, poverty, a lack of education and little or no parish relief, kept this class below the standards that were acceptable to health and happiness and simultaneously exploited their labour. Patrick Brontë tried many times to highlight the problems in the district and eventually persuaded the engineer, Benjamin Babbage to the village to inspect the sanitation, or severe lack of it. Babbage was shocked by what he saw, which included raw sewage flowing down the main street. His report of 1850[8] lists a catalogue of inadequate provisions and a death rate equal to the poor in the east end of London. Average life expectancy was a mere 25.8 years and 41% of children died before the age of 6. Yet, as was happening elsewhere, the towns expanded and the manufacturing industries grew. As people died, others took their places. The mills were full of children as young as 7 who knew little else than work, throughout their short lives.

There is a notable anomaly here between British childhood 200 years ago and the present state of treatment and attitudes towards children. Children in the Brontës' era, especially the working classes, where generally seen as assets to the family, who would contribute to the family finances whenever they were old enough to work and before they left home to start their own families. Those who did not qualify for an education could be working in mills and factories, or their own homes, when as young as 5. Childhood was not viewed by many as an important stage in life, merely as the forerunner to future employment. As the twentieth century progressed and state education developed for all children, living standards rose along with state support for families. After the Second World War, the introduction of the National Health Service (1948) helped to identify areas of need and treat social deprivation and disease. Children developed accordingly with better diets and health. Television and the media entered their lives and parents were under pressure to keep up with demand. More and more mothers began to go out to work, thanks in part to new birth control methods, to provide the goods deemed necessary for their children's benefit. Hugh Cunningham notes that:

> *Children were ceasing to have any economic value and if they did earn any money in a part-time job they kept it for themselves. More important than this, they became the focus for expenditure, parents determining to give their children a better childhood than they themselves had had, and seeing the means for this in expenditure.*[9]

I witnessed, as a child, the start of pocket-money becoming a regular occurrence. We had very little, maybe only six pence (3p) in old money a week, but it soon became an accepted norm in most families. There was a pressure from the media and peers to constantly give children more, to the point nowadays where some children have an enormous amount of money and possessions, way beyond their needs.

The major change we see today is that children, now well-educated to at least 16 years of age, are often at home for the first twenty years of their lives, and beyond. They are no longer expected to be contributors to the family finances, and it is now the parents who go out to work to support the children and not the other way around. Furthermore, modern children are encouraged to be different, opinionated, informed, career minded and many have the freedom to travel and to choose their way in life. These attributes were impossible to the vast majority of children in the nineteenth century. Add to this the current technological age which sees almost every child with their own means of communication and access to the World Wide Web, and there is once again a shift from the child to the adult where childhood seems again, to be shrinking into a few years of infancy.

However, not everyone suffered the fate of the labouring poor in the nineteenth century. Higher up the social scale were professional people who could earn more money, provide better accommodation and keep their children away from the labouring poor. Patrick Brontë's profession placed him in this class, but, although he had status and respect as the church minister, unfortunately, he had no wealth. The position of the sturdy parsonage above and slightly away from the rest of the town, enabled a separation that allowed the Brontë children distance and protection from the working classes. However, I maintain that there was also an element of snobbery involved here. Patrick had extricated himself from his poor birth and childhood and attained a position that he intended to keep. His social rise had been quite phenomenal, and in Haworth he would be able to keep himself and his family somewhat above and beyond the rest of the working population. As a priest he had daily contact with the poor and as a philanthropist he initiated many schemes to help to improve education, sanitation and accommodation in his parish, but he did not give his children free access to the town or encourage socialisation.

There was then a gap between the behaviour and expectations of the children of the working poor and those unemployed, and the children of the professional classes. The Brontë children were not fodder for the mills and had an exceptional childhood protected from the daily grind of work and poverty. The downside of this was an almost complete lack of communication with children of their own age and avoidance of any friendships that could have been allowed to form.

It has been argued repeatedly about the pros and cons of keeping children isolated, home-schooled and away from factors that could harm their health and development. There are no set answers to this dilemma. It suits some children very well and not others. We can only examine it from the Brontë siblings' standpoint and examine what they did, how and why they did it and how beneficial or otherwise their upbringing was at this time and whether it inhibited or enhanced their development.

1825 was the beginning of their intense shared lifestyle, immediately following the deaths of Maria and Elizabeth. We can fully appreciate the adults fear of another child succumbing to illness and death, in some dreadful ongoing cycle. It was perfectly natural to keep them protected and together away from harm. It is a situation that has been mirrored in societies all over the world and children reared in this close and shared development can benefit from each other's ideas and experiences, form close and stable bonds and indulge themselves in learning and playing at their own rate and interests; it is part of the ethos of the Montessori philosophy of education. Whilst Patrick and Aunt Elizabeth will have instilled discipline and an ordered timetable, these children had a very wide and open canvas on which to indulge their imaginations, their education and their play. They were uninhibited by the schoolroom rules that many children have today. There were no distractions that would interfere detrimentally with their daily routine and they always had the escape onto the moors to indulge in healthy games, exercise and natural learning. I suggest that these well-fed, well-catered for and well-educated children, loved and surrounded by each other and their carers had, in some ways, a very pleasant and indulged childhood, one that they repeatedly mourned and hankered after.

However, of course nothing is that simple or straightforward. One could also imply that they were ruled and directed by a strict routine that kept them safe but confined, kept them happy but lacking in the emotional comfort they had received from their mother and elder sisters. They were together as a family but barred and protected from the natural association with other children that would have affected their views and instilled social confidence. Other children, especially of different background and class, would have questioned and affected their views and widened their emotional outlook. This was shown when Charlotte went to Roe Head School and made friends with Ellen Nussey and Mary Taylor. Charlotte's whole outlook changed and the interaction with these two very different females had a lifelong effect on her.

Is it natural or desirable to always be amongst one's own siblings with no alternative viewpoint? We can learn a wealth of information from books and magazines and newspapers but it is not reality; it is not living that life in the real world for yourself. Everything you learn is second-hand and describes lives lived by other people. It negates one's own experiences and inhibits social growth and understanding. When Charlotte stated in her critique of *Wuthering Heights* that Emily had no knowledge of the people passing by the parsonage gate, she was probably correct. None of them had much idea of the lives of the people living so close to them. Knowledge during the years between 1825 and 1831 was almost always second-hand; it was gossip, it was newspapers and letters and books that described people and events, it was not the living experience of the children themselves. No wonder that they developed their own people, places and events, as they were not taking part themselves in regular social interaction. I would argue that it was almost inevitable that they would want to have an element of control of the outside world that they experienced so little of.

In her epic book on the Brontës, Juliet Barker states that after the return from the Clergy Daughters' School and the constant attention of their adult carers, the children would recover their former settled lives:

> *With good food, daily walks in the fresh air of the moors and the re-establishment of a routine of lessons with their father and aunt, the children would gradually return to something like normality.*[10]

One can argue that they developed wonderful imaginations, writing skills and clever and precocious characteristics, but it was not until their mid-teens that they had experience of life outside of the parsonage and Haworth. Then, they were able to look at life in reality and, especially Anne, to see for themselves how other classes and children behaved and developed according to their circumstances.

Unfortunately, when the Brontë children were finally exposed to the outside world they became upset and disorientated. It is almost inevitable that children of their upbringing would react as they did. None of them coped well away from home because it was an alien world that they were unprepared for. It made them ill, unhappy and, in Branwell's case, totally overwhelmed and deeply disturbed. The shyness, the quiet and withdrawn behaviour, the fear of standing out or drawing attention to themselves personified the girls. This was counteracted by Branwell, who over compensated for his shyness with his bombastic and mercurial behaviour that actively sought attention but had no social skills to cope with it.

During the years of enforced home tutoring the children were occupied in many ways. As explained, their developing talents in music and art were encouraged and indulged with Patrick sparing money from his small annuity to employ both an art and music tutor and later to eventually purchase a piano and also to set Branwell up in an art studio. One can see his determination to give his children everything he possibly could to enhance their talents and drive their education. Like so many parents he acted as he thought best for his family and in many ways he succeeded, but they did not develop the social skills that would enhance their adulthood and allow them to mature into fully rounded and capable men and women. Juliet Barker comments that:

> *Like all large families, particularly those with children close together in age, the Brontës were self-sufficient. They had no need to seek friends of their own age in the town when they had companions with the same tastes and enthusiasms in their own home.*[11]

I would argue that in some ways this interdependency was unhealthy and that they remained extremely childish, and childlike, way beyond their teens and well into adulthood. To read Emily's 'diary paper' of 1845, when she is 27 years old and Anne is 25, after they have visited York, is to witness the report of a woman still living in the fantasy world of her childhood. She writes nothing about the sights of York, the massive minster or the shops, ancient monuments or architecture; she talks of 'Gondal' and of her and Anne playing the parts of their fictional heroes and heroines:

> *Anne and I went on our first long journey by ourselves, leaving home on the 30th June, sleeping at York and returning to Keighley Tuesday evening, sleeping there and walking home on Wednesday morning ... during our excursion we were Ronald Macelgin, Henry Angora, Juliet Augusteena, Rosobelle Esraldan, Ella and Julian Egramont, Catherine Navarre and Cordelia Firzaphnold escaping from the Palaces of Instruction to join the Royalists who are hard driven at present by the victorious Republicans.*[12]

It is the inner and outer worlds that they describe in their journals, their poetry and to some extent their novels; the fantasy that is so necessary to indulge when real life is too complicated and difficult. Time and again they are caught up in this imaginary life, Charlotte describes it when she is teaching at Roe Head when she 'escapes' into her fantasy world in the middle of teaching a class of students:

> *Then came on me rushing impetuously, all the mighty phantasm that we had conjured from nothing to a system strong as some religious creed. I felt as if I could have written gloriously – I longed to write. The spirit of all Verdopolis – of all the mountainous North of all the woodland West of all the river watered East came crowding into my mind. If I had time to indulge it I felt that the vague sensations of that moment would have settled down into some narrative better at least than any thing I ever produced before. But just then a Dolt came up with a lesson. I thought I should have vomited.*[13]

Likewise, Charlotte 'sees' the Duke of Zamorna sitting in the school room at Roe Head leaning on an obelisk with his black horse grazing amongst heather under a moonlit African sky.

Anne tries hard to move on to reality but not before she has suffered almost to breaking point during her first foray away from home. Emily too, is dying of home sickness at Roe Head because she cannot cope with ordinary social activities away from the parsonage. Charlotte wrote that:

> *Liberty was the breath of Emily's nostrils; without it she perished. The change from her own home to a school, and from her own very noiseless, very secluded, but unrestricted and inartificial mode of life, to one of the disciplined routine (though under the kindest auspices), was what she failed in enduring... Every morning when she woke, the vision of home and the moors rushed on her and darkened and saddened the day that lay before her... I felt in my heart that she would die if she did not go home.*[14]

Biographers have spent many years praising the Brontës' extraordinary writing skills and imaginations but I would argue that this was at the expense of a normal and fulfilling social experience that would have better prepared them for adult working life. It is all the more amazing that Charlotte, and Anne especially, were able to describe so well and so accurately their observations and personal experiences of life in their novels. Charlotte became the most widely travelled and had the advantage of external friendships and work experience. Anne, determined to prove herself other than the naive and delicate youngest gained the 'age and experience' that she craved and used her acute observation skills and determination to record exactly what she saw, to produce her famous works. At last, she had some first-hand experience to share.

Returning to these six years of enforced companionship one can almost make up a daily timetable for the siblings which incorporates all that the adults thought necessary for their development. We have the description from Nancy Garrs regarding the daily routine and little changed throughout their time at home. One day must have been very like another.

These important years when children are developing a huge range of skills and experience saw them follow this daily timetable, but there were a few other distractions, albeit in the home. The children had plenty of toys and Patrick bought Branwell at least three sets of soldiers. They had wooden animals, dolls and skittles. When it was too inclement to venture out on to the moors, they had a garden surrounding three sides of the house with room for games. Again, their games and toys were played with only by themselves, no other child was involved. When Charlotte first went to Roe Head School aged 15, she was unable to join in with the other girls in the playground as she was unaware of their games or how to play them. At the *Pensionnat Heger*, when Charlotte and Emily were in their early twenties, they still did not mix with the other girls, they preferred their own company and their studies. One can see the drawbacks of this lack of social interaction; it causes distress and an abnormal inability to mix freely with other people. The girls were vocal and interactive at home, but once away from its protection they became withdrawn and unsociable.

It was during the six years together that Charlotte, now the eldest, was able to take control. It is likely that this was with the full approval of her father and aunt, who needed that extra helping hand to help keep the others in order. Also, it is likely that having lost his intelligent and admired eldest girl, Patrick needed a substitute; another female of his own to look up to and be looked after by. This relationship lasted throughout Charlotte's life and she and her father appear to have been very close and yet Charlotte seems to have been the dominant person as she grew older. Charlotte showed tremendous care and worry over her father and seems to have teamed up with him as much, if not more, at times, than her siblings. It appears that both Patrick and Aunt Elizabeth deferred to Charlotte, certainly in adulthood and she, in turn, was able to influence, even manipulate, these two adults.

Anne was now the definite and defined youngest and had, since her mother's illness, been under the constant and close attention of her aunt. There is almost never total harmony amongst siblings and there shouldn't be. It is through the battles of childhood that we learn to cope and behave as adults. We learn our place in the hierarchy and we learn to share, to argue, to develop a sense of humour, if we are lucky, and to realise that others have strong and important feelings and goals that may differ from our own. Inevitably, each child suffers because of their place in the family, and the expectations and treatment of their parents and siblings. Whilst the eldest may be overburdened, deliberately or accidentally, with extra responsibilities, the youngest may also suffer from a lack of the same, and develop an inability to take control of their own independence and behaviour. The youngest is just that, the youngest and they cannot be otherwise. It is almost unavoidable that the older children will look down both physically and emotionally on the youngest. The youngest cannot do as well in any area because the others are always ahead. There develops a helplessness if this state of affairs is allowed to continue as the youngest child ages. The natural maternal behaviour of all of the family, not just the females, brings about a need to protect but control, to cosset yet humiliate, to cherish and ridicule. It is not always the case, but within the Brontë family one can see how this developed and continued throughout Anne's life until she was able to leave home and strike out on her own. Even then, she was not praised and recognised for her bravery, rather she leaves a certain amount of astonishment behind as her family wonders how on earth she will cope. Charlotte writes in awe to Ellen to describe how Anne left home completely alone stating that:

> ... *she thought that she could manage better and summon more courage if thrown entirely upon her own resources.*[15]

This sentence tells us a lot about both of the sisters. Anne is trying to prove that at 19 years old, she can, and will, go it alone and wants to be free of the ties that keep her as the pathetic child. Charlotte, along with the rest of the family, does not see Anne as an adult. They have little or no faith in her ability to survive amongst strangers and they doubt her fortitude and her abilities. This is because she has always been the least noticed and noticeable. She is painfully shy, she has little to say and no lead role in the household. How will she ever succeed as a governess amongst strangers?

The Brontë children's imaginary worlds and their precociousness was not unique then or now. Many children share stories as they learn to read and write. My own brother, the eldest of four, produced a newspaper for us all to read when he was about 10 years old, possibly younger. It is a natural part of one's education and development that you practice what you have learnt or imagined. However, from the age of 4 and for the next twelve years, we went to school every day and interacted with dozens of other children, all different and all with experiences that challenged and questioned our own. We made and lost friends, we learnt to share and play together, we learnt to lose and to suffer and to be frustrated and triumphant. In other words, we learnt to better cope as adults, despite having widely differing ideas and views from our peers and each other. We learnt to question what adults, both teachers and parents, told us. We learnt what was acceptable in society and what was not. We learnt to tolerate society and not be too afraid to venture into it and continue to learn. This is what I suggest the Brontë children missed and it hampered their adulthood. One may be extremely intelligent and very able in the arts, but if you cannot comfortably live in the rest of the society, you are at a major disadvantage. For me, the Brontë siblings coped in some ways with death, but were severely curtailed in coping with life.

Chapter Nine

'The Dark Side of Sisterhood'[1]

As stated, there is very little evidence of Anne's first fifteen years to know how she felt and reacted to being the youngest, but we do know that her position in the birth order separated her out from her siblings and kept her status as less important in many ways than the elder children. We know that she was small, physically weak, asthmatic and the 'prettiest' of her siblings.

In January 1831, there was another major change in the household and in the dynamics of the family. Patrick was aware that the children would soon need the necessary skills to earn a living, especially if he succumbed to any number of illnesses or his 'weak' chest and chronic bronchitis. This meant looking again at schools and how best to continue the children's education whilst keeping them fit and healthy. After much discussion and enquiries, he sent Charlotte to Roe Head School, a girls' boarding school at Mirfield near Dewsbury. The school was owned and run by the Wooler sisters and was a very different place to the Clergy Daughters' establishment. The school still stands today. It is now Hollybank Residential School and is administered by a charitable trust that caters for the special needs of people with severe learning disabilities.

Charlotte was 15 years old and well aware that she was there to learn as much as she could in the next eighteen months. She excelled at this school, after overcoming initial nerves and shyness, and met the two pupils who became her lifelong friends, Ellen Nussey and Mary Taylor. There is no doubt that Charlotte was a highly intelligent and diligent pupil, eager to learn and able to retain knowledge. She had finally broken free of Haworth and the parsonage and thrived in this new environment which was the opposite in every way to her last disastrous school experience.

In many ways, Roe Head broke the bond between Charlotte and Branwell and was the beginning of the end of their writing partnership. Their personal interaction and united partnership very gradually dissolved. Over the next few years where Charlotte blossomed, her brother shrivelled and withdrew. Branwell found life difficult without Charlotte and was probably both worried

Right: A plaque on the wall of the former Thornton Parsonage commemorating the births there of the four youngest Brontë children.

Below: Thornton Parsonage as it looked when the Brontë family moved in, before the right side was extended to form a butchers shop, some time in the twentieth century. It has now been bought by the Brontë Birthplace Trust who are renovating the building with plans to re-open it as an arts and education centre, B&B and cafe in 2025. This will coincide with Bradford's City of Culture award.

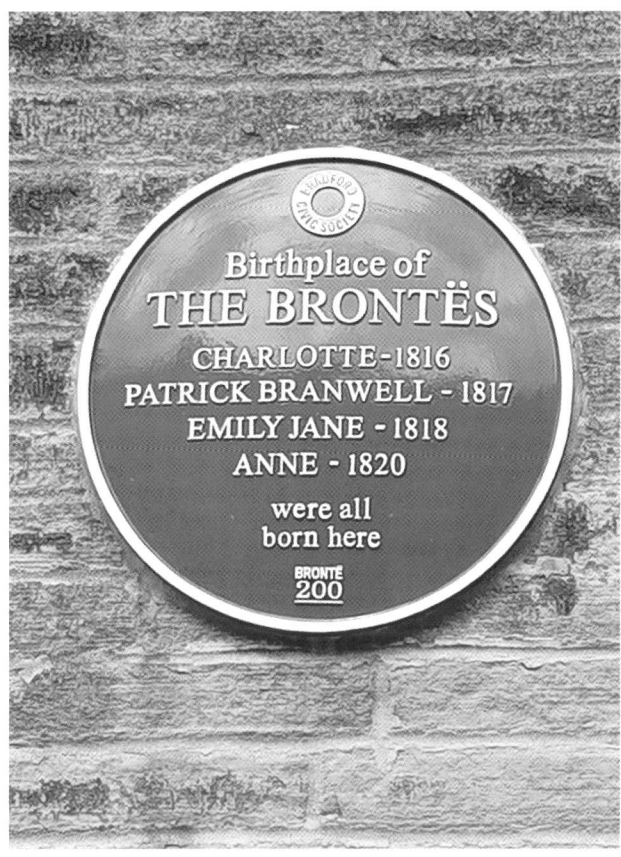

Above: It is said that Mrs Brontë gave birth to her four youngest children in a downstairs room in front of this fireplace.

Left: The font in which the five youngest of the Brontë siblings were baptised. It stood in the Old Bell Chapel where Patrick Brontë was minister during the family's residence in Thornton. It now stands in St James's Church, Thornton.

The remains of The Old Bell Chapel, Thornton, where Patrick was the minister when his youngest four children were all born.

Haworth Parsonage in recent years. Built in 1778, the building has had various alterations and extensions but maintains its former rooms and layout in this photograph showing the original Georgian house.

St Michael and All Angels' Church, Haworth. Patrick was the minister of the former church on this site for over forty years. The church he and his family knew was demolished in 1879, leaving only the tower, the lower part of which dates from 1488. The present church in this photograph was completed in 1882.

The Sunday school, which stands adjacent to the parsonage, was built by subscription and completed in 1834. It was the idea and accomplishment of Patrick Brontë. His four youngest children all taught the local children here on Sundays.

Haworth Moor is a beautiful and wild place and is punctuated with waymarkers to guide travellers, some of whom have been lost on the moors in the past when the dark, the snow, the fog and the rain, have all obliterated their way.

Above: Roe Head School. It is now extended and is the home of Hollybank special needs school at Mirfield, West Yorkshire.

Left: There is now a plaque at Roe Head School, commemorating the three Brontë pupils and Charlotte's time there as a teacher.

This is an old drawing of Blake Hall in Mirfield. This was the home of the Ingham family who employed Anne as a governess in 1839. Her experiences here formed the basis of her book, *Agnes Grey*. The hall has completely gone and is now the site of a housing estate.

A photograph/drawing of Thorp Green Hall, Anne's next and last place of employment from 1840 to 1845. The hall burnt down in the late nineteenth century. Another hall was built a short distance away and after an extensive building project it now forms the current Queen Ethelburga's school, which moved to the premises from Harrogate in 1991.

Whilst a governess with the Robinson family at Thorp Green, Anne attended the nearby Little Ouseburn Church of the Holy Trinity.

The interior of Holy Trinity Church, Little Ouseburn, where the Robinson family had their own pew. Anne would either ride to church in their carriage or walk the two miles from Thorp Green Hall. Branwell would possibly accompany her in the years that he too was employed by the Robinson family. This would be as part of his duties and family tradition, rather than reflecting Branwell's own religious views.

Right: During the time that Anne was at Thorp Green, her father's popular curate, William Weightman, died. He was beloved by many in Haworth, not least the entire Brontë family. The congregation paid for this memorial in his honour. It can be seen today on the inside of the north wall of St. Michael's church, Haworth.

Below: Anne spent summer holidays in Scarborough with the Robinson family. The Spa Bridge, built by and operated by the Cliff Bridge Company, from 1826 to 1957 linked St Nicholas Cliff with a building south across the valley, which housed the Spa waters. Anne would have crossed it many times, including in the days before her death. It was a toll bridge at that time. It is still in use and is managed by Scarborough Council. It offers fine views over the south bay.

This is a picture of the first editions of *Wuthering Heights* and *Agnes Grey* as they appeared in a three volume set in December 1847.

This old drawing shows number 2, The Cliff, and part of Wood's Lodgings, where Anne stayed with the Robinson family. Number 2 is the house in which Anne Brontë died. It is the second cottage from the left. The house looks small but would have extended at the back, overlooking the sea.

Whilst staying in Scarborough with the Robinsons, Anne worshipped at Christ Church, only a few hundred metres from her lodgings, on what is now Vernon Road. It was demolished in 1979 to make way for two modern businesses: Wackers fish and chip restaurant and Iceland frozen foods.

The interior of Christ Church, Scarborough, where Anne's funeral was held as the parish church of St Mary's was under repair and because Anne had worshipped there.

Above: St Mary's and Holy Apostles. The parish church of Scarborough on Castle Road.

Left: Anne was buried in St Mary's graveyard in an area still known as Paradise. This is a photograph of how her grave looked around the turn of the nineteenth century.

This photograph was taken on the 175th anniversary of Anne's death, 28 May 2024, at a memorial service held by the Anne Brontë Association. It shows the plaque placed on the grave by the Brontë Society in April 2013, because of errors on the headstone and its deterioration.

The Anne Brontë memorial space set up in St Mary's Church, Scarborough by the author following the Anne Brontë Conference in 1994. It is in a quiet side chapel and contains information and books.

Above: The Grand Hotel, Scarborough, completed in 1867, stands on the grounds of the former Wood's Lodging houses. This photograph is taken from the Spa Bridge.

Right: The plaque in memory of Anne Brontë on the wall of The Grand Hotel, placed there by Scarborough Civic Society in 1975. It commemorates the site of the house in which Anne died.

Above left: A copy of Anne's first novel, *Agnes Grey*. Published in 1847.

Above right: A copy of *The Tenant of Wildfell Hall*. Anne's second novel, published in 1848, the year before her death. It attracted much criticism at the time of its publication. It is now seen as a seminal work of feminist and social theory. Anne's novels have stayed in print and are now viewed as classics of English literature.

This picture shows a collection of recent books focusing especially on Anne Brontë. All have been published in the last 8 years. They reflect the growing concern that she has not received the respect and acknowledgement that she so rightly deserves.

and pleased that she had new friends and surroundings. He did not have the special relationship with Emily and Anne that he had had with Charlotte and he did not naturally drift to them. He too needed a change and to move amongst lads of his own age and disposition but never really managed this. He still continued to write, but gradually their partnership dissipated and eventually nothing of any worth existed between them. Charlotte also continued to write Angrian tales, but their collaboration had ruptured.

The departure of Charlotte intensified the sisterly bond between Emily and Anne and they began the writing of their 'Gondal Saga'. They still had poor writing skills but their imaginations flourished. The absence of the pressures instilled by the Branwell/Charlotte partnership allowed the two girls absolute freedom to write whatever they wished, uncensored, unopposed and uninterrupted. At 13 years old, it is likely that Anne moved out of her aunt's room and now shared a room with Emily, adding to their closeness and allowing them to collaborate both day and night.

This is why, I believe, that Ellen Nussey came to describe them as, 'like twins', when she first visited their home in June 1833. She noted their strong alliance, which was, in fact, a perfectly normal love and friendship between the only two girls in the house, neither of whom had any outside relationships. I liken writing with someone as similar to playing music together. It creates a bond and each player brings to the partnership something bigger than the individual working alone. The partnership between the two girls grew into the 'Gondal Saga', in which they each 'played their own instruments' but created a unified 'orchestra'.

Unfortunately, a great deal of this saga is lost, although some of the poetry and hints of the story are still extant. The poetry produced by the girls is some of the very finest in English Literature and set a seal on their abilities as authors. Even if the physical writing and grammar were difficult, the ideas and command of language were exceptional.

Charlotte stayed at Roe Head School for three terms, coming back to the parsonage in June 1832. She was given a silver medal to mark her repeated achievements. She had gained two firm friends, something her sisters never achieved, and she settled back into parsonage life and the writing of Angria. However, she now had distractions and obligations that were not present when she and Branwell had been at home together for such a long time. All of Charlotte's skills had improved enormously, not least her drawing and art work, and she also became a proficient and copious letter writer. She was now expected to instruct her sisters in all that she had learnt. So, she now took on the teacher role that further enhanced her status as more experienced, knowledgeable and in charge, of her sisters. At school she had excelled in French and even tried to get her new friend, Ellen, to write to her in her newly discovered language.

What Branwell thought of all these changes is not recorded. He still wanted to maintain a close relationship with his sister, but she was making new and exciting changes in her life.

It wasn't until 1834 that Branwell began to also spread his wings and begin new ventures. The installation of the new organ at his father's church allowed him to learn to play that instrument as well as his flute. He was also tutored later in the year by William Robinson, the portrait painter who had previously given them all art lessons. Unfortunately, Branwell's hopes and ambitions outweighed his skills and he never made a career as a portrait painter, even though he set up a studio in Bradford for some months. He did, however, persuade his sisters to sit for two oil paintings, *The Pillar Portrait,* now in the National Portrait Gallery, London, and *The Gun Group,* copies and engravings of which have passed down over the years, but the original painting is lost. *The Pillar Portrait* is not a wonderful painting, except for its subject matter.

By July 1835, Charlotte had accepted an offer by Miss Margaret Wooler, the owner and superintendent at Roe Head School, to change from pupil to teacher. Part of the contract allowed for her to take one of her sisters who would be educated for free, although some of this expense may have been met through Charlotte's wages. Charlotte, the decision-maker, chose Emily to accompany her and they arrived at Roe Head on 29 July. Charlotte was now one of the mistresses and at 19 years old had a status setting her apart, not only from her pupils but also from her sister. How much Charlotte chose to affect this change of relationship is difficult to assess. It is only known that Emily, removed from her home for only the second time in her life, suffered extreme homesickness that made her so ill that she had to return home. Leaving the school in October, after only three months, Emily's vacant place was filled by Anne.

Homesickness has to be viewed here in the context of the time in which it occurred. The phenomenon goes back to ancient times and is mentioned in both the Bible and the Greek myths. The Israelites wept by the rivers of Babylon for their home of Zion, and Odysseus needed to be recalled home as he missed his wife and family so much. It was usually taken seriously and regarded as an illness. An article in *The American Psychiatric Association,* describes it in these terms:

> *... inappropriate and excessive fear or anxiety concerning separation from those to who an individual is attached.*[2]

It is a highly debilitating state of acute anxiety that can lead to many disabling symptoms including shortness of breath, sweating, palpitations, disturbed mental states, panic attacks and anorexia. It can occur at any time to anyone, but it often associated with soldiers or people kept away from home in troubled circumstances for excessive periods of time. In the nineteenth century it was not dismissed as paranoia but as an illness that was mentally as well as physically debilitating. Nowadays we describe it more in terms of grief, post-traumatic stress disorder and agoraphobia. People can die of it because they are too tired and scared to function and may stop eating or reacting normally to external stimuli. It is partly identified when people say that someone has died of a broken heart.

Emily was, therefore, very ill, and Charlotte was right to be worried. Returning home was for Emily, the only remedy. For Anne, stepping into Emily's place as a child who at 15 years old had never left home or been to school and who was also very shy, it was perhaps inevitable that she too would suffer. Patrick had written in a letter to Anne's godmother, Elizabeth Franks (nee Firth,) that he had not been intending to let Anne leave home. He wrote that:

> '... my dear little Anne, I intend, to keep at home, for another year, under her aunt's tuition and my own'.[3]

It is interesting to note Patrick's description of his youngest child as 'dear little Anne'. Anne did well initially and was well educated in French, German, Latin, History, Geography, English Grammar, Music, Drawing, Needlework and Handwriting. Anne slowly began to suffer but not because the school was in any way too strict, too dismal or physically and mentally taxing, but partly because of the loneliness that ensued for Anne due to Charlotte's superior placement and her rejection of the pupils, including Anne, as worthy of any special attention. It was also partly due to the religious teachings and ideas here that had a strong Calvinistic influence, one that preached predestination.

As explained, Calvinists did not believe in universal salvation, the very doctrine that Anne held dear. She had spent nearly sixteen years believing that she would, one day, be reunited with her mother and sisters, but Calvinism did not allow for anyone to enter heaven who had not been especially chosen by God; the 'elect'. This placed Anne in a religious quandary and it gradually bore down on her sensibilities and caused her intense anxiety. Anne had no-one with whom to discuss her fears. She made two friends, but they were much younger than her and not informed enough to help her in her dilemma. Ann Cook and her sister Ellen, aged 10 and 8 years, were friendly but it was not a natural or healthy friendship, rather one of necessity, as there was no one there of Anne's age. There is no reliable information that the Cook sisters had an enduring friendship with Anne, and Ann Cook died in 1840. Being the sister of one of the teachers may also have ostracised Anne from her fellow pupils and her extreme shyness would have added to her isolation.

Anne's growing fears and religious crisis amplified over the months she spent at Roe Head. She did not waste this time and worked hard at her lessons and appreciated the chance of the education that she had been given, but the growing religious fears and the lack of any special friend of her own to confide in caused Anne's worries to fester. Each time Charlotte and Anne came home for school holidays it made it harder to return.

By 1835, Emily was very busy writing Gondal and Branwell, whilst still deeply involved with 'Glasstown', made several attempts to find a place as a journalist with *Blackwood's Edinburgh Magazine*. He wrote to the editor arrogantly suggesting that he take the place of the deceased James Hogg, 'The Ettrick Shepherd', a character whose writings had greatly influenced all of the Brontës. Branwell wrote in a very high-handed and aggressive manner:

> *Sir, Read what I write ... to you I appear writing with conceited assurance – but I am not – for I know myself so far as to believe in my own originality... Now sir, do not act like a common place person, but like a man willing to examine for himself. Do not turn from the naked truth of my letters ... you have lost an able writer in James Hogg, and God grant you may gain one in Patrick Branwell Brontë.*[4]

Branwell could be bold and rude because he always seemed to imagine that he was very talented. One could argue that he was in some ways, but his arrogance worked against him and spoilt his chances of making his name in literature or art. He was good but not the genius that he imagined himself to be. Perhaps years of adulation and indulgence from his family had given him a false sense of grandeur and ability that was unsustainable.

Charlotte was, by now, becoming thoroughly disillusioned with Roe Head and the pupils, whom she found irritating and slow. She had come to realise that writing was her forte and teaching most certainly was not. Charlotte wrote a diatribe against her situation as a teacher and the lack of empathy and interest she had in her pupils. She wrote how in the middle of day dreaming about 'Angria', she was interrupted by the necessity of teaching pupils who had no intelligence or imagination. She was, however, already beginning to wonder if it would be possible for she and her sisters to open a school of their own where they would have more freedom and more say in their lives. One imagines that Charlotte would have taken a managerial role rather than as a teacher!

In December Charlotte sent off some of her poetry to the Poet Laureate, Robert Southey. He did not reply to her until March 1837 with a very negative reaction. He told her that:

> *... literature cannot be the business of a woman's life, and it ought not to be. The more she is engaged in her proper duties, the less leisure she will have for it.*[5]

It is not often that Charlotte was put in her place but, luckily, Southey was wrong and Charlotte kept his letter, but not his advice.

During June (1837) when Anne was home for a school holiday, she and Emily wrote their 'diary paper' together. This habit found them recording a particular day every four years, sealing the information and only opening it to read again four years later when the next diary paper would be written. It was Branwell's twentieth birthday and the girls recorded the regular goings on at the parsonage, interspersed with happenings in their 'Gondal' world. It is written by Emily and the writing is minute and difficult to decipher. She has drawn a picture of herself and Anne seated at the dining room table. Here one notes again the intermingling of reality with the imaginary world of 'Gondal':

> *... Anne and I writing in the drawing room – Anne a poem beginning 'fair was the evening and brightly the sun' – I, Augustus Almedas life 1st vol – 4th page from the last a fine rather coolish thin grey cloudy but sunny day Aunt working in the little Room papa gone out. Tabby in the kitchen – the Emperors and Empresses of Gondal and Gaaldine preparing to depart from Gaaldine to Gondal to prepare for the coronation which will be on the 12th of July Queen Victoria ascended the throne this month. Northangerland in Monceys Isle- Zamorna at Eversham. all tight and right in which condition it is to be hoped we shall all be on this day 4 years...*[6]

Again, one sees the lack of grammar and punctuation and the 'stream of consciousness' style of tumbling thoughts and lack of coherence. The national event of Queen Victoria's accession is embedded in the more important and immediate happenings in the 'Gondal' world.

By December 1837, Anne had spent over two years as a pupil at Roe Head. Charlotte's bad-temper and lack of empathy and Anne's religious anxiety were compounded when Anne had an attack of gastric flu. (This was sometimes the term given to typhoid, or it may have included asthma or even a latent attack of Tuberculosis.) Like Emily before her, she became gravely ill, but again it took Charlotte some time to realise or recognise it. This separation from her sister and Charlotte's attempts to retain her teacher status did little to acknowledge and treat Anne's symptoms. Even when Charlotte began to feel concerned about Anne and reported it to Miss Wooler, the headmistress did not respond and assumed that Charlotte was over-reacting.

Anne had had two years of Calvinistic doctrine that questioned the core of her beliefs. The belief that fate was pre-ordained by God and that only the 'elected' would go to heaven, was in direct opposition to the Protestant Anglican belief that sinners could be saved and forgiven. It was perhaps the thought of dying and not going to her mother and sisters that made Anne's condition reach crisis point. Her mind was haunted by the prospect of what would happen to her if she died.

Dr Chitham notedly states that:

> *Anne's early religious feelings must be registered ... No one can understand Anne Brontë without empathy with this feeling, whether they agree with her or not. Religion will permeate her life and work, and we shall need to remember this as we follow her through (though at times we find her struggling to equate her own feelings with her religious understanding).*[7]

Eventually, Anne was seen by a local Moravian minister, the Reverend James La Trobe, who visited her several times to offer help and advice.

The Moravian religion, founded in the eighteenth century but able to trace its origins back to the 'Unity of Brethren' in fifteenth-century Bohemia and Moravia, is Protestant in its beliefs with its ideas and doctrine firmly based on the Bible and the Apostles' and Nicene Creeds. The Wesley brothers had met Moravians in the USA in the 1730s and approved of their Evangelical ideas and practices, which are also linked in to the Baptist faith. Anne was, therefore, able to understand and communicate with La Trobe and he was able to calm her fears and was a great help in allowing her to overcome her extreme anxiety. He explained that there was a heaven for all and that she did not need to worry about death, for herself or her loved ones. His reassurance was what Anne needed and it helped to restore and confirm her Christian faith. The Reverend La Trobe is quoted as saying of his visits that:

> *I found her well acquainted with the main truths of the Bible respecting our salvation, but seeing them more through the law than the gospel, more as a requirement from God than His gift in His son, but her heart opened to the sweet views of salvation, pardon, and peace in the blood of Christ ... had she died then, I should have counted her His redeemed and ransomed child.*[8]

Charlotte, finally recognising the severity of Anne's physical and mental decline, blamed Margaret Wooler for not acknowledging and treating Anne much sooner. This accusation greatly upset the headmistress and broke her friendship with Charlotte for some time. Charlotte took Anne home to Haworth after a letter to her father brought about his sudden and nervous summons to go home immediately. Anne never went to school again. She had, however, despite the drawbacks, studied well at Roe Head and in December 1836 she had won a good conduct prize. Miss Wooler also gifted her a book by the famous hymn writer, Isaac Watts, entitled *The Improvement of Mind.* Like Emily, Anne recovered gradually in the warmth and peace of Christmas at home (1837) and regained her close companion and writing partner along with her health.

Emily and Anne were now free to continue 'Gondal' together, and as Anne's health improved, they embarked on more stories and poetry. Around the time of her eighteenth birthday, in January 1838, Anne wrote her beautiful verse, *The North Wind,* demonstrating how far her linguistic and imaginative skills had developed. It begins:

The North Wind

That wind is from the North: I know it well;
No other breeze could have so wild a swell.
Now deep and loud it thunders round my cell,
Then faintly dies, and softly sighs,
And moans and murmurs mournfully.
I know its language: thus it speaks to me.[9]

That same month, Charlotte mended her quarrel with Margaret Wooler and agreed to return to her teaching post. The school had moved to Heald's Hall, Dewsbury Moor, during the Christmas holidays. However, by May, Charlotte too succumbed to the homesickness, loneliness and mental distress that had afflicted her sisters. Juliet Barker suggests that Charlotte was suffering from a similar religious crisis to Anne. There was a close circuit of clergymen in the Mirfield area who had strong Calvinistic leanings. Juliet Barker relates that:

> *The whole circle of Dewsbury clergymen seems to have been hard-line and unduly censorious in its attitudes: Patrick himself had incurred their disapproval with his liberal views on politics and religion... The fact that [Anne] an Anglican clergyman's daughter herself, chose instead to turn to a stranger and a minister of the Moravian church, suggests a rejection of the values of the Dewsbury circle.*[10]

Charlotte's friend, Ellen Nussey, who was also under the influence of Calvinist teachings, had a habit of almost encouraging Charlotte's religious doubts and fears. Charlotte, whilst at times rude and obnoxious in her letters to Ellen, always saw her as a pious and dutiful friend who had little or no sins or faults, except that of letting her family exploit her good nature. Charlotte realised that her religious stresses and her teaching post, which she had come to loathe, were all ruining her health and happiness. She finally returned home in May 1838 to calm her nerves and restore her health.

With his three daughters back at home and none of the children earning a living, Patrick must have been even more worried about the future. As stated, Branwell had finally moved to Bradford around the time that Charlotte returned home from her teaching post. He tried to set up his own art studio, under the tutelage of William Robinson. The family finances were at full stretch and the girls had to find employment. They had all received as much education as Patrick could supply and were adequately experienced to work as governesses or teachers.

In September 1838, Emily took a post as a teacher at Law Hill School, Southowram, near Halifax. This was the first time that she had lived away from home since her disastrous sojourn at Roe Head. Emily tried very hard at her post despite her being obviously miserable and homesick. Although a type of finishing school for older and wealthier girls, Emily's work was with the younger children and she found their demands and the long hours very trying. Charlotte wrote to Ellen with high indignation, describing Emily's work as:

> ... *hard labour from six in the morning until near eleven at night, with only one half hour of exercise between ... this is slavery. I fear she will never stand it.*[11]

However, Emily, despite her family's misgivings, taught there for at least six months, at the beginning of which she wrote some of her finest verse, both personal and as part of 'Gondal'. It would appear that, especially during adversity, loneliness and homesickness, the Brontë sisters wrote some of their most poignant poetry. Again, in the following verses, one sees the romantic and nostalgic emotions of childhood that may have been reinforced by the harsh realities of having to go out to work amongst children and adults so widely differing from her own family experiences. In December, whilst exiled from home, Emily wrote this beautiful poem, to which she did not even give a title. I am quoting it in full for its exquisite evocation of loss and longing and the dreams that can take one away from the heavy burden of work and toil.

Stanzas

> *A little while, a little while,*
> *The noisy crowd are barred away;*
> *And I can sing and I can smile*
> *A little while I've holyday!*

'The Dark Side of Sisterhood'

Where wilt thou go. My harassed heart?
Full many a land invites thee now;
And places near and far apart
Have rest for thee, my weary brow.

There is a spot mid barren hills
Where winter howls and driving rein,
But if the dreary tempest chills
There is a light that warms again.

The house is old, the trees are bare
And moonless bends the misty dome
But what on earth is half so dear,
So longed for as the hearth of home?

The mute bird sitting on the stone,
The dank moss dripping from the wall,
The garden-walk with weeds o'er grown,
I love them – how I love them all!

Shall I go there? Or shall I seek
Another clime, another sky,
Where tongues familiar music speak
In accents dear to memory?

Yes, as I mused, the naked room,
The flickering firelight died away
And from the midst of cheerless gloom
I passed to bright, unclouded day –

A little and a lone green lane,
That opened on a common wide;
A distant, dreamy, dim blue chain
Of mountains circling every side;

A heaven so clear, an earth so calm,
So sweet, so soft, so hushed an air
And, deepening still the dream-like charm,
Wild moor-sheep feeding everywhere –

That was the scene; I knew it well,
I knew the path-ways far and near

> *That winding o'er each billowy swell*
> *Marked out the tracks of wandering deer.*
>
> *Could I have lingered but an hour*
> *It well had paid a week of toil,*
> *But truth has banished fancy's power;*
> *I hear my dungeon bars recoil –*
>
> *Even as I stood with raptured eye*
> *Absorbed in bliss so deep and dear*
> *My hour of rest had fleeted by*
> *And given me back to weary care.*[12]

However, the severe home-sickness and anxiety that had plagued her at Roe Head, again entered Emily's mind, to the point where nothing could alleviate her suffering. Juliet Barker notes that:

> *Between the 12th January and the 27th March, [1839] she [Emily] wrote nothing, indicating a depression of mind that made writing impossible... Deprived of the time to indulge in Gondal fantasies by the rigidity and all-pervasive nature of boarding school life and deprived of the power to write by her home-sickness and unhappiness, Emily broke down.*[13]

However, the years of apprenticeship composing 'Glasstown', 'Angria' and 'Gondal' had borne fruit and their verse, especially Emily's, had adopted what Charlotte later referred to as a 'peculiar music'.[14]

In January, Charlotte wrote a rather long story as part of the 'Angrian Saga', named *Elizabeth Hastings*, which had many of the hallmarks of the later *Jane Eyre*. In February, she received a marriage proposal from Henry Nussey, the clergyman brother of Ellen. Fearing that he was only seeking a housekeeper and having no special affection for him, Charlotte turned him down. This episode may have been reproduced in *Jane Eyre*, when Jane rejects the advances of St John Rivers, to be his missionary wife. With Branwell also at home, having failed in his venture to become a portrait artist, and Charlotte refusing her marriage proposal, all four siblings were at home and the family finances must have been at breaking point.

Anne had, by now, made an important and lasting decision. On 8 April 1839 she made her first venture into the world of work. The youngest child, much to the anguish and concern of her family, had decided that she should take her place as a governess to help the family finances and perhaps to show that she was not the weak and simple child that they all suspected. Charlotte's comments to Ellen at this time demonstrate how little she expected Anne to succeed and her surprise that Anne had actually managed to leave home and gain employment.

I suggest that Charlotte was mocking Anne rather than recognising that her little sister, the unimportant and ineffectual youngest, was actually doing what she herself had so far failed to do. As if in retaliation, Charlotte found herself a post as a governess later that same month with the Sidgwick family at Stonegappe, near Colne in Lancashire.

The sisters' first experiences of working as a governess were equally bad, though for different reasons. Anne was working for the Ingham family at Blake Hall, a large house at Mirfield near Dewsbury. The family were very wealthy and had five children when Anne arrived, but only the two eldest were to be under her care. Anne, in her novel, *Agnes Grey*, gives an account of a governess going to her first post and meeting children such as those she encountered at the Inghams.

Debate as to the autobiography of *Agnes Grey* continues to this day. However, in both of her novels, Anne states that her intention is to 'tell the truth'[14] and her highly intense and accurate writing suggests that she encountered much in reality of what she described in her fiction. In the Ingham's family, the two children, the eldest boy and his younger sister, were in effect out of control and Anne was forbidden to chastise them. The children were rude, loud, ill-mannered and selfish. They refused to do their lessons or listen to Anne's efforts to guide them. They were over-indulged and lazy and Anne had absolutely no backing from the parents, who saw the fault as Anne's lack of skill, not their own failure to supervise or reprimand.

Anne was completely out of her depth but tried for nine long months to keep to her post and teach the unruly children. She was finally dismissed and returned home for Christmas, having gained enormous experience of how some children, and their parents, could behave, in contrast to her own upbringing. It was a shock and a learning experience for Anne and it helped to increase her understanding of difference in families, class and behaviour. Anne was confronted with unbeatable odds, but it gave her courage, rather than an overwhelming defeat, and she was prepared to try it all over again.

Charlotte's experience was different but also traumatic. Again, the children were out of their governess's control but added to this, Charlotte complained that she had a mountainous amount of sewing that overwhelmed her. She wrote to Ellen complaining of the family in the following words:

> ... *as proud as peacocks and wealthy as Jews; the children pampered, spoilt and turbulent.*[15]

However, there seems to have been issues on both sides of the relationship. Charlotte had taken a dislike to her employers and they later described her in terms of 'difficult, recalcitrant and quick to take offence'.[16] They also claimed that Charlotte, on occasion, stayed in bed for the day and left her pregnant employer to look after the children. It is difficult to know the true state of affairs but Charlotte left after three months and did not work away from home again until March 1841, when she went as governess to the White Family at Upperwood House in Rawdon, close by Woodhouse Grove School. That time she lasted for nine months.

Changes were rapidly taking place amongst the siblings. Branwell was in and out of work, first as a tutor to the Postlethwaites who lived at Broughton-in-Furness. Letters he wrote at the time describe drinking bouts and contain sexual innuendo. This gradual dissipation probably began when he was living in Bradford and had finally broken away from home and the influence of his father. With no external schooling or friends of his own age, Branwell was free to indulge himself, but uncontrolled and uninhibited. This was a habit that, unfortunately, he never lost. One could argue that it was possibly an inevitable outcome for a young man who was highly intelligent but vulnerable, mercurial and lacking in self-confidence. Drink, and later drugs, boosted his ego and bought him friendships and encounters with females. Around this time, he wrote to Hartley Coleridge, the son of Samuel Taylor Coleridge, and asked him to look at his poetry. A visit was arranged and the two men had a memorable day together, but no lasting friendship or literary result occurred. Coleridge was a talented writer and orator but had also taken to drink. Branwell was dismissed by the Postlethwaites for his drinking and left in June after only six months. He took up work as clerk at Sowerby station near Halifax, in October and did well. Unfortunately, after promotion to Luddenden Foot as clerk-in-charge, his neglect of duties, owing to drink, again lead to his dismissal. Branwell's life pattern was established and drink was now becoming an addiction that prevented him keeping any steady or lucrative employment. He was 25 years old but had no prospects and few ambitions. Life was passing him by and he had neither the finances nor the inclination to achieve any great career. Wasted talents and lack of life skills sealed his fate.

In August 1839 a new curate arrived in Haworth and brought joy and unexpected happiness into the Brontës' lives. William Weightman was a 25-year-old, amiable young man, in his first appointment since graduating from Durham University. He was amenable, intelligent and flirtatious. Patrick found him first rate and an enormous help and Branwell immediately struck up a friendship. At last, he had a friend who was local and his own age; a man who could possibly keep him entertained and direct his future.

William Weightman obviously had charisma and all of the Brontë siblings became enamoured of his friendship and playful attitude. There was mutual respect and companionship but there has been sustained conjecture as to whether any, or all, of the Brontë sisters fell for his charms. Charlotte became gradually dismissive of him and warned Ellen against him. This could, however, have been to mask her own feelings, and especially if she thought that his attentions were drawn to anyone else. Once again, Charlotte used her acid tongue to ridicule both Weightman and Anne, describing them in church where:

> *He sits opposite to Anne at Church sighing softly – and looking out of the corners of his eyes to win her attention – and Anne is so quiet, her look so downcast – they are a picture.*[17]

This is the only time that we hear of Anne and Weightman as being connected in any overtly direct communication, albeit mainly all on Weightman's part. It is probably the wellspring of the idea that Anne was in love with him and yet there is no proof or further evidence. Was Weightman particularly drawn to Anne and Anne to him? It is quite possible, but there is nothing except this observation of Charlotte's, which is no evidence at all. If Anne was fond, or even in love with Weightman, as some biographers have stated, it began very slowly and neither side made efforts to advance any mutual understanding. When another of their father's curates, Author Nicholls, dared to approach Charlotte with a marriage proposal, Patrick was apoplectic. Whether he would have approved of his 'dear little Anne' in a courtship with a man of similar status, even though Patrick was very fond of him, we cannot know. Before any relationship could develop between Anne and Weightman, two events separated the couple for ever.

Firstly, in May 1840, the persistent and stoic Anne, determined to continue her contribution to the family finances and to prove that she could be a successful governess, took up a post at Thorp Green Hall, near Little Ouseburn, between York and Boroughbridge. Here she had charge of the daughters of the wealthy Reverend Edmund Robinson. This situation was forty miles from Haworth and William Weightman. Anne had very few holidays at home and accompanied the Robinsons on their annual summer holidays to Scarborough. In the following two years, Anne would only encounter Weightman on her short trips home at Christmas and a week in the summer. Secondly, and finally, any possible romance was cruelly interrupted when Weightman died of cholera in September 1842 during an epidemic in Haworth. He was 28 years old and a huge loss to the village and to all of the Brontë family, possibly especially so to Anne.

Other important events had been happening between 1840 and 1842. Charlotte had decided that she hated being a governess and especially that it curtailed her own precious time for writing and drawing. Charlotte had no affinity or empathy for her pupils and consequently made poor relationships with them. She lacked Anne's patience and fortitude or Emily's blunt stoicism. Ever the decision -maker, she decided that the best outcome for all of the girls was to open a school of their own. They had experience, though one doubts how much Charlotte intended to be involved, and they did not like being away from home or in the employment of others. However, around this time, letters from her friend, Mary Taylor, who was travelling on the Continent with her brother Joe, fired Charlotte's enthusiasm for seeking further qualifications and skills abroad. Furthermore, she longed to experience the sights and sounds that Mary wrote so enthusiastically about. As stated, Charlotte had always admired Mary Taylor since meeting her during her first week as a pupil at Roe Head. Mary was a foil to Charlotte and Ellen. Ellen was quiet, biddable and shy. Charlotte was shy but highly intelligent and opinionated. Mary was bold, forthright and dynamic.

Mary's correspondence influenced Charlotte's decision and she argued that it would enhance their prospects of opening their own school if she and Emily were to travel to Paris or Brussels; anywhere abroad where they could enhance their knowledge and perfect their language skills. Anne was at Thorp Green and Charlotte said dismissively that Anne could possibly gain extra experience at some other, later time. It was Emily she wanted with her. Emily, the least happy away from home and already firmly taking over domestic duties in the parsonage, does not appear to have had much, if any, say in the matter.

Charlotte wrote a letter to her aunt in which she used all her powers of persuasion and guile to induce her to lay out between £50 and £100 pounds to fund the continental venture, naming Brussels as the best place to go. In an appeal close to emotional blackmail, Charlotte pleads:

> *Papa will perhaps think it a wild and ambitious scheme; but whoever rose in the world without ambition? When he left Ireland to go to Cambridge University, he was as ambitious as I am now, I want us ALL to go on. I know we have talents, and I want them to be turned to account. I look to you, aunt, to help us. I think you will not refuse. I know, if you consent, it shall not be my fault if you ever repent your kindness.*[18]

Charlotte manipulated her aunt into thinking that the girls were determined to start their own school at some later date, when, in fact, Charlotte had already dismissed the idea despite knowing that Margaret Wooler had made a most generous offer for the girls to take over her school at Dewsbury Moor. This was an amazing proposal that could have seen the Brontë sisters, and Branwell, set up for life. As ever, Charlotte was the decision-maker and her enthusiasm to go abroad appears to have overruled any thought or discussion that the school offer required.

It is at times like this that I have issue with Charlotte. She takes the role of eldest as *carte blanche* authority to make all of the decisions for her sisters and appears to give little, if any, thought as to how they might feel or whether they want to go ahead with her proposals. The £100 that the venture to Brussels eventually cost was a massive amount for the time and came directly from her aunt's savings. A comparison with today shows that £100 in 1840 was the equivalent of over £12,000 today. Charlotte seems to be presumptive of her aunt's good will and kindness, and yet Charlotte never speaks of her in particularly generous or loving terms.

It seems that if Charlotte made her mind up, nothing and nobody was allowed to stand in her way. What she was proposing was not unreasonable if there was a determination to open their own school and had the money and the drive to do so. However, the school project never took place and a lot of money was wasted and heartache ensued for all involved. Whilst one can argue that it gave Charlotte a host of material for her novels and that both girls improved and increased their knowledge and experience, in hindsight, I suggest that it was as expensive, foolhardy, ill-thought out and unrealistic as any of Branwell's ideas and ventures.

Was Charlotte a kind and loving sister to her siblings? Did her actions help or hinder their progress? Did her own needs and preoccupations blind her to the needs of her brother and sisters? I find it difficult to condone some of Charlotte's behaviour, especially towards Branwell and Anne. She dismissed her youngest sister at times, and overruled her distress, as I shall show especially in my final chapter. Branwell became a lost cause, partly through his own behaviour but, I maintain, partly because Charlotte disassociated herself from him when he needed her the most. Like her siblings, Charlotte could write amazing stories and verse and could empathise in fiction, but it was something she was sometimes unable to do amongst her own family.

Chapter Ten

Anne as Governess
The Conflict of Experience

Anne's life as a governess was hard and unremitting. As stated, her first post demonstrated the difficulties of working with undisciplined and obnoxious children. This was new to Anne. Her experience was nurtured by living in an ordered and caring family where life was ruled by strong Christian beliefs that upheld the ten commandments. It included moral obligations, self-control and kindness to others. To suddenly find herself amongst children with no religious or parental guidance of any benefit would have been a profound shock.

How well Anne coped as a governess in her two posts is difficult to assess. She was a small, shy and quiet girl of 19 when she went to live with the Inghams at Blake Hall. The two eldest children (there were thirteen eventually) were a 6-year-old boy, (Joseph) Cunliffe, and his 5-year-old sister, Mary. The younger three girls were still in the nursery. Anne soon discovered that her pupils were completely ungovernable. Anne wrote home about her situation and Charlotte reported to Ellen that:

> *... both her pupils are desperate little dunces – neither of them can read and sometimes they even profess a profound ignorance of their alphabet – the worst of it is the little monkies are excessively indulged and she is not empowered to inflict any punishment – she alternately, scolds, coaxes, and threatens – sticks always to her first word and gets on as well as she can.*[1]

This first letter written home by Anne caused a condescending reaction from Charlotte, who seemed 'astonished' to see what a sensible, clever letter she writes. Again, we see evidence of Charlotte's arrogant dismissal of her youngest sister as barely capable of functioning outside of the home, and even less well than within it!

Anne as Governess

Juliet Barker reiterates a story told by a descendant of the Inghams. On receiving a parcel of scarlet cloaks from South America, the children grabbed them and ran off into the park screaming their heads off and declaring themselves devils. Anne could not get them to return to their lessons and ran in tears to Mrs Ingham. One can understand Anne's dilemma and admire her fortitude faced with this kind of behaviour from young children without discipline or direction. It would be hard to govern such children at any time, then or now, and highlights the necessity for children to have boundaries and moral guidance. We are always warned to avoid seeing autobiography in novels, but I maintain in this case that Anne expressed in *Agnes Grey* a great deal of her first-hand experience of dealing with recalcitrant children and their erring parents.

Anne had had years of watching from the sidelines whilst her siblings fought and argued. She had developed a personality that observed rather than participated and she worked out her own understanding and interpretation of behaviour in both children and adults. She looked for the reasons and the results. In her novels, she did not necessarily condemn or offer her opinion, rather she showed and expressed a scene and allowed the reader to draw their own conclusions. I suggest that this was Anne's strength. To observe but not to comment takes enormous self-control and also puts the onus on the reader to have the sense and ability to understand what the author is saying and demonstrating. It is a brave stance to take and one that not many writers would dare to indulge. It is so tempting to offer one's own opinion when describing a scene or the behaviour of people; Anne stays quiet.

Working as a governess was hard and offered little comfort or status, but it did allow for acute observation and insight into the human condition. This is what Anne discovered and she reproduced what she observed around her in her novels. That is where the truth of her writing lies. She does not make up a tale so much as she allows the reader to interpret what she offers and draw their own conclusions. When we read the scene in *Agnes Grey* where Tom Bloomfield has been with his uncle Robson and is currently intent on torturing and killing a nest of baby birds he has found, Agnes kills them with a stone rather than allowing the child to indulge his sick intentions. However, it is from the uncle that we learn why and how Tom behaves as he does. It is the adults who corrupt the children. His uncle admires Tom's 'manly' behaviour, his berating of his governess, his foul language and his wishing to kill the birds for sport. He says:

> *Damme, but the lad has some spunk in him, too. Curse me, if ever I saw a nobler little scoundrel than that. He's beyond petticote government already: by God! He defies mother, granny, governess, and all! Ha, ha, ha! Never mind, Tom, I'll get you another brood tomorrow.*[2]

Furthermore, Tom's mother chastises Agnes for spoiling her son's pleasure saying:

> *'You seem to have forgotten'*, she said calmly, *'that the creatures were all created for our convenience.'*
> *'I think'*, said she, *'a child's amusement is scarcely to be weighed against the welfare of a soulless brute.'* [3]

Anne is demonstrating how each generation repeats the behaviour of their forebears and perpetuates the myth that man, as opposed to women and opposed to any other creature on earth, thinks that he is supreme master of all he sees, has and does. This is not my opinion; it is how things were at that time and how they had been for generations before. The male human being had ruled and altered and shaped the world to his advantage and was still doing so, perhaps more so, in industrialised Victorian times. Anne was not necessarily supporting a feminist theory here; Mary, and later Martha, are as uncontrollable as their older brother and, as shown above, have similar unreasonable input from their parents. Anne is saying that in a household without morals or mutual respect, there is chaos and the perpetuation of male dominance. She also shows in the book that it is condoned as much by the adult females as the males. It is a state of mind where, in some families, their wealth and privilege had led to a deterioration of Christian morals and a lack of self-control. The adults fail to see the harm that they are causing, but the observant reader can see what these characters cannot.

Anne is using her observations to seek the truth of what is happening in this family. Like a reporter, or journalist, she presents the facts without personal judgement. She is demonstrating the direct cause and effect of parenting that has dire consequences for their offspring.

In his essay on *Wildfell Hall*, Tim Whittome makes a very valid observation about Anne's two novels. He states that:

> *In both novels, but with more 'maternal' authority in 'The Tenant', Anne Brontë presents us with a convincing view of childhood as a fertile field, capable of nurturing both gentler flowers and toxic weeds into adulthood, and with the outcome largely depending on the right or wrong type of parenting.* [4]

Later, in *'The Tenant of Wildfell Hall'*, Anne again demonstrates the dangers of allowing a child to follow in the indulgent and harmful practices of their forebears. Helen Huntingdon will go to any lengths to remove her son from his father, as she can see the damage that is occurring. By the time the child is 6 or

7 years old, there may be no way of altering the pattern of behaviour set by his father and other members of the family.

Anne spent nearly nine months with the Ingham family before she was dismissed by them. One can understand why Anne's efforts, based on her beliefs, were anathema to the family. She never stood a chance. This family demonstrated much of what Anne had learnt from her Bible about the dangers of a lack of spiritual guidance. When people have the wealth to cushion them from the harsh realities of life experienced by the poor and underprivileged, it can be all too easy to dismiss other people's needs and experiences. Joseph Ingham was a Justice of the Peace and his wife was the daughter of the Bradford MP, Ellis Cunliffe Lister. They had money and they had an elevated position in society. Their home was an imposing three-storied high mansion and they should have been happy and contented. In all likelihood they probably were, but from what we hear and see of Anne's experience with the middle classes all is not always as it appears. There are in some families, undercurrents of false grandiose; of believing in their own sense of importance and dismissal of anyone not of their own rank and class. This idea is then perpetuated throughout the generations causing unhappiness and harm to anyone with the misfortune to be employed in their service.

This was Anne's experience in both of her work places. Was she exaggerating, was she bitter and jealous, was she totally unprepared for middle-class wealth and the lives of the privileged? Possibly so, in some ways, but one is drawn again and again to her own words. When Anne insists that she is only trying to tell the truth, it is the truth as she saw it. In her preface to the second edition of *The Tenant of Wildfell Hall* she insists what her motivation was:

> 'I wished to tell the truth, for truth always contains its own moral to those who are able to receive it...'.[5]

That truth is the truth as she saw it and we have to allow for possible anomalies. I have no doubt that much of *Agnes Grey* is Anne's honest record, just as Charlotte gave her honest record of the Clergy Daughters' School in *Jane Eyre*. However, there are always two sides and always other influences and arguments. Anne tying the children to a table when they were too unruly and Charlotte staying in bed; if these accounts are true, it suggests that not everything recorded is as one sided as first appears or quite as straightforward. When we tell the truth, it is the truth as we see and experience it and it is not necessarily how others interpret it. Truth is one of the hardest things to establish, as any courtroom will testify. No two people see the same thing at the same time, in the same way, it is always from their personal point of view. Some philosophers deny the existence of an absolute truth, saying that it is an impossible concept.

However, because it is Anne's truth and very real and unique to her, it does not invalidate it. Her skill lies in recognising that fact and not indulging her opinions. She offers her truth and leaves the reader to draw conclusions from her evidence. The reader can accept or reject it, that is their choice. There is no statement from Anne to force her observations on to others. She offers her 'truth' and leaves interpretation to her readers.

Anne returned home following her dismissal, in December 1839, but, as stated, she was wise enough to realise that although she had failed to control or educate her charges to any degree, she had learnt a great deal about the Ingham's way of life. It was not a way that she approved of, but it was still an important experience; perhaps more so because she could identify the faults using her religion as a yardstick. I don't think that she saw herself as a failure. She had given it a good try and was now more experienced and more capable of trying it again. She was not put off working away from home, unlike Emily and Charlotte. Anne had patience and a liking for children not apparent in her sisters. We see Anne as more empathetic and less inclined to anger and upset. She is more tolerant and more steadfast in her work and less likely to complain. Therefore, ever eager to please her family and relieve its finances, she is willing to tackle the job again.

In her introduction to *Agnes Grey and Poems* (Everyman 1985), Anne Smith pointedly notes something that I believe very likely explains Anne's feelings towards her aunt and older siblings. She quotes Agnes Grey's description of herself in the early pages of the book. Here Anne writes of Agnes:

> *I, being the younger by five or six years, was always regarded as the child, and the pet of the family: father, mother [aunt] and sister all combined to spoil me – not by foolish indulgence to render me fractious and ungovernable, but by ceaseless kindness to make me too helpless and dependent – too unfit for buffeting with the cares and turmoil's of life...*
>
> *... though a woman in my own estimation, I was still a child in theirs; and my mother [aunt/Charlotte] like most active, managing women, was not gifted with very active daughters: for this reason – that being so clever and diligent herself, she was never tempted to trust her affairs to a deputy, but on the contrary, was willing to act and think for others as well as number one; and whatever was the business in hand, she was apt to think that no one could do it as well as herself...*
>
> *How delightful it would be to be a governess! To go out into the world; to enter upon a new life; to act for myself; to exercise my unused faculties; to try my unknown powers; to earn my own maintenance, and something to comfort and help my father,*

mother [aunt] and sister, besides exonerating them from the provision of my food and clothing...[6]

I agree wholeheartedly with Anne Smith's views. Surely, this is Anne talking of her own experience of life within the Brontë household and her need to prove herself as other than the cosseted youngest child. See also Anne's poem, *Self-Communion*.[7]

After the Inghams, Anne applied for more posts and accepted one with the Robinson family at Thorp Green. Again, Anne was living and working within a middle-class family of wealth and prestige. The Reverend Edmund Robinson was a rich, non-participating clergyman and a chronic invalid. He lived at the house and estate of Thorp Green where he was the Lord of the Manor. The estate stood in land close to the village of Little Ouseburn between the towns of York and Boroughbridge, in North Yorkshire. There was no railway connection at this time and travelling was difficult and dangerous. Thorp Green Hall was destroyed by fire in 1895 and in 1912 a new hall was built, next to the original site. It is now the extended premises of Queen Ethelburga's College, a private girls' boarding and day school.

Reverend Robinson's wife, Mrs Lydia Robinson, was the daughter of the Reverend Thomas Gisborne. She was four years younger than her husband, and when Anne arrived they had five children. Anne would be governess to the four eldest – Lydia (14), Elizabeth (13), Mary (12) and Edmund Junior (8). The youngest, Georgina, was eighteen months old when Anne arrived but died during Anne's first year in post.

This was a family who had a large estate, a huge house and the money to sustain their property and lifestyle. Having lived with the Inghams, Anne is less likely to have been overwhelmed than she would otherwise have been, but the sheer size and opulence of the place would have been a new and possibly exciting experience for Anne. She lived in at the house and would be treated with some respect and deference befitting her status as a non-servant. However, the role of governess was one of isolation in so far as she was an employee who could not therefore mix with her employer or their guests, but who had the responsibility of raising their children. She was not a servant as such, but her treatment would be similar.

There is little doubt that Anne took her responsibilities seriously and, in some ways, her task was easier than looking after her previous youngsters. The Robinson children were older and had a modicum of intelligence and behaviour that was less trying on their governess. However, there were plenty of other issues for Anne to deal with. The Robinson girls were not reared for work; their future lay in making marriages to wealthy men who could keep them in a similar, if not better, lifestyle and to increase the family coffers. A title would add to their achievements. To this end Anne would be expected to tutor the girls in the types of skills that would be useful in their future marriages. These included such mundane acquisitions as being able to write a decent letter, sing a few songs, organise their staff, speak a little French, to have good deportment and to play nicely on the piano.

Anne had all of these skills in abundance and many more but most of them would not be required for the education of girls of this class. Edmund was a different matter and Anne probably taught him to a much higher level, including a little Greek or Latin, mathematics and science, as much as she knew herself. Later, she would recommend Branwell as his tutor, a role that Branwell would fill in January 1843. Branwell had been taught well by his father and was more than competent in the classics.

We know more about Anne's time at Thorp Green due to the letters, poetry and drawings she produced and also her accounts of the life of a governess in *Agnes Grey*. Once again, Anne was appalled at some of the behaviour she encountered from both children and adults, but now it was perhaps more subtle and she soon realised that the girls were in fact being raised for marriage and very little else. Marriage was their goal and their fate and they were walking blindly forward into it, as their class and status dictated. Passages from her novel describe the attitude of females reared for the marriage market.

We may see it today, as a form of 'grooming' where these girls had no say in their future and that future was often with men whom they had no liking or affection for. Many marriages were 'arranged' to increase wealth and status, not for love and respect. The girl had to be attractive, coy, innocent and more of an appendage to her husband than a wife. This was not new or strange, it had been the way of life in the upper and middle classes for centuries and still applies in many cultures today. We rarely see a member of the aristocracy marrying a working-class office girl. There is still only small movement between the classes and it is almost always based on wealth. The British royal family, the template for marriage and class behaviour, has only just altered its formula. In Victorian times princes married princesses in marriages arranged with all the precision of a military campaign. One only has to look at the marriages that Queen Victoria arranged for all of her children to see how they spread over the whole of Europe and its aristocracy. Wealth and titles were a priority and the mixing of the classes was rarely seen or allowed. It is ironic that one of the Robinson girls ran away to Gretna Green with an actor she met during the family annual holiday to Scarborough, an event that would have horrified her parents and all who knew the family.

We know that Anne was unhappy in her post as she stated so in her 'diary paper' of July 1841:

Anne as Governess

I am a governess in the family of Mr Robinson. I dislike the situation and wish to change it for another.[8]

It was during these early months that she wrote poignant poems that may have been 'Gondal' related but appear to express more of her own feelings of isolation and homesickness. Again, we can note how a sight or smell can invoke that immediate return to an idyllic childhood moment. In August she wrote the verse entitled *The Bluebell* in which she recalls sunny, happy days of childhood before the cares and woes of work wore her down. She writes how the sight and smell of a lonely bluebell instantly recalls the times when she saw them in abundance in childhood and they recall those happy far-off days.

The Bluebell verses 9 to 12

O, that lone flower recalled to me
My happy childhood's hours
when blue bells seemed as fairy gifts
A prize among the flowers.

Those sunny days of merriment
When heart and soul were free
And when I dwelt with kindred hearts
That loved and cared for me

I had not then mid heartless crowds
To spend a thankless life,
In seeking after others' weal
With anxious toil and strife

'Sad wanderer, weep those blissful times
That never may return!'
The lovely floweret seemed to say,
And thus it made me mourn.[9]

This poem goes further than just the nostalgia of childhood. Ciara Glasscott notes that:

We have a straightforward scenario: the poet's strong association between childhood and flowers (more particularly bluebells) triggers the poet's meditation on the 'blissful times/That may never return'. Moreover, the loneliness of the poet's present

> situation is further amplified by the contrast between their 'thankless life' spent 'mid heartless crowds' and these sweet memories of companionship and playing in nature. This connects with Christine Colon's contention that 'the plight of individuals who are wondrously connected to nature and the power of God when they are young but who gradually lose this bond as they "mature" is a significant theme with Brontë poetry. Therefore, this poem's use of Romantic imagery serves a dual function, as poignant childhood reminiscence provides a contrast with disillusioned adulthood'.[10]

It is fair to say that a great deal of Brontë poetry deals with isolation, loss and grief. The verse of all four siblings, whether as part of their sagas or personal writings, are saturated with nostalgia and melancholy. One needs to wonder at this. Was it the ever-present memories of the loss of their mother and sisters that imbued their emotions and their writing? There appears an excess of woe that, I suggest, can only be explained either by the deaths in the family or their own unrequited loves and losses – Charlotte with Monsieur Heger; Branwell with Mrs Robinson and before that, a possible illegitimate daughter Mary, who died in childhood; Emily with a possible lover, or her own personal emotions; and Anne with the death of William Weightman. These morbid fascinations, mixed with their own mental stresses, are not unsurprising when one considers the number of losses and emotional pain they endured in their short lives. There is also the nostalgia of childhood that so affected them as their 'remembrance of things past'.

Nowadays, we understand more about the effects that these traumas have on people. We are far more aware of the mental and physical reactions people suffer through death and other life-changing events. The British 'stiff upper lip' advice is rarely applied today, or valued. We recognise the need to address suffering and accept it, in both males and females, not hide behind it and try to smother the effects. That is the road to serious mental breakdown.

Therefore, perhaps it was a good and natural thing for the Brontës to express their grief in their writing. It was a form of release and a necessary escape from suffering. Homesickness, again and again, appears as part of the Brontë psyche. In the following, Anne is writing from Thorp Green and longing to be at home.

Lines written at Thorp Green

> *That summer sun, whose genial glow*
> *Now cheers my drooping spirit so,*

Anne as Governess

Must cold and silent be,
And only light our northern clime
With feeble ray, before the time
I long so much to see.

And this soft, whispering breeze, that now
So gently cools my fevered brow,
This too, alas! Must turn
To a wild blast, whose icy dart
Pierces and chills me to the heart,
Before I cease to mourn.
And these bright flowers I love so well,
Verbena, rose and sweet bluebell,
Must droop and die away;
Those thick, green leaves, with all their shade
And rustling music, they must fade,
And every one decay.

But if the sunny, summer time,
And woods and meadows in their prime,
Are sweet to them that roam;
Far sweeter is the winter bare,
With long, dark nights, and landscape drear,
To them that are at home![11]

In my research of the Brontës over the last fifty-five years, I have always found an inescapable melancholia that nothing seems to alleviate. Given any amount of happy and exciting events, one feels that their pessimism will always override any enjoyment. Their glass is always half empty! It is as if they are determined not to enjoy life, as if they feel guilty and wrong if they attempt to laugh or dance or sing. There is this ever-present doom attached to them, that rarely lifts. It seems that only in childhood moments, usually outdoors, that they can celebrate life and living.

In her first year at her post, Anne had only occasional holidays when she could return home for a few days. Thorp Green was, by coach, over forty miles from Haworth, expensive and not easily undertaken, especially in poor weather. There was no train connection to Little Ouseburn or to Haworth from York, Leeds or Bradford during Anne's stay. It was only in her second year with the Robinson family that Anne was accepted enough to accompany the family to Scarborough for their summer vacation. They would have travelled initially in the family coach and later by train. This continued for the next four years and whilst this proved a most enjoyable time for Anne, it still kept her away from her home.

These long separations from the parsonage and Emily interrupted Anne's part in their 'Gondal' partnership to some extent. Emily continued writing at home but Anne had less time and opportunity. When at Thorp Green Anne wrote more personal verse, but both wrote copiously when they were finally able to get together. Unfortunately, we have no letters to and from the sisters during the years Anne spent at Thorp Green, and yet they must have corresponded, possibly frequently. 'Gondal' certainly continued, especially for Emily, who had the time and circumstances in which to write, until she was hauled off to the Continent with Charlotte in February 1842.

1842 was a very difficult year for Anne. When she moved to Thorp Green it once again jeopardised her close relationship with Emily and caused the renewal of Emily and Charlotte's close bond. Charlotte had always favoured Emily and now the two of them were in constant company, day and night. The Brussels venture moved Emily even further away from Anne and helped to reignite the Charlotte/Emily attachment. This would have been a loss to Anne and for almost the whole of that year she saw neither of her sisters. Letters may have passed between them but would be expensive and infrequent and there is no evidence left of any correspondence. Later in the year, the deaths of William Weightman and Aunt Elizabeth could only have added to Anne's loneliness. Having once been so enclosed within her family unit, she was now totally isolated, physically and emotionally.

Fortunately, although Emily worked hard at her Brussels' school and excelled in her studies she did not return there after her aunt's death but stayed at home to manage the parsonage, until her own death in 1848. During these years at home, Emily, now in her mid-twenties, continued with 'Gondal' and concentrated on its characters and events up until her writing of *Wuthering Heights*. Emily had no desire or need to leave home again, and this appears to have been the best place for her. Emily took what would have been her sister Elizabeth's place as housekeeper and spinster child who would always remain to look after her parent, as was the custom at the time. She was under no pressure to seek outside work. She organised the home, as her aunt had previously done, and assisted the servants; the now disabled Tabby and the young Martha Brown. Emily got on well with her father and also had the moors on her doorstep for whenever she felt the need to venture out. She was probably at the happiest point in her adult life.

Anne had far less leisure time and worked hard with her four protégés. She had to use all of her stamina and moral fortitude to repeatedly return to the Robinson household and continue working for them. As the girls grew older their evident interest in their appearance, their clothes and their possessions reinforced their mothers grooming for their lives as rich married women. Whilst Anne knew and had to accept what their fate would be, she also tried to instil some important moral and Christian guidance. These children were typical flighty adolescents who knew the price of everything and the value of nothing. Only surface looks and current issues bothered them. They had so very little insight into life and hardship. Their heads had been filled with the 'idea' of a grand marriage, never to the 'reality' of what that would entail. There is a lovely example of this in *Agnes Grey* when Rosalie describes to Agnes what happened at the ball. Rosalie is there to seek admirers and to assess the male attendees. She states:

> '*Harry Meltham is the handsomest and the most amusing, and Mr Hatfield the cleverest, Sir Thomas the wickedest, and Mr Green the most stupid. But the one I'm to have, I suppose, if I'm doomed to have any of them, is Sir Thomas Ashby.*'
>
> '*Surely not, if he's so wicked, and if you dislike him?*' [Exclaims Agnes]
>
> '*Oh, I don't mind his being wicked: he's all the better for that; and as for disliking him – I shouldn't greatly object to being Lady Ashby of Ashby Park.*' [Rosalie replies][12]

Every word of this passage shows Anne Brontë demonstrating the naivete and danger in this young lady's assessment. She has no understanding of men and no idea of the virtues to look for. She has her sights set on a title. Better to be in an awful marriage with a title, than a happy one with no status. Anne demonstrates this topsy-turvy understanding in her novel when Agnes relates to Rosalie that her sister is to be married:

> '*...and, moreover, my sister is going to be married.*'
>
> '*Is she – when?*'
> '*Not till next month: but I want to be there to assist her in making preparations, and to make the best of her company while we have her.*'
>
> '*Why didn't you tell me before?*'
> '*I've only got the news in this letter, which you stigmatize as dull and stupid, and won't let me read.*'
>
> '*To whom is she to be married?*'

> *'To Mr Richardson, the vicar of a neighbouring parish.'*
>
> *'Is he rich?'*
> *'No, only comfortable.'*
>
> *'Is he handsome?'*
> *'No, only decent.'*
>
> *'Young?'*
> *'No, only middling.'*
>
> *'O Mercy! What a wretch! What sort of a house is it?'*
> *'A quaint little vicarage, with an ivy-clad porch, an old-fashioned garden, and...'*
>
> *'O stop! – you'll make me sick. How can she bear it?'*[13]

Anne is listing the very things that Rosalie thinks she wants and those which she cannot bear to consider. A small home and a husband who is neither rich nor handsome is not something that Rosalie can contemplate in marriage. It sums up the type of girl that Rosalie is and the way that she has been steered by her mother to make a 'good' marriage. Her daughter's happiness is not part of the consideration and as we predictably read, later in the story, Rosalie marries her rich, titled husband and is extremely unhappy. Her selfishness even extends to her child whom she cannot bear to have around her in case she eclipses Rosalie's looks and youth.

A passage in *Wildfell Hall* emphasises how Anne felt about the education and upbringing of both boys and girls and it is reflected in Rosalie's misguided views on marriage. She writes:

> *I would not send a poor girl into the world, unarmed against her foes, and ignorant of the snares that beset her path; nor would I watch and guard her, till, deprived of self-respect and self-reliance, she lost the power or the will to watch and guard herself; – and as for my son – if I thought he would grow up to be what you call a man of the world I would rather he died tomorrow! – rather a thousand times.*[14]

Anne believes in love and respect, in family, friendship and especially in marriage; without it she sees relationships doomed to failure. In the Robinson family, as with the Inghams, she again witnessed the problems that engendered in families where children were not morally guided by their parents. Anne tried to overcome these issues and her five years at Thorp Green did produce results. Her former pupils would write to Anne with their problems and even visited her at the parsonage. Charlotte was astonished to see how much they appeared to cherish their former governess. It must have warmed Anne's heart to discover that her hard work and tolerance had not been completely in vain.

Chapter Eleven

Thorp Green
'A Patient and Persecuted Stranger'[1]

The above quote appeared in a letter from Charlotte to Ellen Nussey in August 1841, describing Anne's current position in her post at Thorp Green. Anne's more than five years with the Robinsons, from May 1840 to June 1845, appears to have come to an abrupt end when she resigned her post that summer. It is hard to establish the reason for this, or even whether or not it was her own choice. Biographers tend to use Branwell's alleged affair with Mrs Robinson as the cause of Anne's departure, but this is not necessarily so. In fact, there are researchers who doubt the whole story of Branwell's attachment to Lydia Robinson, or vice versa.

Anne may have felt that she had done enough to educate her pupils. Lydia Mary was now 19 years of age, Elizabeth (Bessie) was 18 and Mary nearly 17. Did these girls need, or want, a governess any longer? Was there a mutual decision between Anne and her employers that her usefulness was no longer required? These girls were not children any more, in fact Lydia eloped with the actor, Henry Roxby, the following summer. Anne left before the annual trip to Scarborough, possibly because she was no longer needed and would, therefore, be an unnecessary expense. The girls were now young women and needed to be introduced to society as marriage prospects for wealthy young men, not as schoolroom maidens. Anne's role had come to an end and there may well have been a mutual and agreeable leave taking that had nothing to do with Branwell, or any other ulterior motive.

So, this was the end of Anne's experiences as a governess and it is here that I wish to examine what happened to Anne during these six eventful years. She left home in March 1839 to go as a governess to the Ingham family and later the Robinsons. Who was Anne at this time? One thing is obvious to me, Anne was not a governess; she was a naive adult who had virtually no experience of children other than her own siblings, and no teaching experience whatsoever. She was a governess in name only; a governess learning how to be a governess. Governesses had no official training. Any educated young woman could set herself up in the career and many failed because they had little or no idea of what the job entailed and the demands it would have on them. I suggest that *Agnes Grey* is as much about the education of the governess as that of the children in her care. As in her own childhood, Anne had to be silent for much of the time, hampered by her employer's dictates.

Nick Holland states of *Agnes Grey* that:

> *There are many aspects of the novel that are copied straight from the daily life that Anne encountered at Little Ouseburn and beyond: the location and setting of the hall, the number of children and their ages, the character and history of the master and mistress of the house, the sojourns to the seaside. There are also scattered clues as to Anne's life while a governess for the Robinson family, and it was a life of deep contrasts, from swooping highs to crashing lows.*[2]

He notably records that Anne wrote no 'Gondal' poetry whilst at Thorp Green but became much more independent of thought and her poetry becomes much more 'self-reflective and personal'.

I suggest that what Anne did have was courage and determination and she rightly or wrongly believed that these would be sufficient to fulfil her role. Unfortunately, for her and many other women, the role of governess was undefined. A governess could be employed to teach children in their own home, with set hours and leisure times, days off and a decent wage, or they could be totally and utterly exploited by their employers. There is a fascinating book, edited by Joanna Martin and published in 1998, which offers the letters and journals of Miss Agnes Porter, a governess during the latter half of the eighteenth century, who worked for many years at Penrice Castle, which stands on the Gower Peninsula in South Wales. The editor describes Agnes as:

> *... the daughter of a Church of England clergyman, born in 1752 with brains but not looks or wealth. Although she would have liked to marry, her various hopes ended in disappointment. She therefore had to earn her living as a governess, working principally in teaching the daughters and granddaughters of the second Earl of Ilchester. Agnes Porter was neither morbidly religious, as were many of her Victorian successors, nor did she spend her time dwelling on the unfairness of her situation. She emerges as an intelligent, warm and likeable woman ready to make the best of her lot.*[3]

The Brontë Family: Sibling Rivalry and a Burial in Paradise

It was during the late eighteenth century that a governess became a fashionable asset in the homes of the upper and middle classes. Before this time they had mainly been employed by the aristocracy. Employing a governess demonstrated wealth and gave parents freedom to leave the education and guidance of their children in the hands of a suitably accomplished woman. By the nineteenth century the governess was an essential employee in many genteel households. However, the fact that the governess lived in the same building as the family meant that they could be called on to perform any domestic task, night or day, in addition to their governess role. They could be teachers, babysitters, domestic servants, chaperones, needlewomen, sick nurses, companions, and ultimately scapegoats for any problem arising from the behaviour or poor academic performance of their pupils. There was no job description, no contract, no union, not even sisterhood with other servants in the house. The role was exclusive, no matter what the demands. The governess was a separate entity in a peculiar position between the servants and her employers. Anne was in fact a pupil teacher, with only two years formal education. At 19 years of age, she prepared herself to go and do her bit to show that she was equal to her siblings and could venture into the world of work, as they had all done. Possibly to help keep her determination and not lose face before her family, as described, Anne chose to go alone on her journey to Mirfield, to her first post as governess to the Ingham family.

As Anne quickly discovered, the governess often had to teach her pupils with her hands metaphorically tied by the strict instructions of their parents, and the mode of upbringing that these adults believed in and lived by. When Anne found herself out of her own class and amongst those with wealth and title, she had to quickly understand that her pupils were not like her siblings and their parents were not her papa and aunt. More so, the parents and children differed in every household because their circumstances and experiences were dictated by class, wealth, tradition, gender and education. Where Anne had been sheltered in the parsonage by her father and aunt and five older siblings, in a household entrenched in religious beliefs and focused on education, other homes were entirely different. Anne could not use her own learned morals and beliefs in families that did not recognise them. She was powerless and especially vulnerable. She lacked experience and authority and went like a lamb to the slaughter in a household where everything was different to anything she had ever known. This was, of course, a very unhappy and worrying situation for Anne. Without the support and backing of the parents, Anne had no chance of educating or even controlling her pupils. It was furthermore a very lonely existence. Anne had no friend or confidante close by, at either of her posts, with whom she could air her views and anxieties.

I suspect that Anne held rather a naive view of children, perhaps born of her own longing for motherhood and a child of her own. The motif of the adorable child, loved and guided by its parent was not always the case in reality. Anne had to learn that not all parents adored, loved or even wanted their children. Also, that some were so intent on gaining more wealth and status through their offspring, that they would actually submit them to dangers that would blight their children's adult lives.

Anne had to learn how to be a governess before she could call herself one, and that took all of her six and a half years of employment. However, as we know from her novels and poetry, Anne also learnt how to observe the human condition in all of its manifestations. Already a quiet and rather lonely figure, Anne could examine human behaviour from her isolated but special position in her exclusive role. She was constantly with her pupils which meant lots of interaction with their parents, whilst Anne was in the room. The children would meet visitors and their extended family, all under Anne's watchful eye. She could rarely interfere, but she could observe and she did that constantly, storing her observations and experiences away to appear in her writings at a later date. Anne noted the minutiae of human communication and questioned in her own mind how and why people behaved as they did. She observed how differently the male and female were expected to behave and develop in certain societies and how a lack of moral instruction could corrupt and spoil a child's innocence. She recognised and believed that education and an early introduction to Christianity, would help to guide a child on a purposeful course that would help them to grow as moral citizens.

Unfortunately, Anne's character and beliefs did not help her where she had the teaching of children already spoilt and undisciplined. Her first encounter was perhaps the worst, with the Ingham family at their estate in Mirfield, West Yorkshire. Blake Hall was possibly the finest house in the area and stood in its own sixty-four-acre estate. It was owned by Joshua Ingham, a man described as a magistrate and businessman who set himself up as lord of the manor. He was a particularly obnoxious man whom Edward Chitham describes as:

> ... the inheritor of a Puritan and patriarchal tradition in which women were thought of as wholly subordinate... His contempt for women applied not only to the governess, but also the female members of the family.[4]

When Anne went to Blake Hall and met Cunliffe and Mary Ingham, the eldest children of her employer, I imagine that they were the manifestation of Edgar and Isabella Linton, characters of Emily's that may well have been based on Anne's description of her two charges. These children were already beyond the ordered discipline of the schoolroom and Anne had strict instructions not to chastise them. Most children, given these circumstances, could hardly be expected to knuckle down to learning and good behaviour. They had free rein, not only to do as they liked, but also to humiliate and provoke their timid governess. I suggest that Anne was completely out of her depth in this household and was often humiliated and ostracised. Their father's misogyny would already have set an example to his 7-year-old son.

It would appear that the overbearing Joshua Ingham dominated his wife in all things. Mary Ingham is reported to have been kind to Anne, as told to Ellen Nussey by Charlotte, and having a calm and placid nature throughout Anne's stay. However, this calm nature meant that she had little or no command or authority over her wayward children; she eventually produced thirteen, and her lack of significance would only make her children more despotic. Joshua Ingham completely ruled his household and there are stories of him being a cruel and harsh father, especially to his daughters. It is plain to see that these children were damaged long before Anne arrived and she had little, if any, chance to alter the *status quo*.

It is not recorded at what dates Anne arrived or left Blake Hall during 1839. When Charlotte wrote her letter to Ellen Nussey dated 15 April that Anne's pupils were 'desperate little dunces', this was following a letter from Anne some time earlier. However, Charlotte, in her role of elder sibling, and still astonished that her little sister could actually go it alone, remarks to Ellen that:

> ... *you would be astonished what a sensible, clever letter she writes... but I do seriously apprehend that Mrs Ingram will sometimes conclude that she has a natural impediment of speech.*[5]

It was during Anne's stay at Blake Hall that Patrick's new curate, William Weightman, arrived at Haworth, in August 1839. As stated, and despite speculation, there is no actual evidence that Anne felt any emotional attachment to Weightman. The only reference to anything between the two comes from Charlotte describing them in church. Some of her poetry and parts of *Agnes Grey* may suggest that Anne could have had, or may have wished for, an emotional relationship with him, but there seems to be more conjecture than proof. All of the Brontë siblings, their father and his parishioners were delighted with Weightman's geniality and piety. His early death in 1842, when Anne was at her second post at Thorp Green, was a blow to all who knew him.

It is all the more commendable that, rather than retire home and look for a more relaxing and comfortable position following her experience with the Inghams, perhaps as a lady's companion, Anne went straight back into the role of governess with another wealthy family much further away from home. She wrote that she disliked her position with the Robinson family and hoped to change it, but she stayed and over time she won the begrudging respect of her pupils and possibly the praise of her employers.

As recorded, the Robinson family lived at Thorp Green Hall, near Little Ouseburn, twelve miles North of York. Once again this was a wealthy and privileged family and Edmund Robinson saw himself as the local squire. Although an ordained minister he undertook almost no ecclesiastical duties, but preferred the role of sportsman and landowner. His wife, Lydia, was the youngest child of Thomas Gisborne an evangelical minister, so there was certainly some religious knowledge within the household. This may have helped in the children's education and behaviour but they were still unruly and difficult for Anne to teach. There was the advantage of their being older than the Ingham children, in so far as they had better manners and could communicate on a more adult footing.

Although Anne wrote in her 'diary paper' of 1841 that she disliked her situation at Thorp Green, she never did anything to change it. Edward Chitham suggests three reasons for this. Firstly, that having had to leave Blake Hall she was determined to stick to this job, no matter what. Secondly, that she had come to feel possible affection and responsibility for the children and lastly, that the annual five weeks away every summer in Scarborough was a privilege that she could never have afforded for herself. As well as the Scarborough holidays, Anne went home for Christmas and possibly a couple of weeks in the summer. I would add a fourth reason to this list. Anne was now independent, she had a role and a purpose, something that she had been denied her whole life. No longer the youngest and least important, the quiet little girl in the background, she was a woman in her own right who could live and work away from home and survive without the patronage of her family.

Anne was obviously very busy with her duties at work but she did have some leisure time and she made drawings and wrote personal poetry and possibly her hymns and the outline of her first novel. It was only at home, with Emily, that Anne wrote 'Gondal' verse. Anne's verse, written at Thorp Green, was filled with philosophical thoughts and questions. It was here that she began to show her ability to ponder the human condition and use her experiences of human nature to explore the reasons why people behaved as they did and how important moral directions or the lack of them, influenced and affected them. Anne had, through her own upbringing and the assurances of the Moravian faith, come to rely on her belief in universal salvation. However, this belief must have been constantly questioned when she observed people who displayed evil and anti-Christian behaviours. She appears to have been constantly anxious about her faith and suffered ongoing serious doubts and worries, possibly instigated by people and experiences that she observed around her, at work, at home and on holiday. She stated that she had had, 'unpleasant and undreamt-of experience of human nature'.[6]

Sometime before this, Anne had written in her prayer book that she was 'sick of mankind and their disgusting ways'.[7]

This is a very damning statement and not one that we would associate with Anne's controlled and quiet demeanour. It suggests that something of major significance has greatly upset her. To me it sounds more like something that Emily would blurt out, in anger and frustration. This is an Anne one doesn't often see; she usually rationalises and analyses situations until she understands the causes and background and she does this throughout her novels. Remarking on the different ways that each Brontë employed when thinking up and around their characters, Edward Chitham notes that:

> *Emily throws her emotional power at characters she invents and dislikes, such as Edgar Linton, Anne looks calmly and rationally at the alternative, though she does empathise with characters she does not rationally agree with, for example, Rosalie in 'Agnes Grey'.*[8]

We do not know what prompted this outburst of Anne's but a solution may be found in a possible illegitimate child of Edmund Robinson, William Kettlewell, a scandal which is examined by Edward Chitham. It would have added to Anne's store of observations of people and their ungodly behaviour. It may also refer to Branwell whose conduct was causing growing concern and who may also have sired an illegitimate child, who died in infancy.

Anne kept her strength and belief in God by setting herself the task of reading the entire Bible, which she completed over the next two years. Again, this suggests that events were conspiring to make her question her beliefs and to seek reassurance in the Christian faith. It also refers back to the idea of '*solar scriptura*', that the only true word and essence of God was in the scriptures.

Did Anne witness an affair between Branwell and Lydia Robinson? Did she witness debauchery amongst the people she observed at Thorp Green and Scarborough? Was it the attitude of her pupils or violence and upset at home or in the neighbourhood? Was it an offence against nature, similar to the one in *Agnes Grey* where the boy wants to torture the young birds? I suggest that this is the more likely scenario. God and nature where a part of the same spiritual essence for Anne and she wrote of that episode in her novel to demonstrate some of the inherent cruel and evil acts that some people are capable of, although, as ever, she rationalises the reasons for it.

By the end of 1841, and with Anne away from home, Emily and Charlotte appear to have, once again, become close companions. The idea (Charlotte's?)

of starting their own school is now being seriously considered. Anne's opinion does not appear to have been sought, although she mentions the scheme. Charlotte decides that she and Emily need to go abroad to strengthen their language skills and gain certificates and experience to complete their education. Two things puzzle me here. We know that Emily had severe homesickness at Roe Head and that she suffered drudgery and homesickness at Law Hill. The thought that she willingly opted to go abroad for eighteen months is difficult to imagine. Also, Charlotte had always aligned herself with her father as his special daughter and overseer of his health and welfare. Time and again she refused to leave him when asked or required to do so, yet here she was planning to abandon him for a very long time, over 400 miles away.

We know that Charlotte was greatly influenced by her former schoolfriend, Mary Taylor, and aspired to be like her and adopt her courage and independence. However, Mary's family had wealth and Charlotte's did not. Mary had a freedom that she would not compromise for anyone and even remarked on Charlotte's 'sacrifices to the selfish old man'. Mary Taylor was an astute woman and understood Charlotte, possibly better than anyone. She begged Charlotte not to stay at home at the parsonage, year after year, warning her that it would break her health and spirit. Mary was also struck by Charlotte's obsession in carrying out her work within the family. She wrote that Charlotte, 'seemed to have no interest or pleasure beyond the feeling of duty'.[9] This is how she saw Charlotte's determination to be in control, of always having to do everything herself and being unable to delegate.

Then suddenly Charlotte had Mary's letter describing exotic places on the Continent and Charlotte wanted that too. Not for the first, or last time, Charlotte chose to put her own needs and wants before those of her family. Her letter to her aunt is well known and recorded and is, to me, a summing up of a darker side of Charlotte, who will coax, manipulate and cajole in order to get what she wants, irrespective of its effect on others or the expense to her family. She purports to be going along with Miss Wooler's offer of her school at Dewsbury Moor, but has already decided against it. She even tells Emily that she intends for them both to get work abroad after six months in Brussels.

One wonders how much her aunt did come to regret her decision. She did not live to see either of her two nieces again and the whole venture was a costly affair that left the two sisters once more without employment or a school. Was there really a need to go abroad? Did they gain anything that gave them a better chance of starting a school? Charlotte's decision to turn down Margaret Wooler's generous offer to take over Heald's Hall, a venture that could have changed the Brontës fortunes for good and seen a whole new way of life for them all, was unwise. I find it hard to condone Charlotte's behaviour and its consequences, which were damaging to everyone involved. I suggest that the only positive thing that came out of this ill-fated undertaking was Charlotte's masterpiece, *Villette*.

Charlotte and Emily left for Brussels, accompanied by Patrick, in February 1842, a journey that took the best part of a week. Patrick, now 65 years old, had to make the return journey alone, despite his precarious health and poor eyesight. It was to be a sad and lonely year for Patrick, with his girls abroad or working away. His curate, Weightman, died in September and his companion and helper for twenty years, Elizabeth Branwell, died the following month. Only Branwell was at home to comfort his father, although their relationship was perhaps by now not a particularly happy one. Branwell was already using alcohol whenever anything upset him and the deaths of his best friend, Weightman, and his mother substitute, Aunt Elizabeth, may well have had a far greater effect on the young man than has been realised or acknowledged.

In the space of a month, Branwell lost the two people who kept him grounded and offered him love and companionship. By the time Branwell took up his post at Thorp Green in January 1843, he was a sad and grief-stricken man who possibly craved the attention of anyone who would offer him comfort. Whether either or both of the Lydia Robinsons were kind to him or whether their attention was more flirtatious is impossible to know. We do know that Branwell was vulnerable and may have misunderstood or misread any female consideration or affection. He needed someone to show him a way out of his grief and if not, he would, perhaps understandably, turn to the palliative remedies of alcohol and laudanum.

Branwell's downfall into a life of dissolution following his dismissal from Thorp Green, whatever the circumstances, suggests to me a far deeper psychological breakdown linked to the deaths of Weightman and his aunt. He had witnessed Weightman's two weeks of pain and suffering as the young curate slowly died from cholera, visiting him regularly and becoming more and more distraught. Yet, before Branwell could begin to recover, his aunt fell ill, possibly of a bowel obstruction, and died after days of extreme pain and suffering. Branwell wrote at the time to his friend, Francis Grundy, regarding the two deaths. Grundy was upset that Branwell had not been returning his letters and Branwell wrote of the reason why:

> *I have had a long attendance at the death-bed of the Rev. Mr Weightman, one of my dearest friends, and am now attending at the death-bed of my aunt, who has been for twenty years as my mother.*[10]

A few days later he wrote again to say:

> *I am incoherent, I fear, but I have been waking two nights witnessing such agonising suffering as I would not wish my worst enemy to endure; and I have now lost the guide and director of all the happy days connected with my childhood.*[11]

His letters remind us of Patrick's heartbreak over the long nights of pain and distress involving his wife and daughters, when he spent night after night having to impotently watch their suffering.

Returning to the effects of traumatic and sustained tragedy one can at least try to understand some of the reasons for Branwell's adult behaviour. He had lost his guide, not once, but repeatedly throughout his life, including his separation from Charlotte. Branwell did not have the stoicism of his sisters or their ability to cope, at least on the surface, with loss and suffering. Moreover, he had lost his faith and therefore there was no figure or spirit to whom he could go for support, or who could truly understand his dilemma. He wrote a significant reference to what he thought of the Church, in a letter to Francis Grundy in 1842, whilst job-hunting. In answer to a query by his friend, Branwell wrote:

> *You ask me, Sir; why I don't turn my attention in another direction? And so I would but that most of my relations, and more immediate connections, are Clergymen, or, by a private life, somewhat removed from this busy world – And, as for the Church, I have not one mental quality – except perhaps hypocrisy – which would make me cut a figure in its pulpits.*[12]

Perhaps Branwell had also become affected and confused by the numerous religious doctrines around the north of England and further despised his father's continued faith in a God who was doing nothing to help Branwell achieve his goals. Like all males at the time, he was expected to be strong and able to deal with adversity, but that was not part of Branwell's temperament. He needed support and without a religious faith, he found it in those twins of human failing, drugs and alcohol.

Charlotte and Emily returned from Brussels in time for their aunt's funeral. Apart from a short jaunt to York with Anne in June 1845, Emily never left home again, perhaps a pointer that she had done all the travelling and living away from home that she could tolerate. The Christmas of 1842 must have seen a very sad and forlorn Brontë household. By the new year, Charlotte was intent on returning to Brussels, Emily on staying at home, and Anne on returning to her work at Thorp Green. Branwell, once more unemployed, was offered a place with Anne, possibly on her recommendation, as tutor to the young Edmund Robinson, now deemed too old for the teachings of a governess. It must always be remembered that Branwell Brontë was a highly intelligent and educated man. He may have ended his life dissolute, for very many reasons, but I maintain that he had at least the mental capacity of his siblings and showed amazing ability and talent as a child and young man, in many areas of the arts. His gender was, I suggest, his downfall. He had expectations foisted on to him that he could not reach or maintain. He had no male friends or the benefits of a male environment but he was an artist, a poet and a writer of note who never managed to fulfil his early promise. After his death, Charlotte wrote a letter to her publisher, less of grief over his death, than of the mourning of wasted talents. These two siblings, once so close, had severed links long ago. Instead, she wrote:

> *I do not weep from a sense of bereavement – there is no prop withdrawn, no consolation is torn away, no dear companion lost – but from the wreck of talent, the ruin of promise, the untimely dreary extinction of what might have been a burning and shining light... I had aspirations and ambitions for him once – long ago – they have perished mournfully – nothing remains of him but a memory of errors and sufferings – there is such a bitterness of pity for his life and death.*[13]

Once again, we have an example of Charlotte's faint praise, not dissimilar to her denigration of Emily and Anne in her 1850 preface to *Wuthering Heights*. Charlotte could be quite brutal when speaking of her siblings after their deaths, and this example demonstrates not only how alienated Charlotte had become from her brother but how little empathy or sympathy she showed him as a person. Juliet Barker remarks on how poisonous the relationship between the two had become, saying that Branwell had committed 'the unforgivable sin of not living up to her expectations of him'.[14]

As Branwell lay dying, Charlotte witnessed her father's tortuous grief, but this only fuelled her anger and demonstrates an innate jealousy. Did Charlotte believe that her father would be as unmoved by his son's death as she was? She wrote again to her publisher that:

> *My poor father naturally thought more of his only son than of his daughters, and much and long had he suffered on his account – he cried out for his loss like David for that of Absalom – My son! My son! And refused at first to be comforted.*[15]

Thorp Green

The language Charlotte uses in her description of Branwell in these letters is both sad and highly emotive. One feels that she despised, almost hated, her brother in his last years. She demonstrates no feelings of grief, no sadness that he is dead, only the removal of what should, and could, have been. Charlotte's response here is so hard and cold and angry. It is a side of Charlotte that is in line with her dominance over her siblings. She is giving Branwell a telling off, a dressing down, a reprimand for his weaknesses, whilst berating her father's foolish love for a son who had no redeeming features left. To say that he 'refused' to be comforted is almost a criticism of his profound grief.

Branwell went to Thorp Green in January 1843 with Anne and they both stayed until the summer of 1845. As explained, Anne probably left because her services were no longer required, her pupils had grown up. Why Branwell left is not altogether clear. Did he have an affair with his employer's wife? Would a woman in Lydia Robinson's position dally with her son's tutor? Edward Chitham sees Branwell as delusional in his craving for his employer's wife:

> *Mrs Robinson, he seems to believe, was a neglected woman oppressed by her husband, and yearning for a rescuer [himself] to remove her ... where to? From her comfortable home to lodgings in Haworth? Why would a lady on the verge of the aristocracy make such a move?*[16]

Did anything happen between Branwell and young Edmund that caused his dismissal? Did Branwell fall for Lydia Robinson because he craved love and affection from a woman, any woman, because he had lost his aunt and friend so recently? It is worth remembering that there were two Lydia Robinsons in the household – his employer's wife and his daughter! Is it possible that it was the younger Lydia Robinson to whom Branwell became attached? There is a plethora of conjecture. What we do know is that Branwell had been drinking for some years and possibly that was the cause of his dismissal. He certainly drank in earnest for the rest of his short life and his increasing use of laudanum, and possibly pure opium, took a toll on his fragile mental and physical health.

During the two and a half years Branwell was at Thorp Green, one wonders how much communication there was between brother and sister. Branwell appears to have been no more a constant and loving brother to his sisters than they were to him. A lack of surviving letters from either sibling during this time leaves us with no indication that they spent much time together. Branwell was housed in the Monk's Lodge, all that remained of the former monastery that once stood in the grounds, whilst Anne lived in the Hall itself and this may have further ostracised the siblings. It also gave Branwell more freedom of movement to go unnoticed by the members of the household. If he was having an affair with his employee's wife, or daughter, he must have realised that his behaviour was putting Anne's position in jeopardy as well as his own. Branwell appears to have held little affection for his two younger sisters; Charlotte had been his competitor and adversary but her challenges to him had kept him alert and animated. If he loved any of his family it was probably Charlotte, his superior and unattainable elder sister.

Edward Chitham shows a particular interest in Anne's trips to Scarborough with the Robinsons, noting that she spent over half a year there, in total, between 1841 and 1845. This is a time in Anne's life that is often over looked, despite it having a profound effect on her and her writings. As stated, Scarborough was at this time a thriving community, so very different from Anne's experiences at home, school or at work. She lived in rural isolation at Thorp Green and the busy and bustling town of Scarborough was alive with locals, visitors and especially the middle classes. People were taking the spa waters and turning the town into a thriving seaside resort. The sights and sounds of the town added to its castle, museums and galleries, its bays and cliffs and the huge expanse of the North Sea would have deeply affected a sensitive young woman like Anne. It would have greatly expanded her experience and knowledge of people of various classes and backgrounds. This was the Robinsons' holiday venue and Anne would have had more spare time to explore the town and its surroundings. Had Anne written another novel, I suggest that this is where she would have located it and described many of the people and buildings she encountered.

Patrick visited his two children at Thorp Green in the early part of 1843 but neither child records the event. He presumably met the Robinsons and obviously, at that time, there was no disharmony. In the summer, Anne brought home a dog, Flossie, to Haworth, which may have been a present from the Robinsons or perhaps a stray she found in Scarborough, or even a disputed pet between the Robinson children; another incident for Emily to record in her novel!

That summer also saw Anne purchasing her music manuscript book, possibly on a visit to York, and she began to translate hymns, songs and verses that she particularly enjoyed. We know that Anne was fond of music, could play the piano and had a sweet singing voice but what is perhaps less known about Anne is that she was a highly proficient writer of hymns, something her siblings never aspired to. In her essay, 'Singing from the Margins: Anne Brontë's Surprising Poetic Afterlife', Sara Pearson states in her abstract that:

> *Anne Brontë was the only hymn-writer in her family, and her hymns have had a successful afterlife in multiple hymnals from 1858 to 1997. Her hymns have been used by a variety of religious*

> *denominations and sects, in numerous countries, among various groups of people, from children to university students to the sick and suffering ... her hymn 'Believe not those who say', has appeared in over sixty hymnals.*[17]

Pearson tells us that Anne's hymns appear in nine different Christian denominations and also many non-denominational hymn books. This is an area of Anne's writing that has not gained the attention and praise that it deserves. Her hymns demonstrate her religious beliefs and emphasise the Christian ethos to follow the narrow way and to seek God in nature. Anne may have been influenced by one of her favourite poets, the Anglican hymn writer William Cowper (1731–1800).

Cowper was a deeply troubled man. His life was punctuated by episodes of deep despair and depression related to his extreme fear of being rejected by God. After being institutionalised for insanity, he found refuge in Evangelical Christianity. He worried, like Anne, about his salvation and it tormented him for much of his life. Seen as a forerunner to the Romantic poets, Cowper wrote especially about nature and the countryside. Interestingly, his mother died in childbirth when Cowper was only 6 years old.

Anne wrote her famous poem to Cowper, in the November of her '*annus horribilis*' (1842) and in it she tells of her study of his poetry and identification with his themes. The first stanzas read:

> *Sweet are thy strains, Celestial Bard;*
> *And oft, in childhood's years,*
> *I've read them o'er and o'er again,*
> *With floods of silent tears.*
> (Stanza 1)

She describes how she is so affected by his sorrow, saying:

> *All for myself the sigh would swell,*
> *The tear of anguish start;*
> *I little knew what wilder woe*
> *Had filled the Poet's heart.*
>
> *I did not know the nights of gloom,*
> *The days of misery:*
> *The long, long years of dark despair,*
> *That crushed and tortured thee.*
> (Stanzas 3 and 4)

Anne later remarks that he must now in death be safely with God. However, if he is not, then there is little hope for herself. She says:

> *Yet, should thy darkest fears be true,*
> *If Heaven be so severe,*
> *That such a soul as thine is lost,-*
> *Oh! how shall I appear?*
> (Stanza 11)[18]

Anne's Bible, Prayer Book and Hymn Book were probably her most treasured possessions and she read them and used them daily. They offered her reassurance and hope when her faith faltered. As stated, hymns were especially important in the evangelical mode of religion because they reached every member of the congregation, whatever their class, education or status. Many hymns carry messages as well as praise and are still an important way of conveying knowledge of God and help to unite the congregation.

When Anne purchased her music manuscripts, she separated out her songs, religious poetry, personal poetry and her hymns into a manuscript for each. One, entitled 'Hymns' is identified by Pearson as Manuscript X, as labelled by Edward Chitham. Pearson states that this fair-copy book "contains five of Anne's poems that she intentionally wrote as hymns. 'Retirement' (No 14); 'Despondency' (No 17); 'In memory of a happy day in February' (No 18); 'A Prayer' (No 34)' and 'Confidence' (No 41)'.[19]

Pearson identifies them as hymns because Anne gives them a metrical signature. Each poem is headed with either CM, for Common Metre, SM, for Short Metre and LM, for Long Metre. As well as the above five hymns there are others in Anne's repertoire including *Music on a Christmas morning* and *The Doubter's Prayer*. These, and three of her other poems are listed by Pearson: *The Three Guides* and *The Narrow Way*, both published in different issues of *Fraser's Magazine* before Anne's death, and her final poem, excerpted by Charlotte in her 1850 edition, *I hoped that with the brave and strong*. However, over time, lines have been altered and titles changed. Pearson gives the definitive list of Anne's hymns, with their alternative titles as follows:

1. *The Doubter's Prayer/ While faith is with me/ Eternal power of earth and air.*
2. *Music on Christmas Morning.*
3. *A Prayer/My God, O let me call Thee mine.*
4. *The Three Guides/ Spirit of Truth/ Spirit of Faith.*
5. *I hoped that with the brave and strong.*

6. *Confidence/Oppressed with sin and woe.*
7. *The Narrow Way/Believe not those who say.*[20]

These seven hymns, as listed in *The Complete Poems of Anne Brontë,* edited by Clement Shorter, show them as having been written or published between 1843 and 1849. They are, therefore, personal rather than 'Gondal' writings and are mainly written after she left Thorp Green in June 1845. During her research, Pearson discovered eighty-six hymnals containing at least one of these hymns, and there may be more, both in Britain and many other parts of the world.

    I was brought up in the Methodist faith, although I no longer adhere to any religion. I have, however, attended many church services of different denominations and noted Anne's hymns. They are a major part of her legacy and yet are hardly ever mentioned or even known by many Brontë enthusiasts and academics. It is another area of Anne's life and talents that have been hidden in plain sight.

Chapter Twelve

Agnes Grey
The Autobiography of a Governess

Anne's return home must have been a huge relief for her after six years of difficult work far away, but a worry for her father. Branwell's dismissal from the Robinsons followed quickly after Anne left and this meant that all four of Patrick's children were now, once again, at home and none of them were earning any money. The girls had each inherited money from their aunt which they invested in railway shares, but that was for 'a rainy day', an investment against future expense or catastrophe, for example the death of their father.

The siblings were aware of the drain on the family finances. The school scheme had finally been abandoned after they had failed to attract any pupils when they advertised their home as a boarding school for a small number of girls. Reluctant to leave home and work for other people again, the three girls had to find a way to use their talents to earn money. Unfortunately, Branwell's efforts to get another job on the railways failed and he became too unreliable and unstable to earn a living.

Around this time, Charlotte 'discovered' Emily's private papers which included both her 'Gondal' and personal poetry. I suggest that it is doubtful that Charlotte was unaware of her sister's writing talents or of where she kept her manuscripts. One can imagine Charlotte searching through them and insisting that they should be published. We are told that it took many days for Emily to be reconciled with Charlotte after her invasion of Emily's privacy. Whilst the sisters, especially during the writing of their novels, would read various parts to the others and perhaps seek opinion and criticism, although Charlotte later denied this, their poetry was personal or linked to their imaginary worlds. In other words, they were private and only to be shared if and when, the author decided.

It would appear by Charlotte's account of finding Emily's poems that she was not aware of their content:

> *One day, in the Autumn of 1845, I accidentally lighted on a MS, volume of verse in my sister Emily's handwriting. Of course, I was not surprised, knowing that she could and did write verse: I looked it over, and something more than surprise seized me, – a deep conviction that these were not common effusions, not at all like the poetry women generally write. I thought them condensed and terse, vigorous and genuine. To my ear they had a peculiar music – wild, melancholy, and elevating.*[1]

Charlotte continues saying that Emily was not a person that even her closest relatives could intrude upon. She says that:

> *... it took hours to reconcile her to the discovery I had made, and days to persuade her that such poems merited publication.*[2]

I suggest that this is an enormous understatement. Charlotte had completely overstepped the mark. Knowing what little we do of Emily, it is likely that the fallout from Charlotte's 'discovery' was far more devastating, and probably caused a huge rift that lasted for some time. Anne's efforts to calm the storm by offering some of her own work met with an underwhelmed response from her sister:

> *Meantime, my younger sister quietly produced some of her own compositions, intimating that since Emily's had given me pleasure, I might like to look at hers. I could not but be a partial judge, yet I thought that these verses too had a sweet pathos of their own.*[3]

Oh dear, we are back to faint praise! Anne is not even named and her verse is rather like Charlotte's view of her sister, sweet and full of pathos. Anne appears as the peacemaker who will sacrifice her own anonymity and private poetry, to appease her two sisters.

However, whatever the circumstances and the fallout, Charlotte was determined that they should use some of their aunt's investments to have their poems published and recognised. As ever, Charlotte is the driving force and making all of the decisions. In hindsight, she did the world a favour, but I am sure that at the time this was the elder sister deciding what was right and necessary for them all. She had to compromise, however. The 'Gondal' poems came from a secret, private world and were not for publication in their current form. Parts had to be altered and disguised. Also, Emily especially, had no hankering after fame or notoriety and insisted that they publish under androgynous pseudonyms. Both Emily and Anne were insistent about this and, for once, Charlotte had to comply. Being aware that male writers were the authors of almost all published material, the sisters deliberately chose names that suggested masculine writers. Keeping their own initials, each sister chose epicene names to disguise their authorship. Juliet Barker traces the possible origins of these names, Currer, Ellis and Acton Bell, as names familiar within the neighbouring district and people that they would have known. She suggests that the Bell surname may have been linked to the fact that St Michael's Church had recently acquired some new bells; a sound that was heard throughout the day and night at the parsonage.

Whatever the origins of their pseudonyms it is interesting to note that Anne, despite Charlotte's opinion, chose twenty-one of her poems for the anthology. All had been written in the last five years, and none from the 'Gondal Saga'; they were personal or religious verses drawn from her five manuscripts.

By January 1846 the poems had reached, and been accepted by, the small publishing house of Aylott and Jones, off Paternoster Row, in London. At the beginning of March, the sisters sent the required bankers draft of £31.10 shillings for the printing of their volume of verse. No doubt all three sisters were jubilant and eager to see their work in print but it was another few months before the first review appeared. Unfortunately, the focus seemed to centre on questions about the authors rather than their work. However, both *The Critic* and *The Athenaeum* showed interest and the merit of Emily's poetry was singled out.

Surprisingly, despite some favourable comments, the book sold only two copies. This was a valuable lesson, but did not deter the sisters, especially Charlotte, who, having seen their poetry in print and knowing that they all had talent, now had the enthusiasm to move on to novel writing. She felt that they had experience of the pitfalls and processes of publication. She wrote to Aylott and Jones to say that the three 'Bells' were each preparing works of fiction.

Over the following months the sisters wrote voraciously on their novels. Charlotte on *The Professor*, Emily on *Wuthering Heights* and Anne on *Agnes Grey*. We know the trials and tribulations that followed these three novels and their authors, but I want to remain focused on Anne and how and why she wrote *Agnes Grey* and whether or not it was autobiographical.

There has long been dispute amongst biographers and critics as to the links between Anne's first novel and her own experiences. I am not prepared to call it her autobiography but I am sure that many of Anne's personal experiences appear in the story. Like all good authors, she could take an actual event and fictionalise it in her work. It is not wrong or a weakness to do so and I object to critics who seem to assume that one should write absolute reality, absolute fiction or absolute fantasy. For me, the three are not mutually exclusive.

Agnes Grey

How often are writers encouraged to write about what they know and then criticised for being too personal. There is no reason not to acknowledge and admire Anne for introducing her own experiences in the lives and behaviour of her characters. Furthermore, some modern critics describe the novel as a '*Bildungsroman*', where the protagonist changes and develops physically and psychologically, expressing moral growth from childhood to adulthood. Agnes certainly demonstrates the interaction between herself and the world and how that education changes her.

The debate about the amount of autobiography in the book will continue. Unfortunately, it has come to overshadow the books merits. This quote from George Moore during his conversation with his friend, Edmund Gosse, sums up, for me, the true appeal of *Agnes Grey*:

> *Agnes Grey is a prose narrative simple and beautiful as a muslin dress. I need not remind you, Gosse, that it is more difficult to write a simple story than a complicated one ... the first sentences, the eating of the beefsteak is among the first, convince us that we are with a quick, witty mind, capable of appreciating all she hears and sees: and when Agnes begins to tell us of her charges and their vulgar parents, we know that we are reading a masterpiece. Nothing short of genius could have set them before us so plainly and yet with restraint.*[4]

I enjoy *Agnes Grey* especially for the parts that seem so realistic and reflect Anne's possible thoughts and experiences. One of my favourite passages in the whole book is 'the beefsteak' incident referred to by George Moore. It is a short piece that hardly merits the reader's attention but with which I can fully identify. So often, we like a piece of writing or a picture because it is of something that we recognise and can associate with. The passage to which I refer in *Agnes Grey* occurs when Agnes first arrives at her new employment on a snowy day after a long and tiring coach journey. She is very cold, timid and apprehensive. She describes her encounter with her new employer:

> *She led me into the dining-room, where the family luncheon had been laid out. Some beefsteaks and half-cold potatoes were set before me; and while I dined upon these, she sat opposite, watching me (as I thought) and endeavouring to sustain something like a conversation – consisting chiefly of a succession of commonplace remarks, expressed with frigid formality: but this might be more my fault than hers, for I could not converse. In fact, my attention was almost wholly absorbed in my dinner:*

> *not from ravenous appetite, but from the distress at the toughness of the beefsteaks and the numbness of my hands, almost palsied by their five hours' exposure to the bitter wind. I would gladly have eaten the potatoes and let the meat alone, but having got a large piece of the latter on to my plate, I could not be so impolite as to leave it; so, after many awkward and unsuccessful attempts to cut it with the knife, or tear it with the fork, or pull it asunder between them, sensible that the awful lady was spectator to the whole transaction, I at last desperately grasped the knife and fork in my fists, like a child of two years old, and fell to work with all the little strength I possessed.*[5]

This is where Anne is so detailed and so clever at creating the feelings of embarrassment and helplessness that surely most people can empathise with. The reader can recognise the agonising dilemma of Agnes, desperately trying to create a good impression on her first encounter with her mistress and failing miserably. I have complete empathy with this episode. I sat opposite my father at the dinner table for many years and his Victorian beliefs about children and good manners and his intense scrutiny often left me unable to eat. I felt the same on the occasion that my school headmistress, who would sometimes arbitrarily spend lunchtimes in the canteen sitting at one of the dinner tables with the first-year pupils (11 year olds) sat beside me one day and completely killed my appetite. I shook with fear and could barely hold my knife and fork; something that she was very quick to note and broadcast.

Embarrassment is an awful affliction which can cause pain and anxiety to the sufferer. For a shy and timid person, who is overwhelmed in a new and alien situation, one can feel their awkwardness and desire to run away as fast as possible. Scenes like this in *Agnes Grey* bring the book alive and allow the reader to witness events, recognise aspects of the characters and understand their reactions to events. It is perhaps what prompts readers to say that the story is autobiographical; we encounter events so vividly that we attribute them to Anne's own experience. I am sure that some events were witnessed and felt by Anne and used in her novels and there is nothing wrong with that. Unfortunately, when a novel offers realism, a reader can mistakenly assume that everything has been witnessed and experienced by the author but that is not always the case. It is the power of imagination and understanding of behaviour that a good author can conjure up, fooling their readers into thinking that it must have occurred in reality. Jane Sunderland in her essay on the nineteenth-century governess suggests that *Agnes Grey* 'can be cautiously taken as refracted evidence'.[6]

This emphasises my suggestion that *Agnes Grey* does offer a number of passages that indicate that Anne is speaking from her own experience. As previously quoted, Anne Smith especially notes in her introduction to *Agnes Grey and Poems* that Anne is also offering an insight into her childhood and her relationship with her aunt and with Charlotte. When Anne Brontë writes in the words of Agnes, that 'I, being the younger by five or six years, was always regarded as the child, and the pet of the family ... etc',[7] she is, perhaps, describing her own experience.

There is much, especially in the beginning of *Agnes Grey* to make one wonder whether Anne was describing her own thoughts and feelings. Agnes states that she was allowed to do little housework because her 'mother' (aunt/ Charlotte) always saw her as a child, though she was in fact a woman. I reiterate this quote as she goes on to describe her 'mother' in a way that, for me, is a description of Charlotte, taken from life:

> *My mother, [Charlotte] like most active, managing women, was not gifted with very active daughters [Emily and Anne] for this reason – that being so clever and diligent herself, she was never tempted to trust her affairs to a deputy, but on the contrary, was willing to act and think for others as well as for number one; and whatever was the business in hand, she was apt to think that no one could do it so well as herself: so that whenever I offered to assist her, I received such an answer as – 'No, love, you cannot indeed – there is nothing here you can do. Go and help your sister, or get her to take a walk with you – tell her she must not sit so much, and stay so constantly in the house as she does – she may well look thin and emaciated.*[8]

Perhaps I am also guilty of trying to establish a reality when it may not be the case, but all that I read and know of Charlotte's personality and her role as the eldest sibling suggests to me that we are being shown a flicker of Anne's experience at home. Anne stated and insisted that her novels were about telling the truth, the truth as she saw it and experienced it, and I do not see a problem with that. Only Anne could have known how much of her writing contained her own experiences but I maintain that some of her work is very translatable to her thoughts and feelings, especially her poetry. She is careful in her novels to observe without personal comment, and putting her beliefs and ideas into the lives of her characters is a clever and adept way of stating what she needs to say, and sometimes giving an insight into her own life and relationships. However, it may also be seen as an almost accidental result of writing fiction. Writing is personal and it is very difficult to write a book that does not have some input of the author's own experience and understanding. Books can be dated by the names, the outfits, the settings, the types of speech and many other signatures. To write a book that has no author input would be very difficult, maybe impossible.

We do not need to know the details of an author when reading a book. For some time, critics decided that only 'the words on the page' were important and worth studying and that the author was '*persona non grata*'. That may be possible in some cases but, I suggest that a knowledge of the Brontës lives, their childhood, their tragedies, their education, work and their travels, gives, in their case, a much greater understanding and insight into their writing. One can argue that Emily's *Wuthering Heights* is not autobiographical, but a careful reading of it will expose some of Emily's own local knowledge, her religious thoughts and doubts, her love of moorland and her observations on child rearing etc. One can separate an author from their work, but I feel that will sometimes lose something of the meaning of a text and its links with the mind that conceived it. All seven of the Brontë novels contain important aspects of the lives and experiences of their authors, and it is those experiences that make the novels so interesting. The point I am making is that the personal input that an author brings to their work, either by accident or intent, is not necessarily a weakness. In fact, it can be an important and highly effective feature. In Anne's novels, her childhood and her working life were the essence of her writing and simultaneously helped to highlight and identify many of the problems that she observed in the society of the time.

Anne approaches a host of social issues in her first novel, not least the need for an equality of education between boys and girls such as she had herself received. Anne fictionalises some of the issues that had been dealt with by Mary Wollstonecraft in her *Vindication of the Rights of Women* (1772) which advocates equal rights that include female education. It is not known whether or not Anne read Wollstonecraft's book but she understands how, as a governess, she has different roles to play according to the gender of her charges. Anne questions this both morally and politically by showing the results of generations of gender separation and the nurturing of the male into the dominant sex. This is further explored and expounded in *The Tenant of Wildfell Hall.*

In the latter part of *Agnes Grey*, Agnes is staying on the coast and has spent many months of toil and heartache with her employer and their spoilt and wayward children. This break on annual holiday was spent by Anne in reality at Scarborough and it is this seaside resort that Anne describes in her novel where she stays in 'a house at A'. As explained, Anne knew Scarborough well and spent nearly half a year there in four annual holidays with the Robinsons. I want to emphasise here that Scarborough was important to Anne, the highlight of her working year; an escape from some of her duties and a chance to enjoy the summer, the sea and the society. It was not a substitute for her two breaks at home, at Christmas and summer, but an added bonus from her heavy work load.

An annual holiday anywhere in the country would have been a welcome and a change of lifestyle and scenery, it did not have to be Scarborough. The annual visits were a huge bonus for Anne and made her working life much more tolerable. Of course, she enjoyed her time there, but, as I will later demonstrate, that does not mean that she would wish to be buried there away from her family and the home she had always known and loved.

Scarborough in the early 1840s was a small fishing town, but somewhat recognised for its spa waters that had been discovered in the 1600s. They attracted visitors who came to drink from the spa and bathe in the sea; both recommended at the time as health giving benefits. Scarborough attracted a wealthy middle-class clientele and the spa waters spawned a number of attractions to amuse the many visitors. In 1845, the railway was established and it helped to bring thousands of visitors to the town and attract wealth and growth. It already had a ruined castle, built on a former Roman signal station, high above the town, and gradually, especially due to the spa waters, many visitors began to come to the town and it grew exponentially. Theatres, museums, galleries and meeting rooms soon sprang up alongside lodging houses, hotels and shops. Anne would have been able to observe some of the early expansion of the town and to mix amongst the elegantly clad visitors and their servants and children. It was a lively place, especially in the summer months, and she came to know it well. Anne worshipped at Christ Church, not far from the Wood's Lodgings, where the Robinsons rented rooms on The Crescent. The land is now covered by the Grand Hotel, opened in 1867 and, at that time, the largest of its kind in Europe. There was also St Mary's Church high up above the town, adjacent to the castle. This church had been bombarded by Cromwell's troops in the 1600s and was, and still is, partly ruined.

Whilst Anne loved her moorland home, the sea was a new and exciting experience. The wide sands of the town's two bays and the castle promontory between would have offered Anne an abundance of walks and places to observe the ocean. Below and to the side of her lodgings was the harbour where numerous fishermen and fishing boats plied their trade. The contrast with Haworth and the moors was extreme.

Anne gives Agnes a happy ending, which culminates in her encountering the clergyman, Mr Weston and her lost dog, Snap. Both have been in Agnes's thoughts for a long time and Anne provides the wonderful moment when Agnes receives the surprise of her life and all of her dreams are fulfilled. There is no reality here, it is pure fiction, but offered in a simple and undramatic way which is typical of both Anne and her writing:

> *Presently, I heard a snuffling sound behind me, and then a dog came frisking and wriggling to my feet. It was my own Snap – the*

> *little, dark wire-haired terrier! When I spoke his name, he leapt up in my face and yelled for joy. Almost as much delighted as himself, I caught the little creature in my arms, and kissed him repeatedly. But how came he to be there? He could not have dropped from the sky, or come all that way alone: it must be either his master, the rat-catcher, or somebody else that had brought him: so, repressing my extravagant caresses, and endeavouring to express his likewise, I looked round, and beheld – Mr Weston!*[9]

There is no crashing of waves, or thunderbolts and lightning, no grand agonising of soulmates. This is not Heathcliff and Catherine, or Rochester and Jane, it is just a delightful little dog on a beach that makes Agnes happy. Then she turns and sees that the man she has thought about for so long is also there. It is effective in its simplicity and marks Anne, I suggest, as on a par with her sisters by her understated but totally absorbing narrative. She does not write like them, but equally as well. People who try to name their favourite Brontë sibling or favourite Brontë novel fail to accept that they are all different; not better or worse, not more intelligent or less able, they are simply different and should be accepted as such. Comparisons are only valid if they admit difference as acceptable.

One can understand why *Agnes Grey* and *The Tenant of Wildfell Hall* were eulogised by George Moore, many years after Anne's death. He was a prolific Irish novelist and critic who recognised, long before many others, the strength and simplicity, especially of *Agnes Grey*, that marked Anne's writings as outstanding. He wrote of Anne's first novel that it was:

> *The most perfect prose narrative in English Literature.*
> *If Anne Brontë had lived ten years longer she would have taken a place beside Jane Austen, perhaps even a higher place.*[10]

This is high praise and, I suggest, deservedly so, and yet even in the twenty-first century, Anne is still overshadowed by her elder sisters and often viewed as far less an accomplished authoress. The reasons for this are many and I have tried to convey that it was in part Anne's position as the youngest sibling that has contributed to that general opinion. The youngest child has to work so much harder for recognition. They are always the least knowledgeable and experienced by virtue of their youth and if they have a dominant sibling who does not recognise their talents, they are even more likely to be overlooked. Betty Jay noted this in her introduction to her book on Anne, saying that:

> *The literary achievement of the Brontë sisters is difficult to disentangle from the powerful set of myths which has grown*

> *up around the family... In the case of Anne Brontë this problem is compounded by the fact that she has for so long been overshadowed by her two elder siblings, Emily and Charlotte.*[11]

Miss Jay raises the important point that the publication of *Agnes Grey*, only two months after *Jane Eyre* and alongside *Wuthering Heights*, led critics to make unfavourable comparisons. The brutality of *Wuthering Heights* and the passion of *Jane Eyre* naturally drew far more attention and distracted reviewers from the simplicity and focus of the life of a Victorian governess. The timing of the publication of the three novels therefore harmed Anne's reputation as a writer and further pushed her book into the background as a mere addendum to her sisters' novels.

Critics who feel that Anne can only be praised by denigrating her sisters, fail to see that there does not have to be a dominant writer or that one sister is better or more talented than another. Emmeline Burdett makes the point that:

> *A more recent problem has come from those who have tried to redress the balance but have done so in such a way that shows the writer to be less interested in Anne than in seizing every opportunity to denigrate her sisters. Another, and equally problematic modern approach, is when a writer – presumably in a misguided attempt to support Anne – ends up silencing her all over again by complaining bitterly and at length about how Charlotte underestimated her youngest sister.*[12]

I fully acknowledge this criticism but suggest that Charlotte did underestimate her sister and I have tried to show how and where. This book is not a criticism of Charlotte or Emily as writers, but their role as elder sisters. There need not be a power struggle that always places Charlotte in the lead, closely followed by Emily, whilst Anne tags along in the background. The sisters were close – but different – and that is the case that some critics are unable to see or accept. Readers do not have to fall into one camp or another. One may have a favourite author or book, but it is naive and pointless to try and place each against the other. It is like trying to compare green with blue, each has unique qualities and each are completely different, though both are colours. The lives of the sisters may be similar and their writings contain recognisable themes and emotions but they are each a unique person in their own right and their work has to be seen as individual and distinctive.

If I appear to be favouring Anne over her sisters, that is not my intention. I am saying that each child had a place in the birth order that influenced the attitudes and behaviour of everyone else in the family. As in all families, there was and always is, division and upset. There will always be a dominant child and a subservient one and they are often the eldest and the youngest. That Charlotte and Emily were highly talented writers and poets is totally acknowledged by me, but whether they were as able and empathetic as sisters, is where I wish to examine them and question their motives.

I do not find it acceptable to dismiss Emily as some mysterious and withdrawn genius who lives in her own isolated, self-absorbed world where she is too preoccupied to enter into family matters and dilemmas. Emily appears not to have stood up to Charlotte's decision-making or her dominating behaviour, and of all of them, Emily probably had the ability and strength of character to do so. Was Emily as enamoured with Charlotte as Branwell was? Did she protect both her brother and her youngest sister from Charlotte's sometimes harsh and patronising treatment? I suggest that Emily is possibly as much to blame as Charlotte, at times, for not giving Anne or Branwell the support that they needed and deserved. I would also add that Patrick was guilty at times of showing an amazing lack of insight into the behaviour and decision-making of his adult children.

What little extant writing we have of Emily, apart from her poetry, shows her as a rather immature and childlike woman who has taken on a persona that effectively removes her from any major confrontation. She stays at home once she returns from Brussels, and appears to have very little input into the affairs of her siblings. The only time Emily appears to stand up and shout is when Charlotte 'discovers' her poetry and when she also betrays the authors as 'three sisters' when visiting Smith & Elder in London in 1848. Emily craves anonymity but, whilst that is perfectly acceptable, her need to be alone and the impenetrable stoic, does not make her an easy person to be around. That image of Emily has perpetuated after being introduced and multiplied by Charlotte. Charlotte could be, and often was, very outspoken about her two sisters and it is her remarks, often aided and abetted by Mrs Gaskell, that have created the myths around them both and have led to how they are still viewed by many in the twenty-first century.

As Edward Chitham so clearly and rightly claims, Charlotte was the mouthpiece for the Brontë family. Almost all that we know of them is through Charlotte's pen. I also suggest that her influence over her father must also have coloured some of his views and descriptions of life at the parsonage with his family. After the deaths of her siblings, some of Charlotte's words were detrimental to their writing and their characters and whilst she may have had a reason for this, it has coloured the world's view of her sisters and their work, for nearly two centuries. If I criticise Charlotte throughout this book, it is because I dislike the way she treated her siblings even whilst she possibly believed that she was doing the right thing.

I draw attention to Charlotte's strangely defending and condemning 'Biographical Notice of Ellis and Acton Bell' in her 'Editor's Preface' to the new (1850) edition of *Wuthering Heights*. It is a piece of writing that is so damning and so patronising and one which, I am sure, would have grieved her sisters enormously. It needs to be read in full to appreciate what Charlotte is trying to do and say. The following gives a short example of how she disparages her sisters' novels in order to simultaneously promote the authors as naive and misguided women. It is all done in the most beautiful lyrical writing and if it was not for what she implies, it could be seen as a masterpiece of an essay. Charlotte writes a wonderful and wild description of *Wuthering Heights,* which she fails to realise is an almost poetic description of its author and its power; the opposite of what she intended. Charlotte wrote that:

> *Wuthering Heights was hewn in a wild workshop, with simple tools, out of homely materials. The statuary found a granite block on a solitary moor: gazing thereon, he saw how from the crag may be elicited a head, savage, swart, sinister; a form moulded with at least one element of grandeur – power. He wrought with a rude chisel, and from no model but the vision of his meditations. With time and labour, the crag took human shape; and there it stands colossal, dark and frowning, half statue, half rock: in the former sense, terrible and goblin-like; in the latter, almost beautiful, for its colouring is of mellow grey, and moorland moss clothes it; and heath, with its blooming bells and balmy fragrance, grows faithfully close to the giant's foot.*[13]

This is a beautifully written paragraph and Charlotte so uniquely sums up Emily's ability to create her 'monster' Heathcliff. But it was Charlotte's intention to show that Emily was simple, homely and uniformed; too naive to realise what she had done and the terrible story that she had created. She spoke of Emily in the following way:

> *Had Ellis Bell been a lady or a gentleman accustomed to what is called 'the world', her view of a remote and unclaimed region, as well as of the dwellers therein, would have differed greatly from that actually taken by the home-bred country girl... I am bound to avow that she had scarcely more practical knowledge of the peasantry amongst whom she lived, than a nun has of the country people who sometimes pass her convent gates... Her imagination, which was a spirit more sombre than sunny, more powerful than sportive, found in such traits material whence it wrought creations like Heathcliff, like Earnshaw, like Catherine. Having formed these beings, she did not know what she had done... Had she but lived, her mind would of itself have grown like a strong*

tree; loftier, straighter, wider-spreading, and its matured fruits would have attained a mellower ripeness and sunnier bloom; but on that mind time and experience alone could work: to the influence of other intellects, it was not amenable.[14]

I very much doubt that Emily would have grown older and wiser in her choice of subject, but Charlotte is trying to convince the public that Emily was young, innocent and, like all good heroines, died before she could blossom into the acceptable Victorian female.

Anne fared no better in Charlotte's disapproval of *The Tenant of Wildfell Hall*. She states that:

It likewise had an unfavourable reception. At this I cannot wonder. The choice of subject was an entire mistake. Nothing less congruous with the writer's nature could be conceived. The motives which dictated this choice were pure, but, I think, slightly morbid. She had, in the course of her life, been called on to contemplate, near at hand and for a long time, the terrible effects of talents misused and faculties abused; hers was naturally a sensitive, reserved, and dejected nature; what she saw sank very deeply into her mind; it did her harm.[15]

Charlotte continues by saying that Anne 'wanted [as in needed] the power, the fire, the originality of her sister', stating that it was her own reserve that kept her in the shade 'with a nun-like veil, which was rarely lifted'.[16]

We can accept Charlotte's descriptions of her sisters and their works or we can question why she felt it necessary to disparage their vision and their talents. Their novels had not been well received and Charlotte, I suggest, saw this as a slight against herself as much as her sisters. She was of the same stock, had intimate knowledge of her sisters and had also suffered the ignominy of a dissolute brother, whose antics had been well noted and recorded in Haworth. Charlotte must have felt that she had some explaining to do; some words that would placate the critics and help to distance herself from the offences of her siblings. She sought, therefore, to portray her sisters as lacking in awareness, country girls who had no experience of the world and the people in it. They were God-fearing, sedate young ladies who had, thankfully, died before they could cause any more harm.

I suggest that, in defending herself, Charlotte blasted both of her siblings and left a legacy that destined Emily as forever a mystic and Anne as hardly worth the trouble.

Chapter Thirteen

The Tenant of Wildfell Hall
'She Will Not Preach, She Will Exhibit'[1]

I propose that what Anne started in *Agnes Grey,* she continued and expanded in *The Tenant of Wildfell Hall.* The two books are not dissimilar in purpose although they differ greatly in content. Anne continues the theme of observing and highlighting human behaviour. She does not question it so much as identify and expose the good, the bad and the indifferent. Edward Chitham notes that:

> *Truth is her main aim, and she will construct her book in such a way as to show examples. She will not preach; she will exhibit. Wildfell Hall will not tempt her to romanticise except where romance is appropriate. On the other hand, she will not avoid romance. Helen made a terrible mistake in marrying Arthur Huntingdon, a dazzlingly handsome man, but she will correct her life by her second choice, the not always romantic Gilbert.*[2]

I agree wholeheartedly with this statement but I believe that Anne struggled with the concept of 'truth' because of its fluidity. Her close study of the Bible will have demonstrated that it is a concept that shifts and changes and is difficult to assess and is open to question. Anne searched for it and read and re-read her Bible, possibly because the truth of God, Nature and the Holy Spirit were such difficult concepts to explain and understand. As I have previously stated, 'truth' is a strange and unreliable notion that is difficult to analyse or explain. It is never the same and impossible to grasp. One can only understand it from one's own perspective.

In her second novel, written between October 1846 and April 1847, when Emily was also at work on *Wuthering Heights,* Anne uses for the most part the technique of a diary, or journal form. This allows the reader to see events both as the diarist perceived them, and as the person reading the diary interprets them. It also simultaneously allows the reader into the drama, thus permitting them to form their own opinions and conclusions about the characters and the story. It is an effective, indirect method of storytelling that abnegates the need for a narrator. It helps the reader to witness events through the eyes of those intimately involved at the time, but read with the knowledge of hindsight.

Wildfell Hall has less direct personal events than those exposed in *Agnes Grey,* but is perhaps more intimately concerned with adult male and female relationships. Anne has dealt far more with teenagers and adults whilst at Thorp Green, at home and in Scarborough, and is now more disturbed by what she has witnessed and continues to experience. This is not a book examining the problems of childhood and lazy parenting, it is one of adult behaviour and relationships that are difficult, extreme and damaging to all involved. It is the manifestation of Anne's quote that she is 'sick of mankind and their disgusting ways'.

Anne was worried. She was worried that the constant repeated pattern of amoral and dissipated behaviour, fostered in both men and women, was a cycle that many could not escape from. As Anne would know from her intimate dealings with the Bible, 'the sins of the fathers' can be passed down through the generations. The faults of each generation were being blindly and destructively repeated and Anne realised that by damaging the child, their adulthood could be ruined. This philosophy runs through the entire book and dictates the behaviour of its characters. It resembles and critiques *Wuthering Heights* in this way. As Emily demonstrates so vividly the effects of childhood on the later adult, so Anne highlights and demonstrates Heathcliff's threat to see if 'one tree can grow as twisted as another'.[3]

I have often contemplated Mark Twain's book *The Prince and The Pauper.*[4] It is an historical fiction that examines mistaken identity and questions the whole debate of nature and nurture. Are we designed from birth to grow into a particular person, or are we overtly influenced by our upbringing and circumstances? If I had been born into a wealthy, middle-class family, gone to different schools and had different friends, would I be the person I am today? I doubt it. It is back to the dilemma that we have and only can have one upbringing. All our experiences differ from person to person, even within the same family. We are each unique and therefore different from everyone else but we are the product of our experiences. *The Prince and the Pauper* questions what can happen if we are taken and 'swapped' with a person of totally different class and circumstances. We are still genetically the same person, but our whole character and beliefs, experiences and motivation are altered.

Twain lets each boy in the story walk in the other boy's shoes and appreciate the life that each has led. The Prince of Wales has to learn the lessons experienced by the least notable of his subjects and vice versa. It may be a children's story but it exposes deep philosophical questions about identity and experience. Published in Canada in 1882, it was not known to Anne, but she recognised that same questioning of 'what if'. What if young Arthur Huntingdon is left with his father's brutality and without his mother's love and affection. Anne demonstrates a line from one of her favourite poets, William Wordsworth. In his poem, 'My Heart Leaps Up' (1802) he states that: '...the child is father to the man'.[5]

This famous line has become a popular metaphor for representing how the character formed in childhood often stays and develops into adult life. This is what Aristotle predicted and is what Helen Huntingdon fears most; that her child will turn into the brute that is his father. For Helen, there is only one way to avoid that and it is to remove the child from its parent and secrete it away where the father's influence can no longer pervert the child's natural development. One is reminded here of Anne's aunt, Jane Kingston, her mother's sister, who fled her errant clergyman husband in America with only her youngest child. This act would likely have appalled some of the Branwell's neighbours and friends at Causeway Head and made Jane and her daughter's life especially difficult.

One is aware that at the time of writing her book, (1847), wives and children were the property of their husbands and fathers, and that Anne is criticising marriage, the law and the female dilemma. However, *Wildfell Hall* is not as straightforward or naive as this. Leaving her husband and removing her child from its father breaks all the rules of convention and causes the novel, and necessarily its author, to be criticised and pilloried by the reviewers. What is important though is that it also questions the question, can young Arthur escape his father's brutality just by being removed from him? He is 5 years old, he has already seen and heard enough to be influenced. He will soon be 7 and through that first important seven-year cycle. He will not necessarily want to be closeted with his mother in isolation and with only her for company and guidance. Children in this situation may well rebel against the parent who cares for them and yearn after the one that has been removed. There is an extra dilemma here and it is one that today's social workers constantly argue over. Should an abused child be removed from its home or should the abusive parent or parents be removed. Also, what constitutes abuse and when and how should it be tackled? Is more harm done removing the child from the only world that it has known and is that more harmful than the alternative.

As a nurse, I witnessed a number of cases where a child was deliberately kept with its parents because although they were loud, obnoxious and uneducated with poor parenting skills, the child was more traumatised when separated than when they were kept together. Where sexual abuse and violence is involved the outcome may need to be different, but to take a child away from its parent and home at 5 years old can create an enormous risk to their future mental and physical health, as is demonstrated in current research. One does not expect

Anne to examine this dilemma in detail, but I suggest that she is aware of the dangers. Helen does not want to remove her child but she has to make a decision that she assumes, or hopes, will be beneficial to him, and her, in the long run.

There is a realism in *Wildfell Hall* that shows people who are not all good or all bad. Arthur Huntingdon is the product of his upbringing, the same as his friends. He is the adult Tom Bloomfield from *Agnes Grey*, but Anne tries to show that even Arthur, with all his faults, can be saved through her belief in universal salvation. This is another important theme of her novel. Anne believes that no soul is so bad that it cannot repent and therefore be forgiven and enter God's grace. She believes that marriage is for life, as dictated by the Church, and therefore Helen and Arthur are reunited in some way, that saves her body and his soul.

Anne is highlighting the results of her own long struggle with sin and salvation. Her faith in God does not allow her to believe in eternal hell and damnation. All people can be saved, there is no chosen few as dictated by the Calvinists, that so oppressed her. She demonstrates in her novel the belief that as long as Arthur repents for his sins he will be saved. This philosophy is also linked to Branwell's behaviour and his family's fervent hope that despite his addictions and indulgences, he would still be accepted by God. This concept of salvation is based on love, the love of God to provide forgiveness. Anne has loved and been loved, but love is a highly emotive concept and I suggest that Anne understood this and struggled with it, as did Charlotte and Emily. They each examined love from various aspects. They wrote of love between children, between sisters, between people who are attracted but not necessarily for the right reasons. They examined romantic love and violent and aggressive love that comes with possession and the need to defend or own someone. They also dealt with that twin emotion, jealousy.

One of the most violent episodes of *Wildfell Hall* is the terrible assault on Frederick Lawrence by Gilbert Markham; possibly the most unprovoked and shocking episode in the entire novel. It is a truly awful attack; unjustified and borne of extreme jealousy. However, Anne is cleverly showing that Gilbert is not a bad man, he is a man who, at the time, could not control his emotions because love had interfered with them. No one can condone Markham's behaviour but one can recognise the triggers involved. In this scene lies the realism of Anne's work. This is human nature, 'red in tooth and claw',[6] but it is reality. This is not some white knight or handsome hero; it is a man who has fallen in love and does not know what to do about it. When he meets Lawrence on horseback after falsely believing him to be Helen's lover, he is unable to cope and lashes out in a reflex action sparked by his love, anger and jealousy.

The episode has been repeated throughout history, where two men meet and neither understands the other's nature or motivations. Markham has built up his anger against Lawrence, especially after seeing him and Helen together one evening in the garden. Lawrence is evasive and stubborn around Markham because he holds Helen's secret, which he must withhold from everyone in the neighbourhood. Markham has already had one bad encounter with Lawrence but now Lawrence's question ignites his emotions and he can contain himself no longer:

> '*Markham*', *said he, in his usual quiet tone, 'why do you quarrel with your friends, because you have been disappointed in one quarter? You have found your hopes defeated; but how am I to blame for it? I warned you beforehand, you know, but you would not...*'
> *He said no more; for, impelled by some fiend at my elbow, I had sized my whip by the small end, and – swift and sudden as a flash of lightning – brought the other down upon his head. It was not without a feeling of savage satisfaction that I beheld the instant, deadly pallor that overspread his face, and the few red drops that trickled down his forehead, while he reeled a moment in his saddle, and then fell backwards to the ground.*[7]

This act of extreme violence is by the man that Helen will finally marry and yet Anne is able to show the reason, if not the justification, for his action. I suggest that Anne is making a most important point here. People may act through ignorance and emotion and there are times when rational thinking and control are lost. Markham's behaviour is wrong and violent but it is in its unpremeditated action that we see how far his emotional state has been challenged. He is out of control and that may be a bad thing, but it happens and it does not mean that Markham cannot change his character or his actions; in fact, once he knows the truth behind Helen's story, he does just that. People often behave irrationally through a lack of understanding, a lack of self-control or when emotion overtakes reason. Whilst this episode is horrifying in its brutality it is a part of the human condition and, I suggest, it is a brave move on Anne's part to portray Markham as an ordinary man with ordinary, and therefore erratic, emotions.

It is this realism in Anne's work that I find so attractive. The reader is not handed a simple conventional man or woman; they have faults and they have problems and Anne tries to show the reader how much she hopes that bad events and extreme behaviour can be overcome. In the case of Arthur Huntingdon, he too may behave appallingly to his wife, his family and his friends, but even he can realise his faults and hopefully repent. This is Anne's message in her novels; you may have had an upbringing that twisted your view of the world and made you obnoxious, even evil, but as an adult you have choices and therefore whilst upbringing may have forged your character you can change and you can work for the good of others rather than your own self-indulgence and lack of empathy.

One saw this issue especially in Heathcliff – an orphan who was used and abused at *Wuthering Heights* and then chose revenge rather than forgiveness. I have always sympathised with Heathcliff as the child, but far less as the man, because he had a choice. He was bitter and angry, and one could argue, rightly so. However, his own actions were as bad, if not worse, than those of his enemies and so he, as an adult, chose his future and it did nothing to gain him happiness or fulfilment. The same applies to Arthur Huntingdon. He knows that he is abusing his wife and child and he does so without compunction. He chooses not to be kind even though he has the wealth and authority to give them everything they need.

Whilst I have advocated throughout that we are to a great extent the result of our upbringing, what I also wish to emphasise is that as adults, most people have choices and the knowledge to know the difference between right and wrong. However, another philosophy emerges because right and wrong only apply in the circumstances in which one is involved.

The terms right and wrong, good and evil, are all relative to time and environment, law and religion, culture and society. Helen Huntingdon is 'wrong' to leave her husband because the law says so. That does not mean that she is morally wrong or that she has taken the wrong decision. In her case it is the patriarchal society, the law and the religious marriage vows that dictate her position. She is the 'fallen woman' because she has stepped outside of their rules.

Moral law is something that is perhaps a personal understanding of our relationship with others. Those brought up, as Anne was, in Christian faith believed that you should 'do to others what you would have them do to you' as instructed in the book of Matthew 7:12. Most of us are brought up not to fight, not to be abusive and to treat others with respect and kindness. Other religions or cultures may tell their followers to strike their enemies, and fight for lands and possessions, the results of which we see daily through modern media. One can only abide by the rules of the particular society in which one finds oneself. We may applaud Helen Huntingdon from the viewpoint of women in the twentieth and twenty-first centuries for 'slamming her bedroom door', against her husband and champion her for her feminist actions and her protection of her son, but in another time and another place, who can say that she did the right thing or the best thing?

The Tenant of Wildfell Hall

If Helen had not met Markham what would her life, and that of her son, have been like? Anne is saying that Helen felt it morally right to leave her husband to protect her son, and I would endorse that, because Anne shows us that the outcome of rearing a child amongst abuse and violence can have dire repercussions. Anne has obviously thought about this in some depth because her religion gave her a firm belief in the importance of caring for others. Helen may have left her husband but she does not totally abandon him. She sacrifices herself to save her son in a move that condemned her and was against the religious laws of marriage. This was an enormous criticism against both the religious and criminal law of the time. Yet, Anne has insight into the importance of childhood security and love and was acutely aware of how easily the progress of the child could be interrupted and destroyed.

This is linked to Anne's belief in education and religion as the key to the moral guidance of a child and its life as an adult. By education, I suggest, not just that dictated by art and book learning, school and tutors, but education also as life experiences. Unfortunately, Anne's childhood did not include a great deal of life experience. It is perhaps why she was so affected by the people she met when she went out to work. She had, by any standards, a sheltered upbringing augmented by her role as the youngest child. There was plenty of book learning and academic and artistic skills but not a great deal of social interaction and outside friendships. I suspect that when Anne let Helen Huntingdon leave and take her child with her, she was reflecting some of her own childhood and believed that young Arthur would be protected and sheltered in the same way. My point is that this is a fault that can only be rectified by giving Helen friends and acquaintances with whom the child can also be involved. One may recall that one of the obstacles between Helen and her husband arose when he wanted to appoint a governess for the boy, not an unreasonable idea at the time, except that the governess he proposed was his mistress. Anne is cleverly demonstrating how insidious Arthur Huntingdon's manipulation of his wife had become. Helen could not win.

Helen is a mother who doesn't have the love and care of her husband and possibly transfers her affections doubly onto her child. That is good and reasonable whilst he is young, but one wonders how she will manage him when he begins to question her and her motives and wants to make decisions of his own. It is the dilemma of many parents and I do not have the answers. Do children need some 'healthy neglect' – chances to fail, experiences that hurt and upset, but help them to cope? Young Arthur has been exposed to good and bad parenting which has demonstrated extremes rather than a settled and balanced perspective. Will that affect him adversely in the future, or will it demonstrate to him how he should behave if he is to avoid conflict and aggression in adulthood.

I do not intend to fill this book with a diatribe on child psychology or to question too much the rights and wrongs of child-rearing. Every parent has different views and ideas. I have witnessed some appalling lack of child care and also some extensive over indulgence. It is the overindulgence of characters like Arthur Huntingdon and his friends that is the root of their obnoxious behaviour. Helen examines her husband's childhood and the effect of his parents on him. She states that:

> *I lay them both to the charge of his harsh yet careless father and his madly indulgent mother. If ever I am a mother, I will zealously strive against this crime of over indulgence – I can hardly give it a milder name when I think of the evils it brings.*[8]

Whether under or over indulged, both appear to me to be almost as bad as each other. Children do not benefit from either course. However, later in her novel, Anne has Helen record how Arthur, turning from being unable to love his son is now, regrettably, noticing him. Here Anne very astutely describes Helen's fears:

> *He has won his father's heart at last; and now my constant terror is, lest he should be ruined by that father's thoughtless indulgence. But, I must be aware of my own weakness too, for I never knew till now how strong are a parent's temptations to spoil an only child.*[9]

As a mother, I also know and appreciate how difficult it is to love your children unconditionally and yet not overindulge them, and also to let them make mistakes and do things of which you may disapprove. I am also old enough to appreciate the vast changes in child care during my own lifetime. The differences between my childhood, compared to that of my children, grandchildren and great grandchildren, are quite astonishing. That is, I understand, that the world has changed enormously and nothing can stay the same. We rear our children according to our circumstances and our beliefs, at any given time, but it is still a minefield of problems and one can only hope that you have given your child enough education and experience for them to develop into happy and fulfilled adults, always bearing in mind that you also want them to think for themselves and make their own choices. A difficult balancing act, if not an impossible task! No easier now than it has ever been so.

Anne appears to have been the most likely of the Brontës to want children of her own. In *Wildfell Hall* this is perhaps Anne's blind spot. She wants, rather like Helen Huntingdon, the ideal child. She expresses the idea that as long as the child has its mother to love it and care for it, all will be well, a reflection perhaps of her own lost mother-love. She is partly right, but reality is a great deal more complicated. Getting rid of a 'bad' father, or mother, does not necessarily bode well for the child. One can argue that the balance of both is often of most benefit but then many single-parent families, my own included, raise happy and healthy children. It is surely better to have one good and caring parent than two warring ones. Or is it!

There are many instances in Anne's novels that relate to child care and how things taught and witnessed by children affect their later lives. I do not intend to quote reams of examples; these books are there to be read. My purpose is to show that Anne's own childhood and development were overshadowed by her family and also that it was something that she realised and worked through in her writing. Furthermore, the longing of unrequited love could also include that of an unborn child. In Anne's case, someone she could have loved and be loved by, unconditionally.

It is impossible to know how well the Brontë children lived and worked within the parsonage and how each of them viewed their upbringing. My siblings have very divided views on our childhood, each with a very different perspective. After the death of his wife, Patrick had choices. Apart from remarriage or embracing his sister-in-law as a mother substitute, Patrick could have separated his children to live amongst his and Maria's many relatives in Ireland and Cornwall. I suspect that Patrick would possibly have kept Maria, Branwell and Anne, but that the other three could have gone to live with their many aunts and uncles and numerous cousins. Hindsight is a wonderful thing but what a life Branwell could have had in Cornwall, or Emily in the wilds of Northern Ireland! Would they have thrived and lived longer? Maria and Elizabeth almost certainly would have. It is of course impossible to know and Patrick is to be commended for keeping his young family together against all the odds. Interesting to speculate though!

I suggest that the Brontë siblings were, to some extent, a single parent family. Aunt Elizabeth seems to have been closer to Anne and Branwell than the others, but she cannot have been expected to love her sister's children as a mother, although she may well have tried to do so, especially with the youngest child and the only boy. Their parent was always Patrick, and, as stated, he was a very busy minister with a huge parish to govern and a limited income from which to pay for six growing children.

Patrick certainly did his best by them with regard to their education and artistic flares. Unfortunately, we have no way of knowing if he was a particularly doting father after they reached adulthood. I am sure that he loved them, even if the times dictated that there was a lack of demonstrative affection. He mentions them in his letters, interacts with them in their childhood and grieves for their loss. There are times, however, when one wonders how things could occur in the house that he seemed to know so little about. Was he really unaware that Charlotte had written a novel? Where was he when Emily and Anne died? How much aid and guidance did he give to his son and why did he not realise that, as a teenager, Branwell needed the experience and friendship of boys his own age? Why did he indulge Charlotte's whim to go to Brussels? There are many instances when he seems to have lost the ability to understand, or even attend to his children. Was it his age, illness or an overwhelming sense of faith in God to guide his children once they were adults. I wonder how much he approved of or encouraged Anne, living away from home for six years in a job she disliked. How much communication was there between Patrick and his adult children? We cannot know how much each child interacted with their father or what their feelings were towards him. Charlotte appears to have behaved almost as a wife after the death of her aunt. She indulged her father and protected him as much as she could. She also influenced him disproportionately to the others. Charlotte had acted so long as a channel between her siblings and their father and aunt, that after her aunt's death she appears to have taken sole charge of Patrick, possibly in a way that the others may have resented. Charlotte reports in her letters over and again of her father's delicate health and yet he was the one who lived to be 84, surviving his entire family.

One wonders just what the relationship really was between Charlotte and her father. Some saw him as aggressive, dominating and strict; a man who expected his eldest daughter to take care of him to the end of his life and never to marry. Others saw him as a benevolent and interested father, who loved and admired all of his children. When she became the last surviving child, did Patrick abuse her need to care for him and his need for her attention? Or was it the other way round? Perhaps at different times they each took the dominant role. Theirs was a difficult and emotionally charged relationship that seems to have left neither of them happy and contented. Love can be a very difficult emotion, especially at a time when people were not expected to openly state or express their feelings or demonstrate physical closeness.

Unfortunately, during her siblings' lifetimes, Charlotte appears to have built, possibly without meaning to, a barrier between her father and her siblings. Charlotte wants to look after everybody in her family, but she does it through tyranny rather than explanation and consideration. She is in charge and she knows what is best for everyone. This self-inflicted burden makes Charlotte frequently ill herself. She is a highly talented and intelligent woman who appears to have taken on everything in the lives of her family as her own dilemma. She wears herself out worrying about them all but often fails to empathise with their actual fears and needs and creates a lack of communication and understanding that separates her from them all.

This lack of understanding has meant that Anne, throughout the decades, has been denigrated and maligned because Charlotte failed to acknowledge her talents and even attempted to alter or belittle them. Anne was always the youngest and least important for Charlotte, and, as explained, there were reasons for this. Anne was her aunt's favourite niece and this would cause resentment. Anne was cosseted by her father, causing jealousy, Anne was described as the 'prettiest' of the siblings and Charlotte was very aware of her own lack of attractiveness. Anne may have received special attention from William Weightman and it is possible that Charlotte had aspirations on him for herself. Anne was able to form a special bond with Emily, a liaison that Charlotte had had with Emily when they were younger. Emily was the sister that Charlotte most identified with and possibly resented Emily's later close relationship with Anne. Anne had chronic asthma; a visible illness that attracted assistance and sympathy unlike many of Charlotte's continual aches and pains, sickness and fatigue. Anne succeeded as a governess where Charlotte failed miserably. Anne was able to empathise with her brother and keep a semblance of affection. Charlotte dismissed Branwell out of her life as not worth the time or trouble, but this probably hurt her deeply. As the eldest sibling Charlotte had control, especially over the youngest, who could never have her 'age and experience' but there was no doubt a degree of jealousy and resentment.

These are some of the reasons why I believe that Anne did not attract enough sisterly attention from Charlotte and why, when Anne presented her poems to her, Charlotte had little to say by way of praise. Yet, Anne's poetry and hymns are exceptional. They are similar to those of Charlotte and Emily, but have their own music and special choice of language. I suggest that Charlotte always wanted to align herself with Emily and was shocked and disappointed by *Wuthering Heights*. Knowing that Emily could write such amazing poetry, she expected a book far more in keeping with her own novels. *Agnes Grey* barely attracted her attention as being too ordinary and of a subject which Charlotte disliked.

Charlotte wrote to her publisher, W. S. Williams, after he had read her sisters' first two novels, written under their pseudonyms of Ellis and Acton Bell, saying that he was right in his judgment of them and that: 'Ellis will improve, however, because he knows his defects. "*Agnes Grey*" is the mirror of the mind of the writer'.[10]

Dr Chitham reminds us how Charlotte is the spokesperson for the Brontës and Mrs Gaskell speaks through Charlotte. Therefore, Emily, Anne and Branwell have been memorialised only as Charlotte intended and their writing is described and accepted, or rejected, according to Charlotte's taste and discretion. Again, Graham Watson's recent book, *The Invention of Charlotte Bronte*, investigates the portrayal of Charlotte by Mrs Gaskell based on the many letters and interviews she gained access to for the writing of her biography. Recent books have challenged the long accepted lives and myths of the Bronte family and it all appears to be a mixture of truth, lies and conjecture.

A look at Anne's novels and poetry show that Emily and Anne were at least equal to Charlotte and should be acknowledged as such. It is sad that for many years, readers and critics were so swayed by the two biased narrators of the Brontë story; Charlotte had her own reasons for describing her family as she wanted others to see them, and Mrs Gaskell was a novelist who added to Charlotte's tale, and the opinions of others, with her own embellishments.

Perhaps the best way to 'see and understand' Anne Brontë is to examine her poetry and hymns. Her verses can be very personal and give an insight into Anne's thoughts and feelings, even when they are 'Gondal' related. It is perhaps the door to a gainful insight into the life and thoughts of Anne, not known or acknowledged by many readers of her novels. The following is one of her most famous poems/hymns. Here are the first four verses.

The Narrow Way

Believe not those who say
The upward path is smooth.
Lest though should stumble in the way,
And faint before the truth.

It is the only road
Unto the realms of joy;
But he who seeks the blest abode
Must all his powers employ.

Bright hopes and pure delights
Upon his course may beam,
And there amidst the sternest heights,
The sweetest flowerets glean;-

On all the breezes borne,
Earth yields no scents like those;
But he, that dares not grasp the thorn
Should never crave the rose.[11]

Chapter Fourteen

The Final Separation

After the publication of her two novels, in 1847 and 1848, Anne may have been disappointed with some of the reviews, but there were a few months when there was speculation and excitement about becoming authors. However, suggestions that the 'Bell Brothers' may be one and the same person was especially galling to Charlotte who had already begun to distance herself from her sisters' works. Furthermore, she thought that in a letter from her publishers, Smith & Elder, there was a suggestion that she may have hoodwinked them. This was more than Charlotte could tolerate. She was determined to prove that the 'Bells' were three separate writers. With extreme fear and trepidation that she was being thought of as devious and underhand, Charlotte insisted that they all travel immediately to London and prove that they were three separate authors and that there had been no subterfuge. Emily refused to go; she had no desire to leave home for any reason. So Charlotte commandeered Anne and the two set off within hours to visit London and their two publishers.

Again, we have only Charlotte's version of events. She described the difficult journey, the confrontations and the whirl of social activities organised by George Smith. All this left the sisters exhausted and it is possible, though not provable, that it was on this trip that both women were exposed to the Tuberculosis virus and returned home with it, possibly infecting Branwell and Emily. Both brother and sister succumbed to the disease within a few months and by Christmas, Anne was also showing the signs and symptoms that heralded the last few months of her life.

This mad dash to London demonstrates Charlotte's personality and her fear of offending her new London acquaintances. Charlotte had become a snob. She was the highly successful author of the current number one bestseller, but, significantly, she had an undoubtable fear; she was mortified to think that she may be accused of also writing her sisters' novels. Charlotte had very little faith in her sisters' books and agreed with many of the critics who found them coarse and unfit for an unsuspecting reading public. I suggest that it was this that spurred Charlotte into making such agitated haste to reach London and confront her publisher. In a letter to Mary Taylor at the beginning of September, Charlotte described how:

> *It was on the very day I received Smith & Elder's letter – Ann and I packed up a small box, sent it down to Keighley – set out ourselves after tea – walked through a thunderstorm to the station, got to Leeds and whirled up on the Night train to London – with the view of proving our separate identity to Smith & Elder and confronting Newby with his lie.*[1]

Whilst it makes a wonderful episode in her publisher's history and echoes a scene from a novel, the sudden arrival of Charlotte and Anne at the offices of Smith & Elder; two small, plainly clad and demur young ladies with no appointment or invitation, has added to the myths and tales of the Brontë's publishing debuts.

George Smith (junior) the son of the co-founder of the firm, was, naturally, stunned to discover that the Miss Brontë, to whom he had been directing his letters, was in fact Currer Bell. He instantly arranged various social gatherings and events for the two women which overwhelmed and exhausted them. We do not have any record from Anne of what she saw and felt, only Charlotte's description of the whirl of visits that left her with a severe headache and sickness. One suspects that Charlotte suffered from migraines from her numerous reports of sick headaches, especially when excited or under stress. Before leaving the publisher's offices, the gentlemen were all sworn to keep the identity of the 'Bell Brothers', a continuing secret. Charlotte and Anne also visited Thomas Newby, to scotch the rumour that he had probably started. Unfortunately, Charlotte did not record that meeting and Anne, whilst directly involved with Newby, left no written evidence.

During their visit to London, Mr Smith took the sisters to the Opera House to see a performance of Rossini's, *The Barber of Seville.* How must these two plain little country women have felt as they climbed the 'crimson carpeted staircase' amongst the glitterati of London's rich and famous? Charlotte recorded the 'supercilious looks' they received whilst aware that every one of them would have been delighted to be introduced to the author of *Jane Eyre.* The drama of meeting her publishers is a wonderful episode in the Brontë story, beautifully portrayed in Sally Shuttleworth's excellent film, *To Walk Invisible.*

Unfortunately, the next few months were some of the worst times for everyone in the Brontë household. Three weeks after Charlotte was writing to Mary Taylor about their sudden dash to London, Branwell was dead. This followed months of heartbreak, alcohol and opiate addiction and a severe attack of Tuberculosis. How much the alleged 'affair' with Mrs Robinson contributed to Branwell's death is difficult to ascertain. Branwell had been declining slowly for at least eighteen months, almost imperceptibly, masked by his continual presentation of moroseness and hangover, bad-temper and sickness. One supposes that it was his continual appeals for money and his aggressive behaviour that alienated him from the three sisters who would otherwise have taken better care of him. We are aware that Charlotte had given up on him a long time ago but there is little evidence that Emily or Anne were of any help. It's possible that Emily, being taller and stronger, could deal with her brother physically, but whether she or Anne offered him care and affection is unknown. One hopes that they did as by the time of his death all of his father's efforts had been in vain. Branwell's death was sudden and unexpected despite his emaciation and sickness, but the shock that followed was soon displaced by fears that Emily too, was suddenly and dramatically dying of Tuberculosis. The tell-tale signs of cough, shortness of breath and loss of weight were rapid and Emily died only weeks after her brother. The death cycle had again entered the household and as Emily died, the remaining family and servants looked to Anne and saw the same shadow fall across her. Charlotte wrote that after Branwell's death the house was a place of sickness for many months.

As the familiar symptoms began to take hold of Anne, Patrick called for specialist medical assistance and on 5 January 1849, the Leeds physician, Dr Teale, called at the parsonage to examine Anne and offer his clinical opinion. Ellen Nussey was staying there at the time, and she, Anne and Charlotte were all in the parlour. Ellen recorded the event saying that:

> *Mr Brontë joined us after Dr Teale's departure and, seating himself on the couch, he drew Anne to him and said, 'My dear little Anne'. That was all – but it was understood.*[2]

It is here that I offer my greatest criticism of Charlotte as a sister. She had just lost Emily, the sister of whom she later stated that:

> *I could hardly let Emily go – I wanted to hold her back then – and I want to hold her back hourly now.*[3]

The doctor has visited and given his prognosis; Anne was terminally ill. However, Charlotte displays odd behaviour over the last few months of Anne's life which I find both strange and at times, quite astounding. Anne needed help and support from her father and sister more than ever before, and yet Charlotte seemed determined to put obstacles in Anne's way which deeply distressed her dying sister and added to her trauma.

I first visited Anne Brontë's grave, high above the town of Scarborough, North Yorkshire, over fifty years ago. *Paradise* was the name given to the monks' burial ground and walled garden. St Mary's Church, the Anglican parish church of Scarborough, also stands on the former grounds. Anne is buried in its graveyard close to the wall, beside the road that leads up to Scarborough Castle. It is a lovely spot, visited by thousands of people every year. It's headstone, purchased by Charlotte soon after Anne's death, is now worn and barely readable. The Brontë Society placed a slate plaque on the grave some years ago recording Anne's details.

As stated, what puzzled me all those years ago was why Anne was buried there and not with her family in the vault designated to them in Haworth's St Michael's Church. It has taken me years of research to discover what I believe to be the answer. Anne Brontë was the youngest of the Brontë children and was permanently dominated by her siblings. When she became ill towards the end of 1848 only Charlotte was still alive and, as she always had, Charlotte made many of the decisions as to how, where and when, Anne would spend her final months.

Having lost her mother, aunt, brother and three sisters during her lifetime, one would expect that Charlotte would closely assist and cherish her last remaining sibling and, in some ways, one can argue that she did. However, Charlotte was compromised. She had taken it upon herself to protect and support her father for many years as the eldest of his surviving children. Her father's dependency on her and her younger siblings lack of her knowledge and superiority, allowed Charlotte to continue to dictate and manipulate. Charlotte took to the nursing of Anne with enthusiasm and close attention, but I would argue that it was with her usual assumption that she was always right and had to make all of the decisions regarding her care, thus giving Anne little chance to direct her own illness. As a former nurse working at times in both hospitals and a hospice, I can only stress the importance of allowing patients, especially those needing end of life care, to have as much control and input into their treatment as possible. It is an essential part of palliative care.

When Anne received her diagnosis and prognosis on that fateful day in January, it was well known and understood that Tuberculosis was a fatal disease but that it could be alleviated and life prolonged in some measure, if the victim was able to spend time in the open air, away from smoke and the disease and dirt of manufacturing and its by-products. This would ideally be in a warm climate by the sea. Because of the time of the year, it was not seen as advisable for Anne to go to the coast in the first few weeks of her illness. However, as the year progressed Anne began to make plans to travel before she became too incapacitated. She was realistic enough to know that there was no cure, but she was looking for some relief and a possible remission from the inevitable.

It was around this time and following her visit from Dr Teale that Anne wrote her most poignant verses, expressing her horror of death and suffering but then accepting that if this was God's will then she would go to join her mother and siblings in the knowledge that they would all be reunited. Her poem is offered here in its entirety. Ironically, it was Charlotte who gave it its title, after Anne's death. The poem begins with Anne's fears and anxiety as she tries to face the fact that she is going to die.

Last Lines

I hoped, that with the brave and strong,
My portioned task might lie;
To toil amid the busy throng,
With purpose pure and high.

But God has fixed another part,
And He has fixed it well;
I said so with my bleeding heart,
When first the anguish fell.

A dreadful darkness closes in
On my bewildered mind;
Oh, let me suffer and not sin,
Be tortured, yet resigned.

Shall I with joy thy blessings share
And not endure their loss?
Or hope the martyrs crown to wear
And cast away the cross?

Thou, God, hast taken our delight,
Our treasured hope away;
Thou bidst us now weep through the night
And sorrow through the day.

These weary hours will not be lost,
These days of misery,
These nights of darkness, anguish-tost,
Can I but turn to thee.

Weak and weary though I lie,
Crushed with sorrow, worn with pain,
I may lift to Heaven mine eye,
And strive to labour not in vain;

The Brontë Family: Sibling Rivalry and a Burial in Paradise

> *That inward strife against the sins*
> *That ever wait on suffering*
> *To strike whatever first begins:*
> *Each ill that would corruption bring;*
>
> *That secret labour to sustain*
> *With humble patience every blow;*
> *To gather fortitude from pain,*
> *And hope and holiness from woe.*
>
> *Thus let me serve Thee from my heart,*
> *Whate'er may be my written fate:*
> *Whether thus early to depart,*
> *Or yet a while to wait.*
>
> *If thou shouldst bring me back to life,*
> *More humbled I should be;*
> *More wise, more strengthened for the strife,*
> *More apt to lean on Thee.*
>
> *Should death be standing at the gate,*
> *Thus should I keep my vow;*
> *But, Lord! Whatever be my fate,*
> *Oh, let me serve Thee now!* [4]

Here Anne is pleading with God to let her have some time; time to do more and be more. To that end, Anne is looking to go anywhere that will alleviate her symptoms. By April, Anne is desperate to go to any seaside place that will offer the fresh and bracing air that will assist her breathing. Shut up in the cold winter parsonage amongst the worst of the weather, Anne had no relief from her pain and suffering.

A kind offer came from Ellen Nussey for Anne to spend a couple of weeks at her home in Birstall to relieve Charlotte of her nursing duties. Anne was loathe to impose herself on the Nussey family, but suggested to Charlotte that she ask Ellen to accompany her to the seaside instead. Charlotte was appalled that such an imposition be made on her friend. Charlotte actually wrote to Ellen telling her that she must make excuses to Anne. Ellen did just that blaming the weather as a reason to delay and suggesting that June or July would be a better time '*and would also suit Ellen better.*'

Anne was frustrated and becoming nervous that time was running out. She wrote to Ellen herself countering some of the arguments that had been offered. Anne wrote in this, her last letter:

The Final Separation

I hope I should not be very troublesome. It would be as a companion not as a nurse that I should wish for your company; otherwise, I should not venture to ask it... You say that May is a trying month but according to my experience, we are almost certain of some fine warm days in the latter half ... the doctors say that change of air or removal to a better climate would hardly ever fail of success in consumptive cases if the remedy were taken in time... though I suffer much less from pain and fever than I did when you were with us, I am decidedly weaker and very much thinner my cough still troubles me a good deal, especially at night, and, what seems worse than all, I am subject to great shortness of breath on going up stairs or any slight exertion. Under these circumstances I think there is no time to be lost.[5]

Anne is asking in plain English to be taken to the coast as soon as possible, but once again, Charlotte interferes. One notes here a heartbreaking display of the elder sibling who assumes that she is the wisest person and in control of everything and everyone in the household. Charlotte repeatedly used the excuse of not being able to leave Patrick as a reason not to accompany Anne, and yet Patrick had two servants, Tabby and Martha, and his curate, Arthur Nicholls; surely more than enough people for his needs. One wonders why Patrick also did nothing to overrule Charlotte. Perhaps years of her domineering had left him under her direction in almost all issues to do with the family.

As time passed and there was still no sign of a holiday, Charlotte consulted Dr Teale again in an effort to show Anne that it would still be unwise. However, on this occasion the doctor recommended a change of air and Charlotte's efforts to keep Anne at home were thwarted. Patrick finally declared that he could manage without Charlotte's assistance, something he could have done weeks earlier. With all opposition now removed, Charlotte began to slowly make arrangements for their departure.

Whilst I criticise Charlotte over this reluctance to move Anne, I do recognise that she was probably acting under her usual manner of trying to both protect and dominate her sister. Anne was dying and it may have seemed natural and kind to let her do so quietly and undisturbed at home. However, the fact that Anne was so keen to go and so hopeful of a remission in her symptoms should, I suggest, have taken priority.

Charlotte and Ellen finally accompanied Anne to Scarborough, setting out on Thursday, 24 May 1849. They had, as we know, due to various prevarications, left the whole venture far too late. Anne had been too ill to travel on the 23rd, but on the evening of 24 May the three women stayed overnight in York. They even embarked on a shopping trip in the city, which seems rather odd and out of character. Anne had received a gift of £200 from her godmother, Fanny Outhwaite, following her death in February, and it was this money that funded the venture to Scarborough and the shopping trip. This legacy is an issue because it not only paid for the trip, but also gave Charlotte the means to fund Anne's funeral and burial and Charlotte's continued stay on the east coast.

On 27 May, the day after their arrival at Wood's Lodgings in Scarborough, Anne took a turn for the worse and '*asked if it were possible to return home.*' Charlotte decided not. Again, on the actual day she died, at around 11.00 a.m., Ellen Nussey records that Anne again asked if it was possible to go home, 'if we prepared at once' (Ellen Nussey's Diary).[6] A mere three hours later Anne was dead.

I wish to make a few important points here. At no time did Anne request to be buried in Scarborough and she made no will. If it had been her intention she would surely have left instructions to that effect. Anne specifically asked, *twice*, if they could return home and it was denied. Surely, it is natural that Anne would want to be buried with her mother, aunt and sisters in St Michael's Church, Haworth, in the vault that was specifically designated for the family's use. Everything and everyone Anne valued and loved were in Haworth – her father, the servants, her pets and her belongings. If she had been in love with William Weightman, he too was buried in the church. As Adelle Hey pointedly reminds us: 'Anne did not go to Scarborough to die, but for a change of scenery'.[7]

Charlotte and Ellen both claimed that Charlotte chose to 'lay the flower where it fell' but was that Anne's wish? Anne had enjoyed summer holidays in Scarborough when working for the Robinsons, but holidaying somewhere and wanting to be buried there are two very different things. The majority of us now holiday abroad or in favourite places in Britain, but most people want to be buried with or near their families, not in some 'foreign' place. Anne wrote repeatedly of her home and the moors and this was surely where she wanted to remain.

I have issues also with Anne's death scene, as reported by Ellen and Charlotte. Earlier that day Ellen had actually tried to carry Anne down the stairs from their room to the breakfast parlour. It proved an ill-fated attempt which left both Anne and Ellen traumatised. Ellen referred to it years later and it was obviously a scene that had stayed with her. When Anne was returned to their room and laid on the couch she rapidly deteriorated and died a few hours later. Both of her carers describe her death as calm, quiet and uneventful. Charlotte stated that she was happy to let Anne go to God as she felt that he had a right to her.

As I have explained, Tuberculosis is not a disease from which one dies with a sigh and a peaceful sleep, unless you have been treated with drugs such as morphine, to render you relaxed and then unconscious. As previously described, the symptoms of Tuberculosis are horrible and worsen as the victim deteriorates. They include acute shortness of breath, extreme emaciation, anorexia, haemoptysis (coughing up blood) and acute and chronic pain. Anne will have had little or no pain relief and would have found it almost impossible to breath. The doctor who visited that day may have administered laudanum but it would not be enough to relieve her symptoms to any great effect. Descriptions of the deaths of both Branwell and Emily are far more dramatic and there is the sense of suffering and being 'torn from life'. Anne's death scene is described in the terms of a Victorian novel, where the brave victim calmly turns her face to the wall and causes her carers no trouble whatsoever.

I can only speculate, but I suspect that Anne's death was not as calm and peaceful as Charlotte and Ellen maintained. It could well be the case that they were hoping to spare Patrick the heartbreak of Anne's suffering. Anne may well have told her sister to 'take courage' but I suspect that it was earlier during their stay and when Anne was able to talk between rapidly losing her breath.

Charlotte's attempt to sanitise and underplay Anne's death took a further turn when she arranged, with unseemly haste, her funeral and burial in Scarborough. It is sad to note that Patrick received notice of his daughter's death, two days after the event, on the day that she was buried.[8] I consider this a rather cynical *fait accompli*. It was explained away in the words of Ellen who, in a letter to Mrs Ward, the owner of the lodging house, wrote:

> *Miss Brontë thinks it right to spare her father the misery of another internment so soon after the two previous ones.*[9]

I suspect that her father would have been far happier to have his children laid to rest all in the same place, where he could mourn them in his church; his spiritual home.

Why Charlotte chose to have Anne buried in Scarborough is difficult to determine. The cost of burying Anne in Scarborough – the funeral, the service at Christ Church (where Anne had worshipped) the cortège to St Mary's church (which was undergoing repairs) and the grave, were all avoidable expenses. So too was the subsequent headstone. Charlotte had Anne's money and perhaps she thought that it would be fitting to spend it in this way. However, the cost of transporting Anne back to Haworth would have been much less and satisfied everyone involved. Furthermore, Charlotte could have then stayed to support her grieving father.

In the event, Charlotte did the opposite and instead of returning home to the father that she had previously been so determined not to leave, she abandoned him and spent the next three weeks on the Yorkshire Coast, visiting Filey and Bridlington.

Whilst I understand that grief is an awful affliction and that the thought of returning to the empty parsonage, bereft of all of her siblings, would have been very hard for Charlotte, she knew that it had to be done and also that at this time her father really did need her comforting presence. Juliet Barker mentions that in a letter to her publisher, Charlotte states that her father ordered her to stay on the coast. However, Charlotte states only that she is 'ordered', to stay away in her letter to Williams, but does not state by whom. It could just as easily have been Ellen, anxious to stay and give her friend support in her grief.

I think that Charlotte regretted her hasty actions at a later date, but she wrote her explanation to Mr William Smith, the reader at Smith & Elder, about a fortnight after Anne's death stating that:

I have buried her in Scarborough to save Papa the anguish of the return and a third funeral... He and the servants knew that when they parted from Anne they would see her no more. All tried to be resigned. I knew it likewise, and I wanted her to die where she would be happiest. She loved Scarborough. A peaceful sun gilded her evening.[10]

I am not happy with Charlotte's explanation for a number of reasons. Firstly, the costs involved; secondly, she did not go home to her father despite knowing how heartbroken he must have felt. Thirdly, Anne did not expect to die in Scarborough and left no instructions to be buried there. Fourthly, Charlotte loved being alone with Ellen away from home and she would have had to send Ellen away if she returned to Haworth. Fifthly, Charlotte must have known that her father would want the family buried together and that this was probably Anne's wish also. As explained, Anne may have greatly enjoyed her stays at Scarborough but she was working there and not there by choice. Sixthly, it is important to remember that Anne asked, possibly twice, if they could go home as Edward Chitham states from Ellen Nussey's diary. Lastly, the last line of this letter is again a flowery addition that suggests to me that Charlotte was trying to comfort herself and reassure herself that she had done the right thing. It rings of the myth that she ventured out as Emily lay dying and found a sprig of heather on the moors ... in December! Furthermore, there has NEVER been a sun set over the north-east facing town of Scarborough, ever! Again, Charlotte seems to be intent on describing Anne's death as a calm and peaceful letting go into God's care. She wrote to Martha Brown that:

She died very calmly and gently – she was quite sensible to the last – about three minutes before she died she said she was very happy and believed she was passing out of Earth into Heaven.[11]

The Final Separation

I cannot help thinking that Charlotte, and Ellen who was forever influenced and dominated by Charlotte, were trying to convince themselves and others and that it helped to justify the Scarborough burial. These two women were the only witnesses to Anne's demise and had reasons to describe her death in these terms. Both Charlotte and Ellen had prevented Anne's early removal to Scarborough and had contrived to delay her final departure to the coast. Was this Charlotte's way of saying, subconsciously or otherwise, 'I said that you shouldn't have come here. You should have stayed at home'. Or worse: 'You begged to come and have caused all of this upset, so now you can stay here'. My theory cannot be proved or tested, but I feel that it is open to discussion.

As I have stated, I feel that Anne was forever at the mercy of her siblings, especially Charlotte, in death, as in life. The only area that Charlotte had been unable to influence Anne was in her writing. Unfortunately, after her death, Charlotte took control of Anne and Emily's works and altered and interfered with some of the wording. Being unable to alter the text of the first two editions of *Wildfell Hall*, Charlotte actually banned a third edition. This caused an endless problem that is still felt today. Samantha Ellis describes how in 1854:

> ... *a publishing house called Thomas Hodgson brought out a fly-by-night edition of Anne's second novel. They wanted it to be cheap, to squeeze in one volume, so they cut it up to fit. After Charlotte died in 1856, her publishers wanted to bring out their own edition of The Tenant of Wildfell Hall. Not knowing any different, they used Hodgson's hacked-about text. Over a century later, it is usually the one reprinted. There are better versions – the best, I think, is the 1966 one edited by Stevie Davies. But the mutilated editions are still everywhere.*[12]

As the only surviving child, Charlotte had *carte blanche* to do whatsoever she wished with her sisters' belongings, and these included their writings, letters and verses. Emily had told her publisher that she was writing her second novel. What happened to it? Where did all the thousands of words of the 'Gondal Saga' go? Where are all of the diary papers and letters that Emily and Anne wrote to each other? Anne did not intend to die at Scarborough so she is hardly likely to have destroyed her papers before she left.

I think that we have to examine again Charlotte's damming 1850 'Biographical Notice of Ellis and Acton Bell' in her preface to the second edition of *Wuthering Heights* for some of the answers. We know that Charlotte disapproved of her sisters' novels and she begins her preface by again disclaiming the idea that the Brontë novels were all by the same person. She further states that in childhood they shared their writings and showed each other what each had written. However, she later claims that 'but of late years this habit of communication and consultation had been discontinued'.[13]

I suggest that she is again distancing herself and stating that she was ignorant of the content of her sisters' writing and unable to advise them to do things differently. (The ever-elder sister who knows best.) She goes on to describe how her sisters' novels, when finally published, were not critically acclaimed, unlike her own, *Jane Eyre*. Charlotte says that:

> *Critics failed to do them justice. The immature but very real powers revealed in 'Wuthering Heights' were scarcely recognised; its import and nature were misunderstood; the identity of its author was misrepresented; it was said that this was an earlier and ruder attempt of the same pen that which had produced 'Jane Eyre'. Unjust and grievous error!*[14]

She goes on to say that *The Tenant of Wildfell Hall* had also an unfavourable reception and then goes on to agree with the critics, saying:

> *At this I cannot wonder. The choice of subject was an entire mistake. Nothing less congruous with the writer's nature could be conceived ... she had, in the course of her life, been called on to contemplate, near at hand, and for a long time, the terrible effects of talents misused and faculties abused; hers was naturally a sensitive, reserved and dejected nature; what she saw sank very deeply into her mind; it did her harm. She brooded over it till she believed it to be a duty to reproduce every detail ... as a warning to others... She must be honest; she must not varnish, soften or conceal.*[15]

Charlotte is criticising Anne's determination to 'tell the truth'; Anne's own *reason d'etre* for writing her novels. I am sure that Charlotte either misunderstood her sisters' determination to write their novels without her interference or she hoped to point out to the critics that this was their downfall. They needed her help but had failed to ask for it and subsequently their books lacked Charlotte's skill and maturity.

Charlotte's description, as already referred to in her preface, tells us of how she, and probably the whole family, viewed the youngest child:

> *Anne's character was milder and more subdued [than Emily's] she wanted the power, the fire, the originality of her sister, but was well endowed with quiet virtues of her own. Long-suffering, self-denying, reflective, and intelligent, a constitutional reserve and taciturnity placed and kept her in the shade, and covered her mind, and especially her feelings, with a sort of nun-like veil, which was rarely lifted.*[16]

I do not doubt that this is how Charlotte viewed her sister but I question its accuracy in the face of the six years that Anne spent working as a governess. Anne proved that she had stoicism, kindness, empathy and loyalty; qualities which Charlotte often failed to acknowledge or display herself.

Charlotte's interference with her sisters' works after their deaths and her faint praise, all suggest to me that Charlotte had come to believe in her role as eldest child to the point that she felt a given right to dictate and dominate her siblings both in life and death. When they had all died, I wonder how Charlotte came to terms with her role and whether she ever regretted the lack of sisterhood that she lost when she inherited the mantle of eldest child. I do admire a great deal of Charlotte's work and her efforts to perhaps govern her siblings at times when she felt that neither her father nor aunt had the ability to understand their needs and foibles. Unfortunately, Charlotte was not always the best judge of others and her interference was sometimes neither justified nor appreciated. Had Charlotte died before either of her sisters, I suggest that a lot more of Emily and Anne's writings would have survived and Anne would not now be buried in Scarborough.

Whilst I firmly believe that Charlotte loved and mourned her siblings, I also believe that she dominated much of their free will. Her refusal to acknowledge Branwell's pain and suffering until after his death, and even then to speak only of 'wasted talents' rather than his literary input into the Brontë canon, shows a complete lack of empathy and sisterly love and affection. Was this only boy, this longed for and important male, Charlotte's greatest threat? Could she be the most important sibling while ever he succeeded? Was Branwell, along with Anne, their father's favourite children? I suspect so and that Charlotte carried a jealousy over this fact. Branwell's downfall only accelerated and compounded Charlotte's rise. What of Patrick's love for his youngest daughter, his 'dear little Anne', the child he was loathe to let go of? Or Emily, whom he admired as having the strength and fortitude that his son lacked? Charlotte tried very hard to become her father's mainstay and stressed his need for her, but he had other children who had many attributes that his eldest daughter could not attain. One must never forget also that nobody could live up to the 'perfection' of their dead mother and sisters.

I maintain that the Brontë siblings did not live the harmonious and happy lives that we have come to accept. There was sibling rivalry in extreme measures at times and it continued and affected them throughout their lives. They were, like the rest of us, subject to the vagaries of childhood, the arguments and the rivalry that can both nurture and harm the growing child. Edward Chitham warns us to:

> ... be wary of the complacent view of the relations between the three, deriving from Ellen Nussey's meeting with them in 1833, and strengthened by the revisionary anecdotes told by Charlotte to Elizabeth Gaskell. These three sisters are three individuals, with much in common, but much to divide their thoughts.[17]

The Brontë Family: Sibling Rivalry and a Burial in Paradise

I propose that families are, and always have been, an inescapable hotbed of both conflict and harmony; a unit where everyone is seeking to be seen and heard and express their own thoughts and beliefs. Rivalry is at the heart of its function and the birth order of its younger members is the basis for much of its disharmony. Samantha Ellis expresses a similar belief. She says:

> *The more I learn about how Charlotte treated Anne and her work, the sadder I feel. I was so invested in the idea of the three sisters working together, sharing pages, helping each other to get published, supporting each other. I hate knowing that in truth, their story is partly about sibling rivalry, betrayals, recriminations and turf wars. It's tempting to interpret the whole of the Brontës' afterlives – all of the biographies, all the scholarship, all the fan fiction – as part of the same story, with readers and critics getting drawn in, taking sides, defining themselves by which Brontë they feel most sympathy for.*[18]

I often wonder how Charlotte felt after her siblings were all gone. She talks of her sisters in terms of extreme loss, saying of her youngest sibling that 'Anne was the "darling of my life" and "one I would have died to save"'. Yet isn't this the cry of someone who has realised their loss when it is too late to rectify the damage. It echoes Heathcliff.

Charlotte must have realised at some point that she had gone too far. The damage to her siblings' reputations had been done and she was the main perpetrator. She wrote later that she regretted burying Anne at Scarborough. She perhaps realised that it was not what Anne or her father had wanted. She mythologised her sisters as too simple and stubborn to take her advice and her brother as a profligate with no redeeming features. I sympathise with Charlotte's dilemma but criticise some of the decisions she made, sometimes in haste and without referral to those involved. She was, I believe, often full of good intentions that turned out badly for herself and her siblings. It is the curse of the eldest child who so often rules and overrules the rest of the family.

Anne Brontë suffered in her position as the youngest child because her siblings were strong, intelligent and competitive people, determined to hold on to their own place in the pecking order, whilst Charlotte dominated all of their lives. Anne's position in the literary canon has similarly been pushed aside by the critics, most of whom followed Charlotte's lead and denigrated the lesser sibling's ability as a writer.

During the second wave of feminism, academics began to focus on Anne's work and took time to re-examine, re-assess and re-evaluate all of Anne's literary output, not as one of the Brontë sisters, but as a novelist, hymnist and poet in her own right. Had she been an only child, or the only female in the family, her works may have received as much, if not more praise than any other female writer of the time. Her legacy was permanently damaged by the sister who claimed that she 'would have died to save her'. Anne's fate was cast at birth when she became the youngest of the Brontë family and as such, lacked the 'age and experience' that set her apart from her siblings. She has paid the price for her position in the birth order.

We have moved on from the likes of Mary Ward, writing in the prefaces to the Haworth edition of the Brontë novels of 1898, that for Anne:

> *It is not as the writer of Wildfell Hall, but as the sister of Charlotte and Emily Brontë, that Anne Brontë escapes oblivion.*[19]

Anne is a writer in her own right, not a Brontë sister or a youngest child to be fobbed off with faint praise. She had become for over a hundred years, the 'Cinderella' sister and a foil to their genius. As I have repeatedly stated, the siblings were all different. They were not equal, though similar; not a cohesive sisterhood but widely different in looks, personality and beliefs. Each had a different outlook on life nurtured and fed by their position in the birth order and the sibling rivalry between them.

Now Anne's remains lie in the graveyard high above Scarborough town, at the foot of the castle gates, separated from all she knew and loved. One wonders how her closest sister and friend, Emily, would have reacted to this situation. Anne has attained an earthly, physical 'paradise' here and one can only hope that she achieved the spiritual paradise that she craved, with the God that she firmly believed in. Her separation from her family must never be allowed to ostracise the wonderful collection of writing that she left behind, or be viewed as any less than that achieved by her sisters.

The Denouement

However, these three talented sisters do share something. It is far more infinite and everlasting as a memorial and it is way out in the universe. As Paul Chrystal notes in his book *Haworth*: The Brontë sisters are up there in the heavens in force.

1. Charlottebrontë is the name of asteroid #39427.

2. Emilybrontë is asteroid #39428

3. Annebrontë is asteroid #39429.

4. The 60 km-diameter impact crater Brontë, on Mercury, is named in honour of the whole Brontë family.[20]

References

Chapter One

1. Wallace Meri, M.S.W. *Birth Order Blues. How Parents Can Help Their Children Meet The Challenges of Birth Order.* New York, USA: Henry Holt and Company, Inc. First Owl Edition, 1999, p.30.
2. Aristotle. *The Philosophy of Aristotle. A selection with an Introduction and Commentary by Renford Bambrough: With a New Afterword by Suzanne Bobzien.* Signet Classics, Paperback, 2011.
3. Leeman, Kevin Dr. *The Birth Order Book. Why you Are the Way You Are.* Michigan, USA: Baker Publishing Group. Repackaged edition 2015, pp.29–30.
4. Royal Manchester Children's Hospital, NHS. 'Adverse Childhood Experiences (ACE's) and Attachment'. 2023.
5. Wright, Sharon. *The Mother of the Brontës. When Maria met Patrick.* Yorkshire, England: Pen and Sword Books Ltd, 2019, p.5.
6. Eliot, George. *The Mill on the Floss.* London: J. M. Dent and Sons Ltd., 1977, p.245.
7. Crummey, Ciara. 'Early Life Adverse Childhood Experiences (ACE's) and Development', *Journal of Fraser and Allander Economic Commentary*, Volume 6, Issue 3, October 2022.
8. Bucci M., Marques S., Oh D., Harris N. 'Toxic stress in Children and Adolescents', *Advances in Paediatrics*, Volume 63, Issue 1, 2016, pp.403–408.

Chapter Two

1. Rhodes, Philip (Professor of Obstetrics and Gynaecology). 'A Medical Appraisal of the Brontës', *Brontë Transactions*, Volume 16, Issue 2. Taylor and Francis, 1972, pp.101–109.

2. Bowlby, John. *Child Care and the Growth of Love.* Canada: Pelican Books, Second Edition. Reprinted 1987, pp.21–22.
3. Ibid., p.28.
4. Blair, Linda. *Birth Order. What your position in the family really tells you about your character.* London: Piatkus, Imprint of Little, Brown Book Group, 2013, pp.14–19.
5. Ibid., pp.60–61.
6. Bowlby, *Child Care*, p.39.
7. Ellis, Samantha. *Take Courage. Anne Brontë and the Art of Life.* London: Chatto and Windus, Penguin Random House UK, 2017, p.24.
8. Barker, *The Brontës,* p.126.
9. Ellis. *Take Courage,* p.128. Letter from Anne Brontë to Ellen Nussey, 1848.
10. Ibid., p.128. Letter from Charlotte Brontë to Ellen Nussey, 1839.
11. Leman, Kevin. *The Birth Order Book. Why You Are the Way You Are.* Michigan, USA: Revell, Barker Publishing Company, 2015, p.30.
12. Leman, *The Birth Order Book*, p.169.
13. Brontë, Anne. *Self-Communion. The Complete Poems of Anne Brontë.* Clement Shorter (ed.); intro by C.W. Hatfield. London: Forgotten Books, 1920, pp.131–144.
14. Chitham, Edward. *The Novelist of Wildfell Hall. A New Life of Anne Brontë.* Brighton: Edward Everett Root, 2022, p.155.

Chapter Three

1. Wallace, Meri, M.S.W. *Birth Order Blues. How Parents Can Help Their Children Meet The Challenges of Birth Order.* New York, USA: Henry Holt and Company, Inc. First Owl Edition, 1999, p.134.
2. Wallace, *Birth Order Blues*, pp.6–7.
3. Leeman, Kevin Dr. *The Birth Order Book. Why you Are the Way You Are.* Michigan, USA: Baker Publishing Group. Repackaged edition, 2015, p.153.
4. Dearden William. Letter in the *Bradford Observer*, June 1861, p.7. Quoted in Barker, Juliet. *The Brontës.* London: Abacus. Imprint of Little, Brown Book Group, 2010, p.125.
5. Green, Dudley. *Patrick Brontë. Father of Genius.* Gloucestershire: Nonsuch Publishing, 2008, p.19. Letter from Patrick Brontë to Elizabeth Gaskell, June 1855.
6. Eliot, George. *Adam Bede.* London: Zodiac Press, 1952, pp.41–42.

References

7. Green, *Patrick Brontë*, p.94.
8. Brontë, Charlotte. *Jane Eyre.* Norton Critical Edition; Richard Dunn (ed.). New York: W.W. Norton & Company, 1971, p.27.
9. Kübler-Ross, Elisabeth. *On Death and Dying.* New York: Macmillan Publishing Company Inc., 1969.
10. Tennyson, Alfred Lord. *In Memoriam.* A Norton Critical Edition; Robert Ross (ed.). New York: W.W. Norton & Company, 1973, Verse 45, pp.29–30.
11. Ibid., Verse 5, p.6.
12. Hatfield, C.W. (ed.). *The Complete Poems of Emily Jane Brontë.* New York: Columbia University Press, 1941, pp.222–223. B 36, 3 March 1845, R. Alcona to J. Brenzaida.

Chapter Four

1. Barker, Juliet. *The Brontës.* London: Abacus. Imprint of Little, Brown Book Group, 2010, p.147.
2. Brontë, Emily. 'Wuthering Heights' in Pearson, L. H. (ed.) *Case Studies in Contemporary Criticism.* Hampshire, Macmillan Press Ltd., 1992, p.274.
3. Barker, *The Brontës*, p.158.
4. Davies, Stevie (ed.). *Brontë Sisters, Selected Poems.* Manchester, Carcanet Press, 1976, p.23.
5. Burdett, Emmeline. 'An Erring Spirit? Anne Brontë's Words to the "Elect" and The Question of Universal Salvation', in *Walking With Anne Brontë, Insights and Reflections. An Anthology.* Tim Whittome (ed.). Xlibris, 2023, p.453.
6. Brontë, Anne. *The Complete Poems of Anne Brontë.* Clement Shorter (ed.); intro by C.W. Hatfield (1920). London: Forgotten Books, 2018. 'A Word to the Elect', London, 2018, pp.35–37.
7. Barker, *The Brontës,* p.160.
8. Ibid., p.168.
9. Young Minds (2018). Quoted in: Royal Manchester Children's Hospital, NHS, 'Adverse Childhood Experiences (ACE's) and Attachment'. 2023, p.2.
10. Brontë, Charlotte. 'Biographical Notice of Ellis and Acton Bell' (September 1850), *Wuthering Heights.* London: Jonathan Cape / Florin Books, 1932, pp.11–17.
11. Freeman, Joan. *International Handbook of Research of Giftedness and Talent.* Pergamon, 1993, p.675.

12. McConville, Brigid. *Sisters. Love and Conflict within the Lifelong Bond.* Pan Books Ltd., 1985, p.145.
13. Chitham, Edward. *The Novelist of Wildfell Hall. A New Life of Anne Brontë.* Brighton: Edward Everett Root, 2022, p.xiii.
14. Brontë, Emily. 'Wuthering Heights' in Pearson, L. H. (ed.) *Case Studies in Contemporary Criticism.* Hampshire, Macmillan Press Ltd., 1992, p.117.

Chapter Five

1. Barker, Juliet. *The Brontës.* London: Abacus. Imprint of Little, Brown Book Group, 2010, p.175.
2. Ibid., p.179.
3. *Blackwood's Edinburgh Magazine.* Edinburgh: William Blackwood, 1825. Volume XV111, July to December and Volume XX1, January to June 1827.
4. *Blackwood's* 'On the Death of a Daughter', 1827. Volume XX1, No. CXX11, p.226.
5. Barker, *The Brontës*, p.227.
6. Ibid., p.242–243.
7. Freud, Sigmund. Quoted in Lane, Margaret, *The Drug-like Brontë Dream.* London: John Murray Ltd., 1980, p.19.
8. Brontë, Anne. 'Agnes Grey', *Agnes Grey and Poems.* Introduction by Anne Smith. Everyman. Re-issued by J. M. Dent, London, 1997, p.121.
9. Brontë, Emily and Anne. 'Diary Paper November 1834', in Barker, *The Brontës*, p.257.
10. Goethe, Johann Wolfgang. Quoted in Brontë, Charlotte, *Villette.* Introduction by Tony Tanner. Middlesex: Penguin Books Ltd., 1984, p.7.
11. Hamilton, Patrick. *Gas Light.* Play written in 1938; filmed as *Gaslight*, 1944.

Chapter Six

1. Ellis, Samantha. *Take Courage. Anne Brontë and the Art of Life.* London: Chatto and Windus, Penguin Random House UK, 2017, p.125.
2. Ibid., pp.12–13.
3. Barker, Juliet. *The Brontës.* London: Abacus. Imprint of Little, Brown Book Group, 2010, p.258.
4. Ibid., p.257.
5. Hennessy, John. *Emily Jane Brontë and Her Music.* York: Yorkshire Publishing Services Ltd., 2018, p.24.

6. Ibid., p.9
7. Ibid., pp.22–23.
8. Ibid., p.395.
9. Ibid., p.356.
10. Ibid., p.414.
11. Alexander, Christine and Sellars, Jane. *The Art of the Brontës.* Cambridge University Press, 1995, p.9.
12. Barker, *The Brontës*, p.230.
13. Alexander, C. and Sellars, J. *The Art of the Brontës*, pp.25–26.
14. Hatfield, C.W. (ed.). *The Complete Poems of Emily Jane Brontë.* New York: Columbia University Press, 1941, pp.255–256.

Chapter Seven

1. Thormahlen, Marianne (ed.). *The Brontës in Context.* Cambridge University Press, 2012. Essay on 'Mental Health' by Janis McLarren Caldwell, p.344.
2. Barker, Juliet R.V. (ed.). *The Brontës Selected Poems.* Poems by Charlotte Brontë, No. 5, 'Retrospection', p.9.
3. Proust, Marcel. *In Search of Lost Time. The Way by Swann's.* Volume 1, 1913; Reissued with C.K. Scott Moncrief translation. Modern Library, 2012.
4. Novakovich, J. 'Paradise Lost: Theology of Nostalgia and Hope', *Balkan Contextual Theology.* Odak, S. and Grozdanov, Z. (eds.), London: Routledge, 2022, Chapter 18.
5. Barker, Juliet. R.V. *The Brontës.* London: Abacus. Imprint of Little, Brown Book Group, 2010, p.237. Brontë Charlotte, Letter to William Smith Williams, 4 June 1849.
6. Thormahlen, Caldwell, *The Brontës in Context*, pp.347–348.
7. Brontë, Emily. 'Wuthering Heights' in Pearson, L. H. (ed.) *Case Studies in Contemporary Criticism.* Hampshire, Macmillan Press Ltd., 1992, p.154.
8. Eliot, George. *Adam Bede.* London: Zodiac Press, 1952, pp.41–42.
9. Davies, Stevie. *Emily Brontë: The Artist As A Free Woman.* Manchester: Carcanet Press Ltd., 1983, p.167.
10. Brontë, Charlotte. *Jane Eyre.* Norton Critical Edition; Richard Dunn (ed.). New York: W.W. Norton & Company, 1971, pp.257–258.
11. Hughes *et al.* 'Relationships between adverse childhood experiences and adult mental well-being: results from an English national household survey', *British Medical Council Public Health*, 2016, page 7.

12. Royal Manchester Children's Hospital, NHS. 'Adverse Childhood Experiences (ACE's) and Attachment'. 2023, page 1.
13. Young Minds (2018). Quoted in: Royal Manchester Children's Hospital, NHS, 'Adverse Childhood Experiences (ACE's) and Attachment'. 2023, p.2.
14. Daiches, David. *Introduction to 'Wuthering Heights'*. Middlesex: Penguin Books Ltd., 1983, p.29.
15. Hatfield, C.W. (ed.). *The Complete Poems of Emily Jane Brontë*. New York: Columbia University Press, 1941, p.256, Verse 5.

Chapter Eight

1. Shaw, Marion. 'Anne Brontë: A Quiet Feminist'. Version of a paper given at the Scarborough Conference on Anne Brontë, April 1994, p.127.
2. Ibid.
3. Ibid.
4. Ibid.
5. Cunningham, Hugh. *Children and Childhood: in Western Society Since 1500*. Harlow: Pearson Education Ltd., 2005, p.68.
6. Shaw, 'Anne Brontë', p.126.
7. Mirk, John. *Mirk's Festial*. Fourteenth Century.
8. Babbage, Benjamin Herschel. 'Report of the General Board of Health'. London, 1850.
9. Cunningham, *Children and Childhood*, p.186.
10. Barker, Juliet R.V. *The Brontës*. London: Abacus. Imprint of Little, Brown Book Group, 2010, p.165.
11. Ibid., p.128.
12. Ibid., p.531. 'Emily Brontë Diary Paper, 1845'.
13. Ibid., p.296.
14. Ibid., p.274.
15. Brontë, Charlotte. 'Letter to Ellen Nussey', April 1839.

Chapter Nine

1. Ellis, Samantha. *Take Courage: Anne Brontë and the Art of Life*. London: Chatto and Windus, page 125.
2. Various Authors. 'Diagnostic and Statistical Manual of Mental Disorders'. Published by The American Psychiatric Publishing Association, Washington and London, 2013.

References

3. Whipps, Brenda. 'Unwavering Courage and Hope: The life of Anne Brontë; Letter between Patrick Brontë and Elizabeth Franks, July 1835' in *Walking with Anne Brontë: Insights and Reflections. An Anthology.* Tim Whittome (ed.). Xlibris, 2023.
4. Barker, Juliet. R.V. *The Brontës.* London: Abacus. Imprint of Little, Brown Book Group, 2010, pp.270–271.
5. Southey, Robert. Letter to Charlotte Brontë, March 1837.
6. Barker, *The Brontës*, p.315. 'Diary Paper of Emily and Anne Brontë', 26 June 1837.
7. Chitham, Edward. *The Novelist of Wildfell Hall. A New Life of Anne Brontë.* Brighton: Edward Everett Root, 2022, pp3–4.
8. Barker, *The Brontës*, p.327.
9. Barker, Juliet. R.V. (ed.). *The Brontës Selected Poems.* 'The North Wind' by Anne Brontë. Everyman Classics, 1989, p.84.
10. Barker, *The Brontës,* pp.328–329.
11. Palmer, Geoffrey. *The Brontës Day by Day.* The Brontë Society, 2002. Letter from Charlotte Brontë to Ellen Nussey, September 1838, p.42.
12. Brontë, Anne. *The Complete Poems of Anne Brontë.* Clement Shorter (ed.); intro by C.W. Hatfield (1920). London: Forgotten Books, 2018, 'A Word to the Elect', pp.35–37.
13. Barker, *The Brontës*, p.358.
14. Brontë, Charlotte. 'Biographical Notice of Ellis and Acton Bell', *Wuthering Heights.* London: Florin Books, 1932, p.12.
15. Palmer, *The Brontës Day by Day*, p.44.
16. Ibid., p.44.
17. Barker, *The Brontës,* p.429.
18. Ibid., p.425.

Chapter Ten

1. Barker, Juliet. R.V. *The Brontës.* London: Abacus. Imprint of Little, Brown Book Group, 2010, p.360.
2. Brontë, Anne. *Agnes Grey and Poems.* Introduction by Anne Smith. Everyman. Re-issued by J. M. Dent, London, 1997, p.38.
3. Ibid., p.39.
4. Whittome, Tom. 'The Tenant of Wildfell Hall: Finding Treasure and an Overlooked Masterpiece', in *Walking with Anne Brontë: Insights and Reflections. An Anthology.* Xlibris, 2023, pp.380–381.
5. Brontë, Anne. *The Tenant of Wildfell Hall.* Middlesex: Penguin Books, 1982, p.29.

6. Brontë, *Agnes Grey and Poems,* p.xxi.
7. Brontë, Anne. *The Complete Poems of Anne Brontë.* Clement Shorter (ed.); intro by C.W. Hatfield (1920). London: Forgotten Books, 2018, 'Self-Communion', April 1847, London. 2018, pp.131–144.
8. Barker, *The Brontës*, p.421. 'Emily Brontë Diary Paper', July 1841.
9. Barker, Juliet. R.V. (ed.). *The Brontës Selected Poems.* 'The Bluebell' by Anne Brontë. Everyman Classics, J.M. Dent and Sons, 1989, p.86, Verses 9–12.
10. Glasscott, Ciara. 'Is Childhood Then so All-Divine?: Representations of Childhood in the Poetry of Anne Brontë', *Brontë Studies*, Volume 48, Number 45. October 2023, p.312.
11. Brontë, Anne, *The Complete Poems*, p.23. 'Lines written at Thorp Green', August 19, 1840.
12. Brontë, *Agnes Grey and Poems,* p.66.
13. Ibid., pp.61–62.
14. Brontë, *The Tenant of Wildfell Hall,* p.57.

Chapter Eleven

1. Smith, Margaret (ed.). *Selected Letters of Charlotte Brontë.* Oxford: Oxford University Press, 2007, p.33.
2. Holland, Nick. *In Search of Anne Brontë.* Gloucestershire: The History Press, 2016, p.106.
3. Martin, Joanna (ed.). *A Governess in the Age of Jane Austen: The Journals and Letters of Agnes Porter.* London: Hambledon Press, 1998, Flysheet on Book Jacket.
4. Chitham, Edward. *The Novelist of Wildfell Hall. A New Life of Anne Brontë.* Brighton: Edward Everett Root, 2022, p.41.
5. Ibid., p.44.
6. Barker, Juliet. R.V. *The Brontës.* London: Abacus. Imprint of Little, Brown Book Group, 2010, p.537.
7. Chitham, *The Novelist of Wildfell Hall*, p.75.
8. Ibid., p.82.
9. Barker, *The Brontës*, p.292.
10. Ibid., p.474.
11. Ibid.
12. Ibid., p.468.
13. Ibid., p.671.
14. Ibid.
15. Ibid.

16. Chitham, *The Novelist of Wildfell Hall*, p.111.
17. Pearson, Sara. 'Singing from the Margins: Anne Brontë's Surprising Poetic Afterlife', *Brontë Studies,* Volume 48, Number 4. October 2023, p.296.
18. Brontë, Anne. *The Complete Poems of Anne Brontë.* Clement Shorter (ed.); intro by C.W. Hatfield (1920). London: Forgotten Books, 2018, 'To Cowper', November 1842, p.28.
19. Pearson, 'Singing from the Margins', p.298.
20. Ibid., p.301.

Chapter Twelve

1. Barker, Juliet. R.V. *The Brontës.* London: Abacus. Imprint of Little, Brown Book Group, 2010, p.564.
2. Ibid., p.565.
3. Ibid.
4. Moore, George. *Conversations in Ebury Street.* London: William Heinemann, 1924, p.258.
5. Brontë, Anne. *Agnes Grey and Poems.* Introduction by Anne Smith. Everyman. Re-issued by J. M. Dent, London, 1997, p.13.
6. Sunderland, Jane. 'Agnes Grey as a Mid-nineteenth-Century Governess's Life: Anne Brontë's Narrative, Documentation and Critique', in *Walking with Anne Brontë: Insights and Reflections. An Anthology.* Tim Whittome (ed.). Xlibris, 2023, p.258.
7. Smith, Anne. Intro to *Agnes Grey and Poems.* Everyman. RE-issued by J. M. Dent, London, 1997, p.xxi.
8. Brontë, *Agnes Grey and Poems*, p.6.
9. Ibid., p.156.
10. Moore, *Conversations in Ebury Street*, p.253.
11. Jay, Betty. *Anne Brontë.* Writers and their Work series. Devon: Northcote House Publishers Ltd., 2000, Introduction and p.1.
12. Burdett, Emmeline. 'An Erring Spirit? Anne Brontë's Words to the "Elect" and The Question of Universal Salvation', in *Walking With Anne Brontë, Insights and Reflections. An Anthology.* Tim Whittome (ed.), Xlibris, 2023, p.452.
13. Brontë, Charlotte. 'Preface to *Wuthering Heights*', 2nd Edition 1850, in *Wuthering Heights.* London: Collins, 1979, p.31.
14. Ibid., p.28.
15. Ibid., p.23.
16. Ibid., p.25.

Chapter Thirteen

1. Chitham, Edward. *The Novelist of Wildfell Hall. A New Life of Anne Brontë.* Brighton: Edward Everett Root, 2022, p.163.
2. Ibid.
3. Brontë, Emily. 'Wuthering Heights' in Pearson, L. H. (ed.) *Case Studies in Contemporary Criticism.* Hampshire, Macmillan Press Ltd., 1992, p.169.
4. Twain, Mark. *The Prince and the Pauper.* London: Chatto and Windus, 1882.
5. Wordsworth, William. 'My Heart Leaps Up' (1802), in *The Complete Poems of William Wordsworth.* Wordsworth Editions, revised 1994.
6. Tennyson, Alfred Lord. *In Memoriam.* A Norton Critical Edition; Robert Ross (ed.). New York: W.W. Norton & Company, 1973, Canto LVI (56), p.36.
7. Brontë, Anne. *The Tenant of Wildfell Hall.* London: Collins, 1980, p.95.
8. Ibid., p.176.
9. Ibid., p.185.
10. Chitham, *The Novelist of Wildfell Hall*, p.134. The quote is by Charlotte Brontë, as recorded in Chitham's book.
11. Brontë, Anne. *The Complete Poems of Anne Brontë.* Clement Shorter (ed.); intro by C.W. Hatfield (1920). London: Forgotten Books, 2018, 'The Narrow Way', April 1848, p.145. Stanzas 1–4.

Chapter Fourteen

1. Barker, Juliet. R.V. *The Brontës.* London: Abacus. Imprint of Little, Brown Book Group, 2010, p.658.
2. Ibid., p.686.
3. Ibid., p.703.
4. Brontë, Anne. *The Complete Poems of Anne Brontë.* Clement Shorter (ed.); intro by C.W. Hatfield (1920). London: Forgotten Books, 2018, 'Last Lines', January 1849, pp.148–150.
5. Barker, *The Brontës*, p.695.
6. Nussey, Ellen. Diary.
7. Hey, Adelle. *Anne Brontë Reimagined: A View from the Twenty-First Century.* Saraband, 2020, p.35.
8. Lock, John and Dixon, W. T. *A Man of Sorrow. The Life, Letters and Times of the Rev. Patrick Brontë, 1777–1861.* London: Nelson and Sons Ltd., 1965, p.429.

References

9. Nussey, Ellen. 'Letter to Mrs Ward' in Barker J., *The Brontës: A Life in Letters.* Viking Books, 1997, p.236.
10. Brontë, Charlotte. 'Letter to William Smith Williams, 4 June 1849' in *Selected Letters of Charlotte Brontë.* Margaret Smith (ed.). Oxford University Press 2007, p.136–137.
11. Brontë, Charlotte. 'Letter to Martha Brown, June 1849'.
12. Ellis, Samantha. *Take Courage: Anne Brontë and the Art of Life.* London: Chatto and Windus, p.142.
13. Brontë, Charlotte. 'Preface to *Wuthering Heights*', 2nd Edition 1850, in *Wuthering Heights.* London: Collins, p.19.
14. Ibid., p.22.
15. Ibid., p.23
16. Ibid., p.25.
17. Chitham, Edward. *The Novelist of Wildfell Hall. A New Life of Anne Brontë.* Brighton: Edward Everett Root, 2022, p.119.
18. Ellis, *Take Courage*, p.147.
19. Ward, Mary. Quoted in *Anne Brontë: The Other One.* Elizabeth Langland. Women Writers Series. Toronto: Barnes and Noble, 1989.
20. Chrystal Paul. *Haworth: Timelines.* Stockton-on-Tees: Destinworld Publishing Ltd., 2018, p.141.

Bibliography

Alexander, Christine and Sellars, Jane. *The Art of the Brontës*. Cambridge University Press, 1995.

American Psychiatric Publishing Association (various authors). *Diagnostic and Statistical Manual of Mental Disorders*. Washington and London, 2013.

Aristotle. *The Philosophy of Aristotle. A Selection with an introduction and Commentary by Renford Bambrough; With an afterword by Suzanne Bobzien*. Signet Classics, paperback, 2011.

Babbage, Benjamin Herschel. *Report of the General Board of Health*. London, 1850.

Barker, Juliet R.V. *The Brontës*. London: Abacus. Imprint of Little, Brown Book Group, 2010.

Barker, Juliet R.V. (ed.). *The Brontë Selected Poems*. Everyman Classics. London: J. M. Dent and Sons Ltd., reprint, 1989.

Barker, Juliet R.V. *The Brontës: A Life in Letters*. Viking Books, 1997.

Blackwood, William. *Blackwood's Edinburgh Magazine*. Volume XVIII (July to December), Edinburgh, 1825 and XXI (January to June), Edinburgh, 1827.

Blair, Linda. *Birth Order: What your position in the family really tells you about your character.* London: Piatkus. Imprint of Little, Brown Book Group, 2013.

Bowlby, John. *Child Care and the Growth of Love*. Canada: Pelican Books, Second Edition Reprint, 1987.

Brontë, Anne. *Agnes Grey – In Agnes Grey and Poems*. Intro by Anne Smith, Everyman. London: J.M. Dent, Re-issued, 1997.

Brontë, Anne. *The Tenant of Wildfell Hall*. Middlesex: Penguin Books, 1982.

Brontë, Anne. *The Tenant of Wildfell Hall*. London: Collins, 1980.

Brontë, Charlotte. *Jane Eyre*. A Norton Critical Edition, Richard Dunn (ed.). New York, 1971.

Brontë, Charlotte. 'Biographical Notice of Ellis and Acton Bell' (1850), Preface to *Wuthering Heights*. London: Jonathan Cape/Florin Books, 1932.

Bibliography

Brontë, Emily. *Wuthering Heights.* Middlesex: Penguin Books Ltd., 1983.

Brontë, Emily. 'Wuthering Heights' in Pearson, L. H. (ed.) *Case Studies in Contemporary Criticism.* Hampshire, Macmillan Press Ltd., 1992.

Brontë Studies. Taylor and Francis Publishers.

Bucci, M., Marques, S., Oh, D., Harris, N. 'Toxic stress in Children and Adolescents', *Advance Paediatrics*, Volume 63, Issue 1, 2016.

Burdett, Emmeline. 'An Erring Spirit? Anne Brontë's "Words to the 'Elect" and the Question of Universal Salvation, in *Walking with Anne Brontë: Insights and Reflections. An Anthology.* Tim Whittome (ed.). USA: Xlibris, 2023.

Caldwell, Janis McLarren. 'Mental Health', *The Brontës in Context.* Thormahlen Marianne (ed.). Cambridge University Press, 2012.

Chitham, Edward. *The Novelist of Wildfell Hall. A New Life of Anne Brontë.* Brighton: Edward Everett Root, 2022.

Chrystal, Paul. *Haworth Timelines.* Stockton-on-Tees: Destinworld Publishing Ltd., 2018.

Crummey, Ciara. 'Early Life Adverse Childhood Experiences (ACE's) and Development', *Journal of Fraser and Allander Economic Commentary*, Volume 6, Issue 3, October 2022.

Cunningham, Hugh. *Children and Childhood in Western Society since 1500.* Harlow: Pearson Education Ltd., 2005.

Daiches, David. Introduction to *Wuthering Heights.* Middlesex: Penguin Books Ltd., 1983.

Davies, Stevie (ed.). *Brontë Sisters, Selected Poems.* Manchester: Carcanet Press Ltd., 1976.

Davies, Stevie. *Emily Brontë: The Artist as a Free Woman.* Manchester: Carcanet Press Ltd., 1983.

Diary Papers: Anne and Emily Brontë. Preserved at the Brontë Parsonage Museum, Haworth, Yorkshire.

Eliot, George. *Adam Bede.* London: Zodiac Press, 1952.

Eliot, George. *The Mill on the Floss.* London: J. M. Dent and Sons Ltd., 1977.

Ellis, Samantha. *Take Courage. Anne Brontë and the Art of Life.* London: Chatto and Windus, Penguin Random House, 2017.

Freeman, Joan. *International Handbook of Research of Giftedness and Talent.* Pergamon, 1993.

Freud, Sigmund. Quoted in *The Drug-like Brontë Dream,* by Margaret Lane. London: John Murray Ltd., 1980.

Glasscott, Ciara. 'Is Childhood Then so All-Divine? Representations of Childhood in the Poetry of Anne Brontë', *Brontë Studies*, Volume 48, Number 45. October 2023.

Goethe, Johann Wolfgang. Quoted in *Villette,* by Charlotte Brontë. Introduction by Tony Tanner. Middlesex: Penguin Books Ltd., 1984.

Green, Dudley. *Patrick Brontë. Father of Genius.* Gloucestershire: Nonsuch Publishing, 2008.

Hamilton, Patrick. *Gas Light.* Play written in 1938; filmed as *Gaslight,* 1944.

Hatfield, C.W. (ed.). *The Complete Poems of Emily Jane Brontë.* New York: Columbia University Press, 1941.

Hennessy, John. *Emily Jane Brontë and Her Music.* York: Yorkshire Publishing Services Ltd., 2018.

Hey, Adelle. *Anne Brontë Reimagined: A View from the Twenty-First Century.* Saraband, 2020.

Holland, Nick. *In Search of Anne Brontë.* Gloucestershire: The History Press, 2016.

Hughes *et al.* 'Relationships between adverse childhood experiences and adult mental well-being: results from an English national household survey', *British Medical Council Public Health,* 2016.

Jay, Betty. *Anne Brontë.* Writers and their Work series. Devon: Northcote House Publishers Ltd., 2000.

Kübler-Ross, Elisabeth. *On Death and Dying.* Macmillan Publishing Company Inc., 1969.

Langland, Elizabeth. *Anne Brontë: The Other One.* Women Writers Series. Toronto: Barnes and Noble, 1989.

Leman, Kevin Dr. *The Birth order Book. Why you are the way you are.* Michigan USA: Baker Publishing Group, Repackaged edition, 2015.

Lock, John and Dixon, W. T. *A Man of Sorrow: The Life, Letters and Times of the Rev. Patrick Brontë 1777–1861.* London: Nelson and Sons Ltd., 1965.

Martin, Joanna (ed.). *A Governess in the Age of Jane Austen: The Journals and Letters of Agnes Porter.* London: Hambledon Press, 1998.

McConville, Brigid. *Sisters. Love and Conflict within the Lifelong Bond.* Pan Books Ltd., 1985.

Mirk, John. *Mirk's Festial.* A Collection of Homilies from the fourteenth century.

Moore, George. *Conversations in Ebury Street.* London: William Heinemann, 1924.

Novakovich, J. 'Paradise Lost: Theology of Nostalgia and Hope', *Balkan Contextual Theology* (Chapter 18), Odak, S. and Grozdanov, Z. (eds.). London: Routledge, 2022.

Palmer, Geoffrey. *The Brontës. Day by Day.* The Brontë Society, 2002.

Pearson, Sara. 'Singing from the Margins: Anne Brontë's Surprising Poetic Afterlife', *Brontë Studies,* Volume 48, Number 4, October 2023.

Proust, Marcel. *In Search of Lost Time. The Way by Swann's.* Volume 1, 1913. Reissued with C. K. Scott Moncrief translation, Modern Library, 2012.

Rhodes, Philip (Professor of Obstetrics and Gynaecology). 'A Medical Appraisal of The Brontës', *Brontë Transactions,* Volume 16, Issue 2. Taylor and Francis, 1972.

Bibliography

Royal Manchester Children's Hospital, NHS. 'Adverse Childhood Experiences (ACE's) and Attachment'. 2023

Shaw, Marion. *Anne Brontë: A Quiet Feminist.* Version of a paper given at The Scarborough Conference on Anne Brontë, April 1994.

Shorter, Clement (ed.). *The Complete Poems of Anne Brontë.* Intro by C.W. Hatfield (1920). Reprinted by Forgotten Books, 2018.

Smith, Anne. Introduction to *Agnes Grey and Poems.* Everyman Classics. J. M. Dent and Sons, 1997.

Smith, Margaret (ed.). *Selected Letters of Charlotte Brontë.* Oxford: Oxford University Press, 2007.

Sunderland, Jane. 'Agnes Grey as a Mid-Nineteenth-Century Governess's Life: Anne Brontë's Narrative Documentation and Critique,' in *Walking with Anne Brontë. Insights and Reflections. An Anthology.* USA: Xlibris, 2023.

Tennyson, Alfred L. *In Memoriam.* A Norton Critical Edition; Robert Ross (ed.). New York: W.W. Norton & Company, 1973.

Thormahlen, Marianne (ed.). *The Brontës in Context.* Cambridge University Press, 2012.

Twain, Mark. *The Prince and the Pauper.* London: Chatto and Windus, 1882.

Wallace, Meri, M.S.W. *Birth Order Blues. How Parents Can Help Their Children Meet The Challenges of Birth Order.* USA: Henry Holt and Company, Inc., First Owl Edition, 1999.

Watson, Graham, '*The Invention of Charlotte Bronte: Her last years and the scandal that made her.*' The History Press, Gloucestershire 2024.

Whittome, Tim (ed.). *Walking with Anne Brontë: Insights and Reflections. An Anthology.* USA: Xlibris, 2023.

Wollstonecraft, M. *A Vindication of the Rights of Women* (1772). Everyman Library Classics. Bi-Centenary Edition, London, 1972.

Wordsworth, William. *The Complete Poems of William Wordsworth.* Wordsworth Editions, Revised, 1994.

Wright, Sharon. *The Mother of the Brontës. When Maria met Patrick.* Barnsley, Yorkshire: Pen and Sword Books Ltd., 2019.

Whipp, Brenda. 'Unwavering Courage and Hope: The Life of Anne Brontë', in *Walking with Anne Brontë. Insights and Reflections. An Anthology.* USA: Xlibris, 2023.

Young Minds (2018). Quoted in: Royal Manchester Children's Hospital, NHS, 'Adverse Childhood Experiences (ACE's) and Attachment'. 2023.

Dear Reader,

We hope you have enjoyed this book, but why not share your views on social media? You can also follow our pages to see more about our other products: facebook.com/penandswordbooks or follow us on X @penswordbooks

You can also view our products at www.pen-and-sword.co.uk (UK and ROW) or www.penandswordbooks.com (North America).

To keep up to date with our latest releases and online catalogues, please sign up to our newsletter at: www.pen-and-sword.co.uk/newsletter

If you would like a printed catalogue with our latest books, then please email: enquiries@pen-and-sword.co.uk or telephone: 01226 734555 (UK and ROW) or email: uspen-and-sword@casematepublishers.com or telephone: (610) 853-9131 (North America).

We respect your privacy and we will only use personal information to send you information about our products.

Thank you!